Inequality: Economic and Social Issues

Inequalities of opportunity affect a person's life expectancy and access to basic services and human rights through discrimination, abuse, and lack of access to justice. High levels of inequality of opportunity discourage skill accumulation, choke economic and social mobility, and, consequently, depress economic growth. Inequality also entrenches uncertainty, vulnerability, and insecurity; undermines trust in institutions and government, increases social discord and tensions, and triggers violence and conflicts. This book presents wide-ranging perspectives on economic inequality, as measured by differences in incomes and wealth. The contributors to the book explore how the economy is shaped in such a way as to generate differences in economic and social welfare between individuals, regions, and nations. But the book is not limited to economic perspectives: inequality is a many-faceted phenomenon that manifests itself in a number of ways.

Thus, the book begins with a section which highlights some of the 'standard' features of inequality: class, gender, and age. The second section explores the manifestation of inequality in terms of differences in income and wealth. The third section looks at some of the causes of inequality, exploring the effects of discrimination and plunder (by those in power). The final section serves to drive home the point that geographic and institutional factors have an important place as well when it comes to shedding light on what equality is, how it manifests itself, and what its consequences are.

This book will be essential reading for anyone interested in the causes and consequences of economic inequality including those in economics, sociology, politics, and geography.

Mats Lundahl, Professor Emeritus of Development Economics, Stockholm School of Economics.

Daniel Rauhut, PhD in Economic History, Associate Professor in Regional Planning, and an affiliated researcher to Karlstad University, Sweden, and Lisbon University, Portugal.

Neelambar Hatti, Professor Emeritus of Economic History, School of Economics and Management, Lund University.

Routledge Frontiers of Political Economy

Digital Capitalism and New Institutionalism
Daniil Frolov

What Is Financialization?
Taner Akan and Halil İbrahim Gündüz

Unequal Development and Capitalism
Catching up and Falling behind in the Global Economy
Alessandro Donadio Miebach, Henrique Morrone and Adalmir Marquetti

Economic Growth and Long Cycles
A Classical Political Economy Approach
Nikolaos Chatzarakis, Persefoni Tsaliki and Lefteris Tsoulfidis

Income Redistribution, Inequality, and Democracy
A Political Economy Approach
Hwan Joo Seo and Sung Jin Kang

Macroeconomics After the General Theory
Fundamental Uncertainty, Animal Spirits and Shifting Equilibrium in a Competitive Economy
Angel Asensio

A History of Capitalist Transformation
A Critique of Liberal-Capitalist Reforms
Giampaolo Conte

Inequality: Economic and Social Issues
Edited by Mats Lundahl, Daniel Rauhut and Neelambar Hatti

For more information about this series, please visit: www.routledge.com/Routledge-Frontiers-of-Political-Economy/book-series/SE0345

Inequality: Economic and Social Issues

Edited by Mats Lundahl, Daniel Rauhut and Neelambar Hatti

LONDON AND NEW YORK

First published 2024
by Routledge
4 Park Square, Milton Park, Abingdon, Oxon OX14 4RN

and by Routledge
605 Third Avenue, New York, NY 10158

Routledge is an imprint of the Taylor & Francis Group, an informa business

© 2024 selection and editorial matter, Mats Lundahl, Daniel Rauhut and Neelambar Hatti; individual chapters, the contributors

The right of Mats Lundahl, Daniel Rauhut and Neelambar Hatti to be identified as the author[/s] of the editorial material, and of the authors for their individual chapters, has been asserted in accordance with sections 77 and 78 of the Copyright, Designs and Patents Act 1988.

All rights reserved. No part of this book may be reprinted or reproduced or utilised in any form or by any electronic, mechanical, or other means, now known or hereafter invented, including photocopying and recording, or in any information storage or retrieval system, without permission in writing from the publishers.

Trademark notice: Product or corporate names may be trademarks or registered trademarks, and are used only for identification and explanation without intent to infringe.

British Library Cataloguing-in-Publication Data
A catalogue record for this book is available from the British Library

ISBN: 978-1-032-48042-8 (hbk)
ISBN: 978-1-032-48046-6 (pbk)
ISBN: 978-1-003-38711-4 (ebk)

DOI: 10.4324/9781003387114

Typeset in Times New Roman
by Apex CoVantage, LLC

Contents

List of Figures vii
Note on Contributors viii
Preface xi

Introduction: Inequality—A Multifaceted Phenomenon 1
MATS LUNDAHL, DANIEL RAUHUT AND NEELAMBAR HATTI

PART I
Manifestations of Inequalities

1 **The Late Encounter of Inequality and Class** 19
  GÖRAN THERBORN

2 **Gender Inequalities: Progress and Challenges** 33
  ROMANE FRECHEVILLE-FAUCON, MAGALI JAOUL-GRAMMARE AND
  FAUSTINE PERRIN

PART II
Inequalities in Income and Wealth

3 **Piketty and the Distribution of Wealth** 59
  JESPER ROINE

4 **J.K. Galbraith and Inequality: From Confidence to Misanthropy** 75
  BENNY CARLSON

5 **Atkinson on Inequality** 95
  ARNE BIGSTEN

PART III
Discrimination, Plunder, and Inequalities

6 **Discrimination as a Determinant of Economic Inequality** 115
   ALI AHMED, MATS LUNDAHL AND ESKIL WADENSJÖ

7 **The Predatory State: A Case of Extreme Inequality** 137
   MATS LUNDAHL

PART IV
Geographical Inequalities

8 **Regional Inequalities** 157
   DANIEL RAUHUT AND ALOIS HUMER

9 **Housing and Inequality: The Case of Portugal** 173
   SÓNIA ALVES AND PEDRO GUIMARÃES

10 **Liberty, Equality, Fraternity, and Globalization** 191
   ARNE BIGSTEN

   Index *207*

Figures

1.1	Frequency of 'inequality' as a keyword in English-language books, 1800–2019	20
1.2	Frequency of 'class' as a keyword in English-language books, 1800–2019	21
1.3	The Inegalitarian Turn from the 1970s. Shares of national income of the top 1 percent and the bottom half of the adult population in the United States	27
2.1	Gender perception of occupations	39
2.2	Part-time job in EU28, 2002–2022	40
2.3	Employment by the number of children in EU28, 2009–2022	41
2.4	Average weekly hours spent in childcare, 2016	43
2.5	Men and women at risk poverty in 14 EU countries, 2020	46
3.1	Top one income share in 20 countries 1870–2010. A U-shaped development over the 20th century due to fluctuations in capital (at least in the first half of the century)	63
3.2	The income share of the P90–99 group, relatively flat over the 20th century due to capital incomes being less important than for the very top	64
8.1	Two-dimensional ranking of services of general interest and Maslow's hierarchy of needs	167
9.1	Temporal segmentation of housing policies in Portugal	178
10.1	Four policy dimensions	193

Note on Contributors

Ali Ahmed is Professor of Economics at Linköping University, Sweden, and serves as Researcher at the Ratio Institute in Stockholm. His work is predominantly centered on the economics of discrimination, focusing on the unequal treatment of vulnerable groups in various markets and societal contexts. Ahmed primarily employs experimental methods in his research, including field, online, and lab experiments. His research interests extend beyond discrimination to include behavioral economics, financial economics, Islamic economics, the economics of religion, and sustainable development economics. Ahmed's interdisciplinary approach has led to his research being published in a diverse array of journals within the fields of economics, psychology, and sociology.

Sónia Alves holds a BSc in Geography, a master's degree in Urban Planning, and a PhD in Sociology. She is Research Fellow at the Institute of Social Sciences of University of Lisbon, Lisbon, Portugal, and Visiting Researcher at BUILD—the Department of the Built Environment, Aalborg University, Aalborg, Denmark. Her research is guided by several overarching and often intersecting themes in the fields of human geography, housing policy, and urban planning—fields that offer perspectives necessary for grasping a complex reality.

Arne Bigsten is Professor Emeritus of Development Economics at the School of Business Economics and Law at the University of Gothenburg, Gothenburg, Sweden. His research has concerned poverty and income distribution, trade and globalization, industrial development, foreign aid, and institutional reform. He has been Visiting Professor at universities of Oxford, Nairobi, Keio, New South Wales, and Auvergnes and has done work for the World Bank, United Nations, Sida, WIDER, OECD, African Development Bank, EU, UNIDO, and the IMF. He has published a dozen books and numerous articles, mainly on African economic development.

Benny Carlson is Professor Emeritus of Economic History at the Lund University School of Economics and Management, Sweden. His fields of interest include the history of economic ideas, the spread of economic and social ideas, mainly between the United States, Germany, and Sweden, and the economic and social integration of immigrants in a comparative perspective, mainly involving the United States, Canada, Great Britain, and Sweden.

Note on Contributors ix

Romane Frecheville-Faucon is a PhD candidate at the Bureau of Theoretical and Applied Economics (BETA) at the University of Strasbourg, Strasbourg, France. Her research interests focus on the impact of the state on women's economic independence. Specifically, she examines the impact of public services and public employment on women's access to the labor market and their precariousness in Europe.

Pedro Guimarães is Assistant Professor at the Institute of Geography and Spatial Planning of the University of Lisbon. He is co-coordinator of the ZOE—(Urban and Regional Dynamics and Policies) research group at the University of Lisbon's Centre for Geographical Studies. His research explores processes of urban transformation, with a nonexclusive focus on the interaction of the commercial sector and urban dynamics. With several publications in international journals, he was awarded the University of Lisbon/Caixa Geral de Depósitos Scientific Prize 2021 in the scientific area of Geography and Territory.

Neelambar Hatti is Professor Emeritus, School of Economics and Management, Lund University, Sweden. His research interests include gender issues, institutions, growth, trade, decentralization, poverty, and corruption. Among his publications are 25 volumes on new world order (1987–2007), jointly edited with Hans Singer and Rameshwar Tandon. His other publications include *Unwanted Daughters: Gender Discrimination in Modern India* (2011), (coedited with T. V. Sekher and Hans Singer) and *Politics and Poverty of Politics* (2018) (coedited with Daniel Rauhut). More recently, he has coauthored several studies with Rameshwar Tandon and Krishnaswamy Hariharan: *Control of Resources* (2017), *Globalization Syndrome* (2017), *Third World Perspectives on Technology* (2018), *Trade Policy for the Third World* (2018), *International Monetary Interdependence in the New Century* (2019), and *Trade in Services in the New Century* (2020).

Alois Humer holds a doctorate in Geography/Regional Research and Regional Planning from the University of Vienna, Vienna, Austria. He is leading a working group at the Institute for Urban and Regional Research at the Austrian Academy of Sciences. Before that, he was leading another working group at the University of Vienna (2020–2023). He has been Fellow, for example, at Aalto University in Finland (2017–2020). Since 2018, he is a senior expert of the European Commission in the field of Regional and Urban Policy. His interests include geography of welfare policies and European regional development.

Magali Jaoul-Grammare is CNRS Research Fellow at the BETA Laboratory (Bureau d'Economie Théorique et Appliquée) at the University of Strasbourg. Her research topics are cliometrics and economics of education. She is particularly interested in gender and social inequalities in educational pathways and their impact on the labor market and economic growth. Her analysis focuses on France in the 19th and 20th centuries.

Mats Lundahl is Professor Emeritus of Development Economics at the Stockholm School of Economics, Stockholm, Sweden. Among his research fields are development economics, international economics, agricultural economics, economics of discrimination, economic history, political economy, economic biography, history of economic doctrines, and music. Lundahl has written or edited 81 books.

Faustine Perrin is Associate Professor at the Department of Economic History at Lund University School of Economics and Management, Lund, Sweden. Her research interests focus on understanding the long-run development process with a particular focus on the role played by female empowerment and gender equality. She has worked extensively on the dynamics of human capital accumulation and the fertility transition within the French context. She has also worked on various research projects focusing on the interplay between gender equality and economic development within the Swedish context.

Daniel Rauhut is Associate Professor and holds a PhD in Economic History at Lund University. He has worked as Senior Lecturer and Researcher at Swedish, Norwegian, and Finnish universities and research institutes and is currently affiliated Researcher at the University of Lisbon, Portugal, and University of Karlstad, Sweden. Rauhut has participated in many EU-funded research projects on, for example, migration, social welfare, and regional development, and his research interests cover issues related to ideas on poverty and inequality, social welfare, as well as to economic thought.

Jesper Roine is Adjunct Professor of Economics at the Stockholm School of Economics and Deputy Director of the Stockholm Institute of Transition Economics (SITE), Stockholm, Sweden. His main research field is long-run income and wealth inequality, and he has published several articles in international journals in this field, including the *Handbook of Income Distribution* chapter on 'Long Run Trends in the Distribution of Income and Wealth'. He has also written a summary and guide to Thomas Piketty's *Capital in the Twenty-First Century*.

Göran Therborn is Professor Emeritus of Sociology at the University of Cambridge, Cambridge, the UK, and Affiliated Professor of Sociology, Linnaeus University, Sweden. He has pursued a range of research interests, and his works have appeared in 25 languages. His publications include *The Ideology of Power and the Power of Ideology* (1980), *Why Some Peoples Are More Unemployed than Others (1986)*, *European Modernity and Beyond* (1995), *Between Sex and Power. Family in the World, 1900–2000* (2004), *The Killing Fields of Inequality (2013)*, *Cities of Power* (2017), and *Inequality and the Labyrinths of Democracy* (2020).

Eskil Wadensjö is Professor of Economics at the Swedish Institute for Social Research (SOFI), Stockholm University, since 1980. He was Dean of the Faculty of Social Sciences 1996–2005; has been member of several governmental commissions in Sweden; and contributed with studies for EU, ILO, OECD, the Nordic Council, and the European Council. He was president of the Swedish Economic Association 1992–1993 and of the European Association of Labour Economists 1993–1999. His research interests are the economics of migration, labor economics, and social policy. Current research topics are the effects of immigration, discrimination, unaccompanied refugee minors, integration of migrants, occupational insurances, older workers' retirement, and the youth labor market. He has published many articles, books, and chapters in books.

Preface

The present volume, *Inequality: Economic and Social Perspectives*, is a companion volume to our *Poverty in the History of Economic Thought: From Mercantilism to Neoclassical Economics* (2020) and *Poverty in Contemporary Economic Thought* (2021), both published by Routledge. In the previous two volumes, we discussed how economists have analyzed poverty, its causes and cures, during different epochs. However, since the mid-20th century, the focus to a large extent has shifted from poverty to economic inequality. Differences of class, gender, ethnicity, and geographical locations all affect the chances of individuals in life and the degree of inequality that they may experience. Therefore, in the present volume, we discuss both single economists and their contributions and different aspects of class, gender, ethnicity and geographical location, and how these are related to economic inequalities.

We would like to thank the contributors for their effort. Working with them has been the most stimulating experience for us as editors. We also want to thank Andy Humphries for his patience and support during the different stages of the process from the first idea of the book to the final product, together with the Routledge production team. Once again, working with you has been a great pleasure.

We hope that the present volume will constitute an easy and accessible introduction to some of the different aspects of inequality and how these can be analyzed by economists and other social scientists.

Mats Lundahl
Daniel Rauhut
Neelambar Hatti
Stockholm and Lund, 30 November 2023

Introduction

Inequality—A Multifaceted Phenomenon

Mats Lundahl, Daniel Rauhut and Neelambar Hatti

The history of mankind has been characterized by various forms of scarcity (see Albritton Jonsson and Wennerlind, 2023 for a history of the capitalist period), and the perennial companion of scarcity has been inequality. Since time immemorial, elites have used various means, from ancient religions to modern philosophies, to legitimize inequalities within and across societies. This is an issue which is extremely important also in our own time since you often hear that '[a]cross the globe, especially in the wealthy economies of the West, the gap between the rich and the rest has widened year after year' (Milanović, 2023, p. 78). This statement, however, is true with modifications. While income equalities have increased *within* countries in recent decades, the extent or inequality *between countries* has decreased (Drèze and Sen, 2013; Milanović, 2023). If you take a 200-year perspective, however, the picture is the opposite one: an enormous increase of the income inequality *between* nations but possibly a decrease *within* nations, altogether an increased inequality between all the people in the world, to be set against a steady decrease of the number of people living in absolute poverty, that is, a defined minimum income level, in the world (Roine, 2023, pp. 138–139).

To complicate matters further, the inequality concept is far from clear-cut. Inequality can be measured in a variety of ways. Nor is the border line between positive and normative aspects clear. Is the issue one of what the world looks like or what it ought to look like? What causes inequality, and which are its consequences? Once you start to think about it, inequality as a study object quickly becomes almost immense.

It is difficult to say where the world is heading. The struggle against inequality is, however, not an impossible one. You cannot deny the existence of mechanisms that tend to uphold and increase inequality, as the essays in the present book demonstrate, but there are also mechanisms that can be used to close the gap between rich and poor, as demonstrated for example by the recent works by Joseph Stiglitz (2012), Thomas Piketty (2014, 2020, 2022), Anthony Atkinson (2015) and Daron Acemoglu and Simon Johnson (2023), respectively. Inequality issues are acquiring increased importance, as manifested in the decision of the Royal Swedish Academy of Sciences to award the 2023 Sveriges Riksbank Prize in Economic Sciences in Memory of Alfred Nobel to Claudia Goldin for her work on the economics of gender labor market inequality (Committee, 2023).

While inequalities are usually measured in economic terms, by income or wealth, they are determined by a host of noneconomic factors as well—gender, age, origin, ethnicity, disability, sexual orientation, class, religion, and place, and not least by political factors (Atkinson, 1984). How do governments perceive inequality problems and what do they do about it? These factors lead to inequalities of opportunity, which continue to persist, within and between countries. Inequality has increased in most countries over the past three decades, and in some parts of the world, these divides have become very pronounced. In many cases, there has been a particularly sharp increase in income concentration at the top end of the distribution. Wealth concentration at the top end of the distribution is still more acute—on average roughly twice as high as the concentration of income. Trends in income distribution are more mixed across emerging economies, but many of them have also experienced rising inequality over the same period (Piketty, 2014).

Moreover, the common procedure to use income as a proxy variable when quantifying social inequality has some implications. To contend that the only way to create a socially just society, that is, a society without any social inequality, is to ensure that people have the same incomes is a highly ideological statement, which is questioned, and challenged, by all those not sharing these ideological premises (Rauhut, 2011). However, the measurements and impacts of inequality go beyond income and purchasing power. Inequalities of opportunity affect a person's life expectancy and access to basic services such as health care, education, water and sanitation. They can curtail a person's human rights through discrimination, abuse and lack of access to justice. High levels of inequality of opportunity discourage skill accumulation, choke economic and social mobility and human development and, consequently, depress economic growth. Inequality also entrenches uncertainty, vulnerability and insecurity; undermines trust in institutions and government and increases social discord and tensions and trigger violence and conflicts (Drèze and Sen, 2013; Milanović, 2023).

During the last two centuries, inherited wealth has grown faster than earned wealth, which makes inequality develop in the wrong direction. This stimulates a society, where the preferred path to wealth is inheritance or marriage rather than labor (Piketty, 2014). A basic criterion for a just society is that all members of the community should have the same opportunities and all members of the community should be treated equally (Rawls, 2001). The findings by Thomas Piketty (2014) suggest that society is moving away from a labor-based path to wealth and instead favors a nepotistic path. Indeed, this will increase economic and other inequalities. However, Thomas Sowell (2016) notes, from his conservative position, that social disparities do not *per se* equal social inequalities or social injustices. Disparities in opportunities should be fought, as they generate inequalities as well as injustices, but to use affirmative action programs or income distribution schemes will exacerbate the problems; affirmative action programs will discriminate more qualified candidates and income distribution schemes through progressive taxation penalize the hard-working.

Is this necessarily true and desirable? As shown in the two and a half dozen essays in Blanchard and Rodrik (2021), an anthology which concentrates on how to combat inequality, this is often taken for granted. Not all scholars, however, think of inequality as being necessarily bad. For example, the Hindu philosopher Swami Vivekananda (1863–1902) argued that the proposition of equality between all of mankind was untenable. It was nothing but a fanatical millenarian idea which could make people work harder in anticipation of a better tomorrow, but true equality had never existed and would never exist on the earth. Vivekananda contrasted it with the Hindu insistence that all men are different and constitute 'unity in variety', an idea embodied in the caste system (Sharma, 2013, pp. 141–142). 'Unity', he writes, 'is before creation, diversity is creation. Now if this diversity stops, creation will be destroyed' (cited by Sharma, 2013, p. 176). The formative forces of nature manifest themselves through 'struggle, competition and conflict' (Sharma, 2013, p. 142).

Vivekananda is, of course, not alone. It does not take any 'Eastern mystique' to defend inequality. Materialist arguments do the trick too. It just depends on how you think about it. Thus, Adam Smith argues that social inequality may make people work harder to become better off, that is, social inequality is an incentive to change the life of the individual (Rauhut, 2021a). The 1998 Nobel Laureate, Amartya Sen, advances a similar argument but emphasizes that opportunities to change his/her life should be open to all individuals, not just to those privileged. This is an idea highly influenced by the social liberal philosopher John Rawls and his thoughts about social justice and public reasoning (Rauhut and Hatti, 2021). However, as the unprivileged and poor always will outnumber the privileged and rich, social inequality may also trigger greed and the ambition to soak the rich (Bengtsson and Rauhut, 2021). Seen from this perspective, the strive to fight inequality is accompanied by redistribution schemes which prolong poverty and dependencies of lagging groups (Sowell, 2016, 2019). From a libertarian perspective, a forced redistribution of incomes through the tax system will not counteract social inequality (Nozick, 1974). Such a perspective clashes with the prescription to fight inequality suggested by, for example Piketty (2014), where progressive income taxes and higher taxes on capital incomes and fortunes are seen as instruments to weed out inequality over time.

When you discuss inequality, it is necessary to define why inequality is wrong. We must also clarify whether we want to reduce inequality because it is bad in itself or because the consequences of inequality are bad. Moreover, we must be clear about whether there is an objectionable inequality and an unobjectionable inequality, that is, there may be inequalities that are acceptable under some circumstances while some inequalities can never be acceptable. In a Rawlsian perspective, an increase of inequality should lead to attempts to improve the well-being of those worst off in society (Van Parijs, 2021). Just increasing the incomes of the poor will not reduce inequality; you must address inequality with other than simple income measures as well and focus on equity instead (Scanlon, 2021). Other analysts advocate radical interventions. The state should regulate different markets to ensure that different groups have equal access to services, welfare, education, work, etc. (Allen, 2021). From Sen's perspective, social inequalities are unobjectionable while inequalities in opportunities are objectionable (Rauhut and Hatti, 2005, 2021). Of course, behind these different strategies, we find different political ideologies (Rauhut, 2011).

Aim and Scope of the Volume

The point of departure of the suggested volume is economic inequality, as measured by differences in incomes and wealth. All the chapters relate to this fact. The book is about economics—about how the economy is shaped in such a way as to generate differences in economic and social welfare between individuals, regions and nations. However, as should be clear from the foregoing, when it comes to the causes and expressions of these differences, we feel that the attention cannot be limited simply to economics.

Inequality is a many-faceted phenomenon that manifests itself in several ways. Income and wealth differences are one—arguably the most important one—but far from the only one. Hence, the suggested volume adopts a somewhat eclectic approach—intentionally so—to highlight different characteristics and causes of inequality: an approach that attempts to extend the economic perspective to include several factors that complement and interact with the economy.

The purpose is not to try to be exhaustive. That would require a major 'handbook' effort, something which is outside our scope. Instead, what we attempt to do is to illustrate the very fact that inequality is a phenomenon which cannot be isolated to one or a couple of dimensions. By presenting a selected number of different approaches with roots in different parts of the vast field of social science, we want to point to the complementarity of various types of analysis. This is important not least from the policy point of view. We stress the multidimensionality of the phenomenon of inequality, a complication which is necessary to come to grips with if you want to narrow the differences between the well-to-do and those less well off. If you want to design efficient tools to combat and reduce inequality, it is important to grasp all the relevant components of the particular situation and not fall back upon more or less mechanically conceived solutions based on a merely partial analysis, likely to generate effects that differ from those intended by the policymaker.

The Contributions

The book begins with a section that highlights some of the 'traditional' features of inequality: class and gender. The second section deals with the manifestation of inequality in terms of incomes and wealth differences. Thereafter, we turn to the causes of inequality. The third section explores the effects of discrimination and plunder (by those in power). The final section serves to drive home the point that geographic and institutional factors have an important place as well when it comes to shedding light on what equality is, how it manifests itself and which its consequences are.

Manifestations of Inequalities

In his chapter on the fundamental issue of class and inequalities, *Göran Therborn* notes that the concepts of class and inequality are not as intimately related as one may think. They belong to different semantic fields—fields which were kept apart during most of the 20th century. The respective frequencies of their use in the English-language literature since 1800 describe two curves which do not coincide at all. Therborn traces the use of the equality/inequality dichotomy back to the American, French and Haitian revolutions of the late 18th century and its roots in Christianity, naturalist anthropology and the articulation of individuality in the free trade doctrine. Socioeconomic inequality, however, remained secondary to political, legal and gender inequality until very recently. Even the rise of capitalism and worker organization failed to trigger much interest in it. The concept of class, in turn, began to be used in 17th- and 18th-century France. It was used by French economists and spread to British colleagues like Adam Smith and David Ricardo. Gradually, the term made it into the political language of the 19th century.

Therborn notes the absence of both class and inequality in post-World War II sociology and the substitution of terms which dodged the class issue as well as the reaction against this by later sociologists. The resurrection of inequality studies has not come from sociology but from economics, notably from the works of Amartya Sen. However, Therborn points to a neglected contribution by the Swedish sociologist Walter Korpi, which interprets politics in the Western democracies as class struggle, a struggle between labor and capital which decides the mix of egalitarian and inegalitarian policies and hence the extent of inequality. Contrasting the fields of class and inequality, he also backtracks to Marx' analysis in the *Critique of the Gotha Programme* which he relates to modern, Neo-Marxist, approaches.

The rediscovery of inequality as a research topic began with the recognition of persistent poverty in the United States and Western Europe in the mid-1960s, but the topic was pushed into the background for a couple of decades from 1980, when neoliberal economic policies were introduced in the West. As the income gap between the rich and the poor widened, however, inequality has again become a 'hot' topic, and several economists, above all Thomas Piketty, have begun to connect the notion with that of class.

The chapter by *Romane Frecheville-Faucon, Magali Jaoul-Grammare*, and *Faustine Perrin* offers a comprehensive overview of gender inequalities prevalent during the 20th and 21st centuries. By gaining a comprehensive understanding of gender inequalities and taking active measures to address them, societies can strive toward being a more inclusive and egalitarian society and foster sustainable and prosperous developments for all. By empowering women and girls and ensuring their equal participation in the workforce and in decision-making processes, societies can unleash their full potential and reap the benefits of their talents and contributions. In turn, this will combat inequalities based on gender.

The chapter highlights the strides made through the implementation of legal frameworks and policies. Efforts to address gender inequalities and promote equality have been made throughout the past century. The expansion of women's rights, educational opportunities, and career advancements has played a pivotal role in reducing gender disparities. However, despite these positive developments, formidable obstacles remain that impede the achievement of complete gender equality and leaving women susceptible to adverse consequences in their daily lives and render them more vulnerable to economic shocks.

Although the women's rights movement has made significant strides in the past, there are still numerous areas where women face disadvantages. Various aspects of contemporary society contribute to the perpetuation of gender inequalities, manifested in unequal pay, limited employment opportunities for women, discriminatory practices and persistence of gender stereotypes. The chapter shows that while gender inequalities have decreased substantially during these periods, there are persistent barriers that continue to hinder further progress.

Inequalities in Income and Wealth

The starting point for Jesper Roine's discussion of Thomas Piketty's approach to inequality is that inequality is too often measured simply in terms of income, while the wealth component is forgotten. However, as Piketty has stressed, inequality has both a flow and a stock dimension. This observation constitutes the foundation of his monumental *Capital in the Twenty-First Century* (Piketty, 2014). Piketty was, of course, not the first economist to note that household incomes consist of both earned (labor) income and the return on the capital assets owned by the household. However, the initiation of the so-called top income project by Piketty and Anthony Atkinson at the beginning of the new millennium made it possible to trace the development of the share of the national income earned by the top income earners. A U-shaped pattern emerged, with a declining share over the first half of the 20th century followed by a flattening-out and a rise from around 1980, a finding which was related to the relatively high importance of capital incomes in the highest bracket, although the pattern differs between countries.

Roine summarizes the main contents of *Capital in the Twenty-First Century*. He notes Piketty's definition of capital as all assets owned by the households. No distinction is made between capital and wealth. Roine explains how Piketty arrives at the conclusion that the share of capital income increases over time and that the role of inheritance increases along with the importance of capital. Finally, he presents Piketty's suggestion of how an efficient tax on capital should be designed.

Finally, Roine examines the main criticisms against Piketty's views—against the theoretical framework, the interpretation of data and the role of capital itself— as well as Piketty's response to his critics. In the end, he concludes that the role of capital in the creation of inequality is contested, but Piketty must be credited for having brought it into the center of the debate—a debate which is likely to go on for a long time to come.

Benny Carlson examines John Kenneth Galbraith's views of inequality. Galbraith was a heterodox economist, so it does not come as a surprise that he would tackle the unfashionable inequality theme. Focusing on three of his main books, *The Affluent Society* (Galbraith, 1958), *Economics and the Public Purpose* (Galbraith, 1974) and *The Culture of Contentment* (Galbraith, 1992), Carlson traces how his views changed over time. In *The Affluent Society*, Galbraith singles out the distribution of income as the most important issue to be dealt with in modern society. He questions the conventional wisdom about what causes income differences and stresses that after World War II, little had been done to reduce them. The issue of productivity had overshadowed that of redistribution. He also emphasized the need for more public goods at the expense of private consumption.

In *The New Industrial State*, the emphasis is on the role of the large multinational corporations and their cooperation with governments in the industrial countries, while the importance of inequalities was played down. Seven years later, however, Galbraith would come back to the theme in *Economics and the Public Purpose*. There, he divided enterprises into two groups, on the one hand the small firms working in a competitive environment and, on the other hand, the large corporations able to control both the market and the state: a division which accounted for a lot of the inequality observed in society. The bargaining power of the former group had to be increased, and Galbraith sketches a recipe for how the economic policy should be reshaped to reduce inequality.

In 1992, in *The Culture of Contentment*, Galbraith struck out against the *laissez-faire* policies of Ronald Reagan and George W.H. Bush—policies that had only served to increase the gap between the well-to-do and those with lower incomes. He did not endorse the idea that lower taxes for high-income earners would benefit those lower down in society. Nor would growth do the trick. On the contrary, what was needed to come to grips with poverty and inequality was progressive taxation and public expenditure. However, as Galbraith saw it, the willingness to undertake such measures was low indeed. It would take a major military or economic failure to change the mood.

Anthony Atkinson's work on inequality covers both theory and empirical studies. All of it is surveyed by *Arne Bigsten*. Atkinson held that inequality issues had been unduly marginalized in economics and fought hard to bring them in again. Inequality was intrinsically related to justice, and a deeper understanding of it could contribute to the solution of social problems. However, it was important to measure it correctly. To this end, Atkinson, in 1970, developed his own measure, what became known as the Atkinson index, based on a social welfare function, a measure that would have a profound impact on later inequality studies.

Atkinson mapped the development of inequality within countries over time, but he was also interested in global inequality and poverty. Acknowledging that measurements were necessarily imperfect, he argued that there was still enough knowledge to make action possible. For this, however, you also had to understand what causes inequality. Historical episodes were important, but theory was needed as well. Unfortunately, no unified approach exists, so, given the exact problem to be dealt with, different types of models have to be compared.

The main reason for studying inequality is to find ways of reducing it. Atkinson devoted considerable energy to the design of policies for this within the context of the welfare state, notably on not only the design of tax systems but also methods for counteracting undesirable effects of technological change and reducing unemployment, increasing the equality of capital ownership, universal social security coverage and the introduction of a basic income for all the desirability of international solidarity: the case for international development aid. Altogether, Anthony Atkinson devoted a lifetime to the understanding and combat of inequality, the subject that he thought should be regarded of the core of economics.

Discrimination, Plunder, and Inequalities

That discrimination contributes to inequality goes without saying. In their chapter, *Ali Ahmed, Mats Lundahl* and *Eskil Wadensjö* examine how economic theory can be used to unearth the mechanisms to produce discrimination, to identify the winners and losers from it and to construct recipes for the eradication of discrimination. They stress the fact that economics is far from being a unified social science, and hence the need to apply different theories as different situations call for it. Two notorious cases are examined: the South African apartheid system and the American discrimination of blacks by whites. The chapter ends with an examination of a number of contemporary cases of ethnic discrimination of minorities.

The apartheid system lends itself well to the application of disaggregated neoclassical general equilibrium analysis, since this permits the identification of the main actors in the economy in a long-term perspective. The analysis takes place in three stages. The first one extends from the arrival of the Dutch in the Cape area to the mineral discoveries in the late 19th century, when the Europeans deprived the Africans of their land. The second one deals with the increased demand for labor in the European sector of the economy as a result of the rush for diamonds and gold and the attempts of white workers and farmers to minimize the competition of Africans for mining jobs. The third and last period analyses the twofold attempt to keep Africans out of skilled jobs on the one hand and of reducing the influx of them to white areas on the other.

The second case highlighted by Ahmed, Lundahl and Wadensjö is that of race discrimination in the United States, viewed notably through the eyes of Gunnar Myrdal (1944) in his monumental *An American Dilemma*. There, Myrdal applies an unconventional interdisciplinary approach, based on the rejection of the static and comparative static equilibrium concept, where the dynamic interaction of a wide array of economic, social and political factors produces a circular, cumulative spiral which either serves to produce discrimination and a low standard of living for blacks or sends society off in the opposite direction, in a positive cumulative movement which improves their situation and reduces the prejudices that foster discrimination. Myrdal's book proved instrumental in the political struggle for black civil rights, but racial discrimination did not come to a complete end, which calls for the continued examination, with the aid of different theories, of above all the racial situation in the US labor market.

Discrimination, unfortunately, is not just a thing of the past. The phenomenon is still with us today. Ahmed, Lundahl and Wadensjö exemplify this sad fact by pointing to the experiences of the Rohingya in Myanmar, the Uyghurs in China, the Dalits in India, Palestinians, and women in Afghanistan. These cases all reveal patterns of racial, ethnic and gender-based oppression, and they all reveal mechanisms which resemble those of the systemic discrimination in South Africa and the United States dealt with here.

A predatory state is a state where the ruler (or the ruling clique) attempts to maximize his private income by preying on the citizens. *Mats Lundahl* lists several historical instances of predatory rule, a phenomenon which tends to be ubiquitous both in time and in space, most recently and most forcefully manifested by Vladimir Putin's Russia. He presents some statistics which point to extreme concentration of income and wealth in the hands of kleptocrats. Kleptocratic regimes rest on the redistribution from the prey to the predators, to the detriment of growth. To be able to rob the citizens, the ruler must remain in power. For this, he needs help. He must determine how many should be allowed to share the spoils. There is, however, a trade-off between income and security. The former can only be increased at the expense of the latter and vice versa, which in turn makes it attractive to invent devices which can shift the trade-off in such a way as to make for more of both: obfuscation, 'ideologies' concocted to mobilize the support of the citizens, as well as outright repression.

The methods of predation rest on control of the state apparatus, notably of taxation. The tax system is devised to maximize revenue and hence favors taxes whose collection costs are low, like taxes on foreign trade, debasement of the currency, tax farming and of course outright confiscation and blackmail. The state may also be involved in smuggling and illegal trade. Alternatively, borrowing is resorted to, abroad or at home. Developing country kleptocratic regimes attempt to get as much foreign aid as possible. The use of government revenue is not revealed. Explicit budgeting is avoided. Public and private companies are milked for funds.

Predation has negative effects on the economy. Most important in the present context is that it concentrates incomes and wealth to a small minority. Efficiency and growth suffer when the allocation criteria used are biased in favor of activities that further the interests of the latter. The economy becomes more informal since the citizens attempt to avoid being robbed by not revealing their activities.

Geographical Inequalities

Regional inequalities and how they may materialize are discussed by *Daniel Rauhut* and *Alois Humer*. They discuss three regions, all in the backwaters of economic growth and prosperity, and how the geographical location affects the increasing gap between the 'urban' or 'metropolitan' regions, on the one hand, and side, rural, remote and peripheral regions, on the other. A person's life chances and quality of life depend on social class distinctions but even more so on the region where he or she grew up. The starting point when discussing regional inequality is always the urban and metropolitan regions, that is, the situation in the other regions is compared to the situation in the urban or metropolitan regions. How disrupting these inequality problems and challenges are from a geographical perspective depends on where the boundaries between different types of territory are drawn when analyzing inequality in a regional perspective.

The problematization of regional inequalities has usually gone hand in hand with the legitimization and/or delegitimization of some political powers, especially when 'justice' is related to such issues as regional development, production and accessibility of welfare services and infrastructure, as well as public participation. The marketization of welfare services and infrastructure as well as public sector retrenchment in advanced economies hit mainly weak regions. The market cannot make a profit in peripheral, remote and lagging regions; the 'third sector' cannot accumulate sufficient money for investments and hence is unable to meet the needs of the population. Rauhut and Humer conclude that if the state cannot level out regional disparities, who will?

Rauhut and Humer link their argument to an argument which the Swedish economist Gunnar Myrdal put forward in the 1950s. He argued that economically expanding regions will attract capital and labor from lagging regions; investments are made in prosperous regions simply because investments have been made there before and the migrants are in their prime working age with attractive human capital and skills. Lagging regions, on the other hand, will drop behind even further as the flow of human resources and capital tends to favor the more prosperous regions. In other words, polarization between regions will increase (Lundahl, 2021b) and so will the inequality at the individual level in the lagging regions.

In their contribution, *Sónia Alves* and *Pedro Guimarães* discuss inequality in housing, using Portugal as an example. The mechanisms underlying the increased housing inequality and housing segregation are discussed together with the efficiency of the policy measures launched to address these problems. A central theme within the policy studies literature, including that on housing policy, has been how to come to grips with how problems are understood, defined and shaped in processes of agenda-setting, asking what impacts policy design choices have (in terms of beneficiaries and tools)—and specifically whether they reinforce or mitigate inequality within both residential space and society as a whole.

The analysis shows that housing subsidies and social housing programs have been in existence for over a century but that they have emerged because of different housing models derived from policy agendas and policy goals belonging to different political regimes (both authoritarian and democratic) and political parties (both left- and right-wing). Although social housing, rent controls, etc., have helped to respond to chronic housing crises, and addressed problematic housing costs, the coverage and efficiency have varied significantly. Some groups have been excluded from support that has been made conditional on income or other criteria (such as behavior).

One could expect that different governments, with different ideological directions, would have addressed the housing inequality in different ways. However, Alves and Guimarães conclude that the policies to stimulate housing construction have failed under most governments. Instead, an unequal distribution of housing subsidies and opportunities to obtain housing has prevailed, which has had a negative impact on equality and social cohesion.

In the final chapter, *Arne Bigsten* discusses inequality in the context of the increased globalization of recent decades. His yardstick is that of the French Revolution: liberty, equality and fraternity, and he analyzes the changes of global inequality and their impact on feelings of freedom, national and international fraternity. Bigsten's point of departure for the discussion of changes in inequality is Branko Milanović's (2016) analysis of the factors behind increased inequality within countries in the West from around 1980 as well as the determinants of inequality between countries from the mid-20th century. He poses the question whether freedom is threatened. Unfortunately, the answer may be 'Yes', since almost three-fourths of the world population lives in autocracies. The outlook for fraternity is not too bright either. Increased populism in Western countries has contributed to an increased tension between globalists and nationalists. The old national cohesion has eroded.

The increased inequality in the age of globalization poses strong policy challenges. International trade has potentially welfare-enhancing effects, but for these to materialize, those who lose must be compensated. Trade must be made competitive and not subservient to national political interests. Migration is even more difficult to handle. No mechanisms exist for compensating the losers, and the issue is highly politically charged. Financial globalization is also difficult to regulate in a meaningful way since countries tend to compete instead of cooperating. Finally, the positive effects of globalization tend to be concentrated to urban agglomeration while rural areas may suffer.

The resistance to globalization has largely come from populist groups who feel that they have not made any gains and that the winners are elite groups who have furthermore been able to manipulate the political machinery, and these groups have gained strength in recent years. This calls for the construction of institutions and mechanisms that can deal with the negative side of globalization and bring people together instead of polarizing them.

What Can We Learn?

Inequality has been a persistent issue throughout human history, and it has been a subject of interest for economists since the birth of political economy as an independent discipline. The question of inequality is multifaceted and has been approached from different perspectives by different schools of economic thought. The classical school of economics, which includes, for example, Adam Smith (Rauhut, 2021a), David Ricardo (Gehrke, 2021) and John Stuart Mill (Rauhut, 2021b), believed that the market mechanism tends to reduce inequalities. The classics argued that the invisible hand of the market ensures that resources are allocated efficiently and lead to economic growth and prosperity. However, Karl Marx, a vehement critic of capitalism, contended that capitalism inevitably leads to greater inequality. He believed that the bourgeoisie exploits the proletariat by extracting surplus value from their labor (Lönnroth, 2021).

Toward the end of the 19th century and the beginning of the 20th century, neoclassical economics emerged as a dominant school of thought. Economists such as Alfred Marshall, Knut Wicksell, Gustav Cassel and Eli Heckscher focused on poverty rather than on inequality. Society had an obligation to fight poverty but not inequalities (Olsson, 2021; Lundahl, 2021a; Carlson, 2021a, 2021b). Later conservative economists, such as Milton Friedman and Friedrich Hayek, believed in the efficiency of markets and advocated minimal government intervention in the economy. They argued that free markets lead to optimal outcomes and that government intervention distorts market signals (Bengtsson and Rauhut, 2021; Backhouse, 1991). In this context, the New Welfare Economics school can be mentioned as well (Bergh, 2021).

However, the 2008 financial crisis exposed some limitations of neoclassical economics. The crisis was caused by excessive risk-taking by financial institutions and inadequate regulation by governments (Piketty, 2014). It led to a loss of confidence in free markets and a renewed interest in alternative economic models (Milanović, 2023). Three such approaches are post-Keynesian economics, feminist economics and ecological economics. Heterodox economists argue that neoclassical economics is too narrow in its focus on efficiency and growth and neglects issues such as inequality, social justice and environmental sustainability. Institutional economics is also a part of the heterodox economics (Syll, 1999), and it discusses inequality aspects (Daniels, 2021).

Inequality is not only an economic issue but also a social and political one. High levels of inequality can lead to social unrest, political instability and reduced economic growth. Therefore, it is essential to address inequality through policies that promote social justice and equality of opportunity (Sen, 1973, 1998). The formulation of efficient policies in turn presupposes that the extent of inequality is measured correctly. It is not enough to look at flow variables—labor income—but stocks—capital—must be brought into the picture as well (Hatti and Rauhut, 2017).

The present work highlights the contributions of three leading modern economists, John Kenneth Galbraith, Anthony Atkinson and Thomas Piketty, who, following the example of their illustrious predecessors in different ways, have pointed to the continued importance of the inequality issue. They have provided methods for the measurement of inequality, for the analysis of the mechanisms which cause national and international economic and social differences and for the formulation of efficient policies to reduce the gap between the rich and the poor.

Our volume concentrates on the issue of equality and inequality, and most of the contributions deal with domestic inequalities of different kinds. However, it is important to be able to think of equality (and inequality) also as part of a larger setting. The concept of equality is intimately related also to the fellow fundamental human values of liberty and fraternity. What does the larger world that we are living in look like and how does it impact on the trinity at the bottom of the French Revolution? The world has shrunk. Globalization has become a bone of contention in recent decades. The movement of goods and factors across national borders has led to economic gains but has also produced losers; that is, it has created new inequalities, a fact that calls for the design of compensation mechanisms.

Mechanisms similar to the ones that produce inequalities between countries also create inequalities between geographical regions and between urban and rural areas within countries. Regions which from the outset have an advantage of some kind vis-à-vis other regions, and hence a higher income, frequently strengthen their relative position over time. It is no coincidence that Bertil Ohlin's (1933) monumental treatise on trade has the title *Interregional and International Trade*. Barring policy-induced impediments to international trade and factor movements, the mechanisms at work—increasing or decreasing the extent of inequality—are fundamentally the same.

Inequality manifests itself in different ways. Two of the most notorious contexts are gender and housing. The differential treatment of men and women runs like a thread through human history, more during earlier periods, but it still persists in our own time.

Substantial progress has been made in the struggle for equality, but many issues remain to be resolved. What should be obvious to everyone—the equality of the sexes—is still a controversial issue in contemporary society when it comes to practical action. The need for political action and formulation of efficient policies has not disappeared.

Housing is another obvious case of inequality and segregation. Programs designed to put an end to segregation in the housing market frequently fail, regardless of which the political constellation is that put them forward. Again, there is a need for a proper analysis of the causal mechanisms of segregation which may serve as the starting point for the design of adequate remedies.

The housing issue points directly to the more general problem of systematic discrimination of certain groups in society, not least racial discrimination, a phenomenon which tends to have disastrous effects for large groups of people. It is a phenomenon with many roots—some economic, others not. In the present volume, an effort has been made to demonstrate the usefulness of different types of economic theory in the analysis of both the causes and the effects of racial discrimination.

One of the most extreme forms of income inequalities is caused by plunder—plunder by the state or the ruler. Kleptocratic regimes have been one of the eternal companions of mankind, from Antiquity to the present. Vladimir Putin has a wide array of sources of inspiration to fall back upon. There seems to be virtually no end to the ingenuity when it comes to inventing new ways of cheating the citizens, which are systematically connected to the acquisition and retention of political power, and which have several negative effects on the economy at large and on the welfare of the citizens.

But, will the faithful Marxist argue: 'Isn't inequality simply a class issue?' The answer to that question is, however, not as clear-cut as it may seem. In the historical perspective, inequality and class have described very different trajectories. The two concepts have lived different 'lives', as it were. Surprisingly, it seems as if it is only in recent years that the two have been appearing together in a systematic fashion in the analytical literature.

The main purpose of the present volume has been to demonstrate that inequality is a multifaceted phenomenon which does not lend itself to an analysis in just a few dimensions. The number of ways to approach the mechanisms which produce it and the effects that they produce are large indeed. The vast majority of them are designed to focus on one or two particular aspects, and we are likely to see more such attempts in the future. No grand synthesis is in sight, which may be both a weakness and a strength. The overall picture is that of a jigsaw puzzle. We know a lot, we have an idea about what the picture might look like in the end, but we have not turned all the pieces yet.

References

Acemoglu, D., and Johnson, S. (2023). *Power and Progress: Our Thousand-Year Struggle Over Technology and Prosperity*. London: Basic Books.

Albritton Jonsson, F., and Wennerlind, C. (2023). *Scarcity: A History from the Origin of Capitalism to the Climate Crisis*. Cambridge, MA and London: Harvard University Press.

Allen, D. (2021). Time for New Philosophical Foundations for Economic Theory? In O. Blanchard and D. Rodrik (eds), *Combating Inequality: Rethinking Government's Role* (pp. 41–47). Cambridge, MA: MIT Press.

Atkinson, A.B. (1984). *The Economics of Inequality*. Oxford: Oxford University Press.

Atkinson, A.B. (2015). *Inequality*. Cambridge, MA: Harvard University Press.
Backhouse, R. (1991). *A History of Modern Economic Analysis*. Cambridge, MA: Blackwell.
Bengtsson, I., and Rauhut, D. (2021). Hayek, Welfarism and the Deserving Poor. In M. Lundahl, D. Rauhut and N. Hatti (eds), *Poverty in Contemporary Economic Thought* (pp. 13–27). London and New York: Routledge.
Bergh, A. (2021). Poverty and New Welfare Economics. In M. Lundahl, D. Rauhut and N. Hatti (eds), *Poverty in Contemporary Economic Thought* (pp. 145–157). London and New York: Routledge.
Blanchard, O., and Rodrik, D. (2021). *Combating Inequality: Rethinking Government's Role*. Cambridge, MA and London: MIT Press.
Carlson, B. (2021a). Gustav Cassel on Poverty: Growth, Not Grants! In M. Lundahl, D. Rauhut and N. Hatti (eds), *Poverty in the History of Economic Thought: From Mercantilism to Neoclassical Economics* (pp. 147–164). London and New York: Routledge.
Carlson, B. (2021b). Eli Heckscher on Poverty: Causes and Cures. In M. Lundahl, D. Rauhut and N. Hatti (eds), *Poverty in the History of Economic Thought: From Mercantilism to Neoclassical Economics* (pp. 165–178). London and New York: Routledge.
Committee for the Prize in Economic Sciences in Memory of Alfred Nobel (2023). *Scientific Background to the Sveriges Riksbank Prize in Economic Sciences in Memory of Alfred Nobel*. 9 October. www.kva.se/app/uploads/2023/10/scibackek239kn6hg4dgb.pdf. Downloaded 25 October 2023.
Daniels, P. (2021). Veblen, North and the Institutional Economics on Poverty. In M. Lundahl, D. Rauhut and N. Hatti (eds), *Poverty in Contemporary Economic Thought* (pp. 69–88). London and New York: Routledge.
Drèze, J., and Sen, A. (2013). *An Uncertain Glory. India and Its Contradictions*. London: Allen Lane.
Galbraith, J.K. (1958). *The Affluent Society*. Boston: Houghton Mifflin.
Galbraith, J.K. (1974). *Economics and the Public Purpose*. London: André Deutsch.
Galbraith, J.K. (1992). *The Culture of Contentment*. Boston: Houghton Mifflin.
Gehrke, C. (2021). David Ricardo on Poverty. In M. Lundahl, D. Rauhut and N. Hatti (eds), *Poverty in the History of Economic Thought: From Mercantilism to Neoclassical Economics* (pp. 56–75). London and New York: Routledge.
Hatti, N., and Rauhut, D. (2017). What Lessons Can Be Learnt? In D. Rauhut and N. Hatti (eds), *Politics, Poverty and the Poverty of Politics* (pp. 99–124). New Delhi: B.R. Publishing Co.
Lönnroth, L. (2021). Marx and His Followers on Poverty. In M. Lundahl, D. Rauhut and N. Hatti (eds), *Poverty in the History of Economic Thought: From Mercantilism to Neoclassical Economics* (pp. 89–104). London and New York: Routledge.
Lundahl, M. (2021a). Knut Wicksell and the Causes of Poverty: Population Growth and Diminishing Returns. In M. Lundahl, D. Rauhut and N. Hatti (eds), *Poverty in the History of Economic Thought: From Mercantilism to Neoclassical Economics* (pp. 128–146). London and New York: Routledge.
Lundahl, M. (2021b). Poverty and Circular, Cumulative Causation. In M. Lundahl, D. Rauhut and N. Hatti (eds), *Poverty in Contemporary Economic Thought* (pp. 47–68). London and New York: Routledge.
Milanović, B. (2016). *Global Inequality: A New Approach for the Age of Globalization*. Cambridge, MA: Harvard University Press.
Milanović, B. (2023). The Great Convergence, Global Inequality and Its Discontents. *Foreign Affairs*, 102(4), 78–91.
Myrdal, G. (1944). *An American Dilemma. The Negro Problem and Modern Democracy*. New York: Harper & Row.
Nozick, R. (1974). *Anarchy, State and Utopia*. New York: Basic Books.
Ohlin, B. (1933). *Interregional and International Trade*. Cambridge, MA: Harvard University Press.

Olsson, C.A. (2021). Alfred Marshall, Poverty and Economic Theory: A Historical Perspective. In M. Lundahl, D. Rauhut and N. Hatti (eds), *Poverty in the History of Economic Thought: From Mercantilism to Neoclassical Economics* (pp. 105–127). London and New York: Routledge.
Piketty, T. (2014). *Capital in the Twenty-First Century*. Cambridge, MA: Belknap Press.
Piketty, T. (2020). *Capital and Ideology*. Cambridge, MA: The Belknap Press of Harvard University Press.
Piketty, T. (2022). *A Brief History of Equality*. Cambridge, MA: The Belknap Press of Harvard University Press.
Rauhut, D. (2011). *Den besvärliga fattigdomen*. 2nd ed. Lund: Studentlitteratur.
Rauhut, D. (2021a). Adam Smith—A Champion for the Poor! In M. Lundahl, D. Rauhut and N. Hatti (eds), *Poverty in the History of Economic: From Mercantilism to Neoclassical Economics* (pp. 29–43). London and New York: Routledge.
Rauhut, D. (2021b). Saving the Poor: John Stuart Mill on Poverty and the Poor. In M. Lundahl, D. Rauhut and N. Hatti (eds), *Poverty in the History of Economic Thought: From Mercantilism to Neoclassical Economics* (pp. 76–88). London and New York: Routledge.
Rauhut, D., and Hatti, D. (2005). Amartya Sen, Poverty and Capability Deprivation. In D. Rauhut, N. Hatti and C.A. Olsson (eds), *Economists and Poverty* (pp. 275–296). New Delhi: Vedam Books.
Rauhut, D., and Hatti, N. (2021). Capability Deprivation and Poverty: Amartya Sen Revisited. In M. Lundahl, D. Rauhut and N. Hatti (eds), *Poverty in Contemporary Economic Thought* (pp. 168–181). London and New York: Routledge.
Rawls, J. (2001). *Justice as Fairness—A Restatement*. Cambridge, MA: Belknap Press.
Roine, J. (2023). *Därför är ojämlikheten viktig: Om rika, fattiga och alla däremellan*. Stockholm: Volante.
Scanlon, T.M. (2021). Why Does Inequality Matter? In O. Blanchard and D. Rodrik (eds), *Combating Inequality: Rethinking Government's Role* (pp. 59–64). Cambridge, MA: MIT Press.
Sen, A. (1973). *On Economic Inequality*. Oxford: Oxford University Press.
Sen, A. (1998). *Development as Freedom*. Oxford: Oxford University Press.
Sharma, J. (2013), Cosmic *Love and Human Apathy: Swami Vivekananda's Restatement of Religion*. Noida: HarperCollins Publishers of India.
Sowell, T. (2016). *Wealth, Poverty and Politics*. New York: Basic Books.
Sowell, T. (2019). *Discrimination and Disparities*. New York: Basic Books.
Stiglitz, J.E. (2012). *The Price of Inequality*. New York and London: W.W. Norton & Company.
Syll, L.P. (1999). *De ekonomiska teoriernas historia*. Lund: Studentlitteratur.
Van Parijs, P. (2021). What Kind of Inequality Should Economists Address? In O. Blanchard and D. Rodrik (eds), *Combating Inequality* (pp. 49–57). Cambridge, MA: MIT Press.

Part I
Manifestations of Inequalities

1 The Late Encounter of Inequality and Class

Göran Therborn

In current imagination and speech, 'inequality' and 'class' are often easily associated with each other. Classes express inequality, and inequality is a likely manifestation of class. However, the two concepts arose in different semantic fields and were kept apart for most of the 20th century by their different, though in both cases controversial, relationships to prevailing 'Western' socio-economic and political discourse, inside as well as outside academia.

1.1 The Discovery of Inequality

Inequality has been a late and rare discovery, in particular, as a contemporary issue of social justice. Until equality was 'invented' (Rosanvallon, 2011, Part I), inequality could not be taken note of. The coexistence of the rich and the poor was indeed widely noticed but as a natural or God-given *difference* among humans. A notion of human equality converged from several sources in the Atlantic revolutions of the United States, France, and Haiti. One was religious, in the equality of human souls, common to Christianity and Islam and most explicitly expressed in Paul's letter to the Galatians (3, pp. 27–28): 'There is neither Jew nor Gentile, neither slave nor free, nor is there male and female, for you are all one in Christ Jesus'. This was a vision of humanity secondary to the hierarchical tradition of the Catholic Church, but important to 17th-century and 18th-century Puritanism. In the 18th century, there also developed a secular equivalent in the naturalist anthropology of Buffon, as part of his grandiose 36-volume Natural History. His essay *De la nature de l'homme* (1749) stressed the basic similarity of the whole human species. Another source was the 17th-century European development of natural law, starting from reflections on humanity in 'the state of nature', before the Fall of Sin, before institutions of property and authority. The general conclusion was that then humans were equal (Alfani and Frigeni, 2016, p. 45f.). A third major source was the articulation of individualism of free and equal individuals doing reciprocal exchange on the emerging pre-industrial markets of the Netherlands, France, Britain, and British America (Rosanvallon, 2011, Chapter 2; McPherson, 1962).

Equality became a keyword of the Atlantic revolutions, but mainly as equality in contrast to pre-capitalist inequalities, of feudal seigneurial rights, feudal privileges, monarchical prerogatives, and, in Haiti primarily, slavery.

Socio-economic inequality did emerge as a secondary concern but on the margins and for long undertheorized. One might date its appearance to 1753–1754, when the Academy of Dijon put out its prize question, 'What is the origin of the inequality among men, and if it is authorized by natural law', and with Rousseau's winning response to it, which also enticed other critical contributions (Clouatre, 1992, p. 412f.). However, the target of Rousseau's (1754) critique was 'moral or political inequality' in the first stage of which 'the state of rich and poor was authorized' through the institution of private property. The marginality of socio-economic inequality in the European Enlightenment is exemplified by its central, collective *oeuvre*, the *Encyclopédie* (1751–72). Its entry on *inégalité* (1765) says 'Word much used in Astronomy to describe many irregularities . . . in the movement of the planets' (here quoted from Alfani and Frigeni, 2016, p. 47f.). During the period 1789–1830, there was a sudden surge in prints on equality (*aequalitas*) in a large European database to 334 items from 17 in 1750–1788, and also on distribution, from 120 to 366. *Inaequalitas*, on the other hand, stayed well below, ranging from 3 in the 17th century, to 50 in 1750–1788, and then going down to 31 for 1789–1830 (Alfani and Frigeni, 2016, p. 32).

The relative lack of interest in inequality has continued until recently. Thanks to Google Ngram Viewer, we can follow the trajectory of this interest in the keywords of books in several languages in the huge database of Google from 1800 to 2919 (see Figure 1.1). There is a general pattern in French, English, German, Italian, and Spanish, which is little or virtually no interest in inequality from 1800 until the 1960s, then a steep rise in publication, with periods of stalling in the years around 1980 and from about 2000 until 2010, that is the years of the neoliberal counter-reformation and of the heyday of unfettered capitalist booming. The Spanish data show a declining interest for 2004–2012, followed by a rise to a new top in 2019. In the German language, there is a peak in 2007 and substantial decline to 2018, while in English, French, and Italian, the curve stops in 2019, at its highest altitude so far. Through more than two centuries, the interest in inequality has been all the time much larger in British and, second, US book publishing than in other languages.

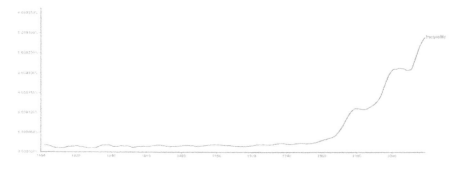

Figure 1.1 Frequency of 'inequality' as a keyword in English-language books, 1800–2019

Source: books.google.com/ngrams. Downloaded 18 November 2023

The American and French revolutions were committed to 'equality' principally as White non-'servant' and non-pauper men's freedom from aristocratic and monarchical authority and privileges. This left no relevant space for socio-economic inequality. There was, however, a theoretically strong case against persistent legal and political gender inequality, and it generated embryonic Feminism, first of all in the United States. But women remained too marginal for inequality becoming a central issue for long.

It may appear surprising that the rise of industrial capitalism and of the working-class movement did not give rise to a large interest in inequality—although it has to be admitted that Google Ngram is far from being a perfect indicator of social interest. However, the disjuncture between the discourse on inequality and the social divisions of the 19th-century industrial capitalism highlights the originally different semantic fields of inequality and class.

1.2 The Rise of Classes

The continuing conceptual disconnection between inequality and class is illustrated by their recent divergent keyword publication curves. While the inequality curves have gone up in the last 50 years, from a very low base, those of class have been going down since their national peaks or high plateaux, the American in 1905–1933, the British in 1995–2003, in all English in 1911–1919 (see Figure 1.2), and the French and the Italian and German since 2006. Spanish publishing interest topped in 2016, while attention to inequality continued upwards.

The perception of society as consisting of rich and poor and/or of categories of people with different hierarchical functions *is* ancient and virtually universal of societies since the Bronze Age. The Indian castes and the continental European estates have many relatives across the globe and its recorded history. Class is, of course, one of them but a different one, as a product of emerging capitalist modernity, never presented as part of a permanent divine order. The concept was developed in France from the mid-18th century soon followed in Britain and was consolidated as

Figure 1.2 Frequency of 'class' as a keyword in English-language books, 1800–2019

Source: books.google.com/ngrams. Downloaded 18 November 2023 a respectable signifier of both social scientific and political language by the 1820s. It had to overcome and replace the prevailing European conceptualizations of social differentiation in terms of ranks and orders and, on the continent, estates. It also had to assert and/or assure its autonomy from simultaneously developing naturalist taxonomies. Linnaeus published his very influential *Systema Naturae* in 1735 and his *Classes Plantarum* (The Classes of Plants) in 1738.

Social class emerged gradually in French political thought and practice in the 17th century, referring to social groupings without hierarchical qualities. Resurrecting an old Roman use of *classes*, for some tax collection, the population was divided into wealth or income classes overriding estate rank. In mid- and late 18th century, French political economy, by Cantillon, and the Physiocrats Quesnay and Turgot, developed the concept further, linking it to production, in their protagonizing analyses of commercial agriculture and their attacks on '*feodalité*' with its ranks and seigneurial rights. In somewhat variable forms, the French economists operated with a three-class system of landlords, (tenant-)farmers, and workers, defined purely by their economic functions. From the very beginning, modern class was a force for social change, to the Physiocrats for the development of market agriculture, the foundation of wealth in their view (Clouatre, 1992; Wallech, 1992). It should be noticed that class emerged before or outside industry, which Quenay considered a 'sterile' activity (Wallech, 1992, p. 276), but within agrarian capitalism.

In Britain, Adan Smith and his colleague in the Scottish Enlightenment John Millar kept the old concept of ranks, but in the 1790s class began to spread, including, in 1797, perhaps the world's first middle-class tax grievance. 'The burden of taxation presses so heartily on the middle classes of society, so as to leave the best set of the community little to hope and everything to fear from' wrote an author in *Monthly Magazine* (Briggs, 1956, p. 68). (The background was the novelty of an income tax to contribute to financing the wars against the French Revolution.)

A post-agrarian-centred class configuration arose in Britain, theorized in political economy by David Ricardo (1817), with his three-class analysis of landlords, capitalists, and workers and of the determinants of their remuneration in rent, profits, and wages, respectively. In polite political language, 'the capitalists' were replaced by 'the middle class(es)'. Both variants were focused on class conflict and social change and directed against the landlords or 'the Upper class', dominating Parliament, and the beneficiaries of the Corn Laws, the tariffs on corn imports. It was the British 'middle class' which initiated modern class politics in successful struggles for (limited, with minority suffrage) parliamentary reform and for repeal of the Corn Laws (Briggs, 1956). Working-class politics came later, from the late 1830s, as the first mass movement for (male) universal suffrage, Chartism. It was defeated.

Classes were conceptualized as major forces of social change, the working class and the 'middle class', or 'bourgeoisie' (most eloquently in *The Communist Manifesto)*. With de-industrialization, the weight of the working class has diminished, whereas a rising middle class is widely hailed as a saviour of the Global South, while portrayed as being threatened by extinction in the North (Therborn, 2020). In the Marxian tradition, class analysis is always focused on the capital-labour relations, on the one hand, on the configurations of different kinds of capital and, on the other, on how different occupations of employment are related to capital authority, in E.O. Wright's later writings (1997, Part I) also to 'scarce skills'.

A different class perspective, closer to the problematic of inequality, was launched by Max Weber (1922/1964, p. 678ff). In his grand treatise, *Wirtschaft und Gesellschaft (Economy and Society)*. '*Klassenlage*', class position was Weber's new concept, defined by individual life chances, so far as they were determined by the goods or labour market. 'Property and propertylessness are . . . the fundamental categories of all class positions' (Weber, 1922/1964, p. 679). 'Class position is . . . ultimately market position' (Weber, 1922/1964, p. 680). It was distinguished from 'status position' (*Ständische Lage*), which referred to rankings of 'honour' or prestige.

Class and inequality were for long kept marginal and separate in institutionalized sociology. The International Sociological Association was founded in 1949, under UNESCO auspices. This was in the early years of 'the American Century' and the Cold War, when 'industrial society', where inequality was hard to see, replaced 'capitalism' in polite academic language. Capitalism, class, and class struggle were deported to behind the Iron Curtain.

The International Sociological Association has 57 organizational Research Committees which frame its research activities. Not one is dealing with inequality or with class. Instead, the ISA has a committee on 'stratification'—a geological term of social layering—without any links to social relations. The strata were hierarchical layers of occupations with gradations of prestige or of individuals with different amounts of education or income. Sociological stratificationists were interested in processes of individual 'status attainment' and in 'social mobility', the liberal idea of (in)equality. 'Class' was here investigated mainly as father's or parents' social position and to what extent it had been left behind by individual social mobility (Ganzeboom et al., 1991). Through its increasing methodological sophistication, RC 28 on Social Stratification and mobility has become a sort of flagship of mainstream sociology, the one closest to the prevailing model of economics.

Stratificationism is still entrenched in many departments of sociology, but various other schemes of class have emerged, without linking up with the historical concept of class. So, for example, in the Weberian sense of market position (*Klassenlage*), it has become a standard descriptive category of one kind of inequality, along gender and race, which has inspired an interest in the 'intersectionality' or interaction of the three categories, a concept first launched by the US law professor Kimeberlé Crenshaw (1989).[1] The occupational class scheme becoming dominant in mobility studies, developed by John Goldthorpe and associates, has been challenged by i.a. Daniel Oesch (2006), adding three 'work logics' to employment status as explanatory variables of life chances and political behaviour, technical, organizational, and interpersonal. The most ambitious and influential alternative is that of Pierre Bourdieu (1979) in which classes are situated in a three-dimensional space defined by the volume and composition of the economic, cultural, and social 'capital' individuals own. It is a field of 'class struggle' for 'power over the classification schemes and systems of class positioning [*classement*]' (1979, p. 559). Bourdieu was above all interested in symbolic domination, and his great book is appropriately called *La Distinction*, and not *Inégalités*.

The concentration on stratification and social mobility has not prevented sociologists from studying inequality, including in penetrating ways, such as, for example, Charles Tilly's *Durable Inequality* (1998). But the sociological obsession with stratification is probably one reason why the post-2000 surge of inequality studies has mainly come from economics.

1.3 The Different Problematics of Inequality and Class

Class started as a concept for the agents of key economic functions in efforts to understand the emergence of a new economic system and developed into broad popular use denoting the main actors of the new politics of the new economy and society, mainly the middle class and the working class. Class operated primarily on an analytical field, the normativity of which was submerged into the economic structure—capitalist or socialist—to which the speaker/writer was committed.

Inequality derives from reflections on the human condition of individuals in the famous 18th-century prize essay question of the Academy of Dijon, as well as in the great theoretical developments in the late 20th century by John Rawls (1971) on justice by and Amartya Sen (1992) on (in)equality. Coping with human diversity, inequality first of all has to clear its relationship with difference (see Table 1.1).

Equality has so far been best formulated by the Nobel Laureate Amartya Sen as the equality of capability to function fully as a human being (Sen 1992, Chapter 3, 2009, Part Three). This definition underlines that social inequality should be understood in much broader terms than income and wealth. One way of specifying its multidimensionality is to start from the question: what is a human?

Humans are organisms, and *vital inequality* is varying the social constructions of human health and life expectancy.

Humans are also persons, with selves, living in interpersonal relation, characterized by hierarchy, discrimination, humiliation or by recognition, respect, tolerance, that is by *existential inequality* or equality.

Third, humans are goal-directed actors, with very different resources, income, wealth, education, contacts, power, in sum more or less divided by *resource inequality*. The three dimensions of inequality are interrelated and interact, or 'intersect', but they have their own dynamics and are irreducible to each other.

For inequalities to be perceived, felt, and, even more for them to be acted upon, there has to be a *commonality* of unequals. There is no commonality between

Table 1.1 Bases of Difference and Inequality

Difference	Inequality
Given (by God or nature) or chosen (style)	Socially constructed (dis)advantages
No necessary relation between compared entities	Some assumed fundamental commonality among the unequals
Descriptive, can also be evaluative	Normative, referring to a lack of equality, inequality

Source: Therborn (2013), Chapter 3

humans and fish and therefore no inequality. The elementary commonality of human (in)equality is being human, the basis of the norm of human rights. Nation-building and nation-state construction are about creating a commonality of the nation, a real as well as an imaginary national community.

How do the three dimensions of inequality outlined above relate to the conventional trinity of class, gender, and race? The latter, through their roots in social structures of class, gender, and race, are forces and practices impacting all the three dimensions of inequality. The categories are a way to investigate and to specify the effects of the dimensions on human lives.

We may try to sum up the differences between the social *problématiques* of semantic fields of inequality and class in a simple table (Table 1.2). 'Class' here stands for its use in the political economy tradition from the Physiocrats and the Ricardians to Marx and Marx-inspired scholarship.

The different fields of class and inequality were highlighted in Marx' *Kritik des Gothaer Programs* (1875), a programme for the unified Workers Party of Germany, merging—at a congress in Gotha—the reformist current of Ferdinand Lassalle and the Marxists. In his very sharp critique, Marx paid central attention to formulations about distribution and 'just distribution' and of the 'equal right' 'of all members of society' to the fruits of labour [*Ertrag der Arbeit*]. He had two main arguments. One was that the distribution of the means of consumption (*Konsumtionsmittel*) was determined by the distribution of the means of production in the (capitalist) mode of production. 'Are the elements of production distributed in that way, the current distribution of the means of consumption follows by itself.' Marx wanted to replace the programme demand of 'removal of all social and political inequality' thus, 'with the abolition of the class differences, all social and political inequality deriving from them will disappear by themselves' (Marx, 1875/1969, pp. 22, 26).

The second main point of Marx's critique is rooted in his conception of communism, which was not one of equality but of emancipated individuals freed from the 'servile subordination [*knechtende Unterordnung*] under the division of labour', where 'Everyone [contributed] according to capacity, everyone [receiving] according to needs'. From this vision, Marx pointed out another difference between the field of distributive (in)equality and that of class. Class is too crude a category for the former, as it does not adequately cover human diversity from different work capacity to different social relations: 'One worker is married, the other not; one

Table 1.2 Inequality and Class

	Class	Inequality
Field	System of political economy: capitalism	Human society
Mode	Agency, conflictual	Condition
Social status	Collective	Individual
Concept character	Analytical/interpretative	Normative and investigative
Conceptual use	Predictor of macrosocial change	Explanandum, mutandum

has more children than the other etc. etc.' (Marx, 1875/1969, p. 21). Marx here anticipates an argument developed by Amartya Sen (1992, p. 120) a century later.

Marx was not dismissive of demands and struggles for reforms within capitalism, such as shortening of the working day, public inspection and regulation of labour conditions, etc. But within a Marxist perspective, there was no intellectual space for a concern with inequality as a specific field of economics or politics. Inequality was inherent in the capitalist mode of production and would disappear when the class struggle had terminated capitalism.

Neo-Marxist theorizations of class in the late 20th century were not much concerned with distributive outcomes either, seen as self-evident consequences of capitalism. Their main foci were patterns of class structuration with a view to their potential for social change (Projekt Klassenanalyse, 1973; Wright, 1985, 1997) and the configuration of the power of the dominant class (Miliband, 1969; Poulantzas, 1968; Therborn, 1978).[2] Outside of his large empirical class study project, however, Wright (1979) uniquely also made an investigation of income distribution, showing how the US class structure patterned the income distribution in the United States.[3]

Turning to class, there were two main barriers to connecting this notion with inequality. One was the Marxian assumption that for all practical purposes, inequality was not only inherent but also invariant under capitalism. The other was Marx' and his followers' post-capitalist horizon, with class struggles leading to socialism. In this double perspective, criticizing and combatting inequality were no worthwhile major tasks, either for radical academia or for radical politics. For a left-wing social-democratic current, also Marx-inspired, these assumptions were no longer tenable.

An early connecting key contribution was the Swedish sociologist Walter Korpi's (1983) *The Democratic Class Struggle*. Current politics in rich capitalist democracies should 'fruitful[ly be] viewed as an expression of a democratic class struggle, i.e., a struggle where class, socio-economic cleavages and the distribution of power resources play central roles'. 'Class' refers to 'categories of individuals delineated on the basis of their relations to the means of production' (Korpi, 1983, pp. 21–22). The outcome of the conflicts between capital and labour, each with their resources of power, decided (with other factors) the variation of egalitarian and inegalitarian policies. Korpi's approach has had great international influence on social policy studies with his approach to comparative welfare state research and focus on (in)equality 'in specifying the characteristics of the welfare state, the *degree* of equality and inequality ... among citizens stands out as a basic variable' (Korpi 1983, p. 185, emphasis added).

In contrast to categorical variables, such as socialism-capitalism, emancipation-exploitation, or legal (in)equality, social (in)equality is a more or less ordinal variable. In the politics of the working-class movement, and also of Feminism and anti-racism, this distinction generated important divides between, on one hand ruptural politics, concentrated on qualitative, categorically defined change and, on the other, negotiating, gradualist politics giving priority to ordinal amelioration.

A class-conscious radical social democracy, such as the Swedish one of the late 1960s–1970s, in a sense summed up theoretically by Korpi (1983), dismantled the barriers between Marxian class perspectives and inequality concerns by highlighting the intra-capitalism variations of inequality and by decoupling everyday class struggles from an end-game of capitalism. However, radical Social Democracy was by the 1980s a declining intellectual and political force, less dramatically and less geopolitically significant than that of Communism as carrier of orthodox Marxism but hardly incomparable in ideological depth and social scope. Class analysis, freed of economist reductionism and of fixation with revolutionary change, had to be pushed, also from other angles.

For the long-neglected or forgotten inequality to become a field basically equal to class, other social and intellectual changes were necessary, and they were at the door.

1.4 The Inegalitarian Turn and the Rediscovery of Inequality

Polarizing inequality of poverty among prosperity was noticed towards the end of the post-World War II boom. By the mid-1960s, the persistence of poverty among affluence in the North America and Western Europe had begun to be recognized, largely thanks to Michael Harrington's book *The Other America. Poverty in the United* States (1962), and in the UK by Brian Abel-Smith's and Peter Townsend's *The Poor and the Poorest* (1965). In Sweden, the same year, an official Low Income Investigation was begun, which soon mutated into a large, long-term, generously financed research programme on the levels of living.

However, the incipient egalitarian concerns were stopped by the international neoliberal counter-reformation from around 1980 (see Figure 1.3). In two decades,

Figure 1.3 The Inegalitarian Turn from the 1970s. Shares of national income of the top 1 percent and the bottom half of the adult population in the United States.

Source: https//:Wid.World World Inequality Database. Downloaded 19 November 2023

virtually all the economic equalization in the Global North after World War II was wiped out, spearheaded by the United States. Transmitted by the IMF, the World Bank, and private consultants, a drastic economic reversal of equalization swept the whole world in the decades around 2000 (Alvarado et al., 2018).

The precarious legitimacy of the neoliberal dispensation was continuously contested by the losers among the popular classes and was soon lost or undermined through a series of economic crashes in Southeast Asia, in Latin America, and finally in the United States itself in 2008. Little wonder then that inequality became a major public concern. By 2014, inequality was considered 'a very big problem' by population majorities in Africa, Europe, Latin America, and the Middle East and by more than 40 per cent of the populations of the United States and Asia. It was even considered 'the greatest danger in the world' (among a list of five) by pluralities in Europe and the United States (Pew Research Center, 2014). Inequality has been a recurrent theme at the World Economic Forum in the 21st century, as causing risks of 'social fragility', and 'Fixing inequality' has even been put on as an Agenda in Focus by the WEF (in 2017). After Amartya Sen (laureate in 1998) there has been a string of Nobel Laureates in economics investigating inequality: Joseph Stiglitz, Angus Deaton, Abijit Banerjee, Esther Duflo, and Claudia Goldin.

The normative dimension of inequality and its currently wider scope than income distribution have their roots in broad social and political movements, as well as in social philosophy, with the extraordinary theorizations on social justice by Rawls and Sen in particular. There are the vast international movements from the 1960s onwards against patriarchy and racism—which the latter even in explicit institutional form survived the liberation of Auschwitz for surprisingly long, in the United States and in South Africa. Furthermore, there is the revival of human rights, with their strong normativity of politics—including geopolitical weaponization—which emerged out of the late de-escalation of the Cold War and, in Latin America, out of the defeat of radical change attempts by ruthless military dictatorships.

1.5 Thomas Piketty and the Revolution of Historical Political Economy

To 20th-century mainstream economics, capitalism, class, class conflict, and inequality[4] have largely been non-existent or taboo. Also in this century, prominent US economists were issuing dire warnings against concerns with inequality. Most straightforward was perhaps the Chicago Nobel Laureate Robert Lucas in 2003: 'Of the tendencies that are harmful to sound economics, the most seductive, and . . . the most poisonous is the focus on questions of distribution' (quoted by Anthony Atkinson, 2015, p. 15, a latter-day exception).

Into this competitive but self-contained little world, mostly consisting of mathematical models, a barrage of heavy empirical missiles has been fired by an iconoclast with an extraordinary self-confidence and hard-work capacity nourished by a French elite education: Thomas Piketty. Its explosive force was amplified by its timing, starting shortly after the ignominious crash of North Atlantic financial capitalism in 2008.

Herewith the fields of class, in the historical sense of political economy, and inequality has been fruitfully connected by the work of Piketty and his associates.

Inequality, in a multidimensional sense, is the explanandum et mutandum, what is to be explained and changed, and class, together with other social cleavages, constitutes the major forces of resistance and of change. Class cleavages are then deployed in a 'broad sense, understood as resulting from the mobilization of social identities more or less imbricated in the socio-economic structure' (Gethin et al., 2021, p. 23).

Thomas Piketty's (2013) *Capital in the 21st Century* started a revolution of political economy where the concepts of inequality and class played a central role as analytical tools. The reach of the revolution is hardly known yet, but the studies of inequality and class have certainly been revolutionized by an intellectually very powerful attack on mainstream, US-dominated economics, with its 'infantile passion for mathematics and purely theoretical, and often ideological, speculations to the detriment of historical studies and rapprochement with other social sciences' (Piketty, 2013, p. 63). After getting his US economics PhD of 'some relatively abstract mathematical theorems' (Piketty, 2013, p. 63), Piketty was inspired by the great French *Annales* school of long-term transdisciplinary historiography. Appearing right after the financial crash of 2008 and in the midst of rising anger against the speculative inequality by many deemed a major cause of the economic crisis, the book became an international bestseller, despite its almost 1,000 pages.

Piketty's, and his large and highly capable team's, work is focused on distribution, mainly of income and wealth but also of carbon emissions (Chancel and Piketty, 2015; Chancel et al., 2022, Chapter 6), with a view to contributing to a 'just society' (Piketty, 2013, p. 62)—in other words on inequality. Characteristics of the *oeuvre* are above all two things. One is methodological innovation, finding sources and analytically managing and combining their raw data, for example fiscal data and inheritance data on high incomes and wealth, using national accounts for estimating income distributions, electoral surveys of 50 countries for identifying social cleavages, linking income distribution and consumption to carbon emissions, and using social structural data and voting records from the 36,000 French communes to get at the historical evolution of political cleavages. A second characteristic is the vast scope of empirical investigations, marshalling big data, global, historical, and multidimensional (e.g. Piketty, 2019; Chancel and Piketty, 2021; Gethin et al., 2021; Cagé and Piketty, 2023). The productivity of the group, whose books range between almost 600 pages (Gethin et al) and almost 1,200 (Piketty, 2019), is without comparison.

Piketty (2013, p. 949) is very conscious of the historical location of his work, after the 'bipolar battles of the years of 1917–1989', which is probably a significant background to the scholarly fruitful link-up, at last, between gradual social inequality and categorical, if often blurred, class cleavages and conflict, a connection which jarred in the 19th-century Gotha brief party merger of monarchist reformism and Marxist revolution.

In his latest book with his partner, Julia Cagé, Piketty concludes from a study of voting behaviour and social structure in France in 1789–2022: 'The principal result of our study is no doubt the following: social class has never been as important as today for understanding voting behaviour' (Cagé et Piketty, 2023, p. 844).

1.6 Conclusions

In contemporary speech, 'class' and 'inequality' may sit close to each other, class as a manifestation or an aspect of inequality and inequality as an expression or outcome of class. However, they originated in different semantic fields. Class developed in political economy as a concept for a new set of economic and political actors in a rising market economic system. The 'middle class' and the 'working-class', in that order, became the most talked and written about classes. Inequality grew up in the shadow of the 18th-century 'invention' of human equality, which primarily asserted itself against monarchical prerogatives and aristocratic privileges. In the new societies of the Atlantic revolutions, and in the ensuing bourgeois societies of Europe, there was virtually no interest in socio-economic inequality. This continued into the post-World War II expansion of social science, at least until the late sixties to early seventies. Concepts of capitalism and class, central to 19th-century respectable social science in Germany, France, and Britain, virtually disappeared.

Nor was there much direct inequality concern in the Marxist or otherwise socialist movement, which had its eyes focused on emancipation from capitalism into a socialist and communist society, taking inequality as an obvious feature of capitalism, bound to disappear with it. This perspective continued into the swell of neo-Marxist class analysis in the 1970s–1980s, when class structures were analysed for decoding their power configurations and their potential for social change through class conflicts.

Inequality as such is a recent public interest of the 2000s, following from the brusque neoliberal reversal of 20th-century equalization onto soaring economic inequality. By then, the socialist horizon of the radical movement, the only social current interested in class, had largely disappeared, and the class struggle had become resistance against the ongoing tendencies of ever more inequality. Scholarly, an enormously productive link-up of class and class conflict with inequality was established by the massive innovative work of Thomas Piketty and his team. How far his revolution of political economy—where 'economics [is] a sub-discipline of the social sciences, alongside history, sociology, anthropology, political science, and others' (Piketty, 2013, p. 945)—will reach remains to be seen, but it is already a revolution of both class and inequality studies.

Notes

1 Crenshaw's original aim was a critique of US antidiscrimination law and judicial practice for failing to take into account the interaction and overlapping, the intersectionality of race and gender, and their interrelated manifestations of power and subordination. The lens of antidiscrimination law was focused either on black men or on white women. Intersectionality has since become a central Feminist concept for analysing pluridimensional discrimination and marginalization, and even an international intellectual movement (Cf. Carbado et al., 2013).
2 For the record, it should perhaps be added that the present author made an explicit distinction between class analysis and studies of distribution, also leaving out the latter in his study of the Swedish class structure (Therborn, 1981).
3 Wright (1994) did also publish a collection of essays under the title *Interrogating Inequality*, but apart from a brief section on achievement and exploitation, it deals mainly with class, socialism, and Marxism.

4 On inequality, there is one great mid-century exception, Simon Kuznets' (1955) Presidential address to the American Economic Association in 1954, on 'Economic Growth and Inequality'.

References

Abel-Smith, B., and Townsend, P. (1965). *The Poor and the Poorest*. London: G. Bell & Sons.
Alfani, G., and Frigeni, R. (2016). Inequality (Un)Perceived: The Emergence of a Discourse on Economic Inequality from the Middle Ages to the Age of Revolution. *Journal of European Economic History*, 44(1), 21–67.
Alvarado, F., Chancel, L., Piketty, T., Saez, E., and Zucman, G. (2018). *World Inequality Report*. Paris: World Inequality Lab.
Atkinson, A. (2015). *Inequality*. Cambridge, MA: Harvard University Press.
Bourdieu, P. (1979). *La Distinction*. Paris: Les Éditions de Minuit.
Briggs, A. (1956). Middle-Class Consciousness in English Politics, 1780–1846. *Past & Present*, 9, 65–74.
Buffon, G.-L. (1749). *La nature de l'homme*. Paris: L'Imprimerie Royale.
Cagé, J., and Piketty, T. (2023). *Une Histoire du Conflit Politique*. Paris: Seuil.
Carbado, D.W., Crenshaw, K.W., Mays, V., and Tomlinson, B. (eds) (2013). Intersectionality. Mapping the Movements of a Theory. *Du Bois Review*, 10(2), 303–312.
Chancel, L., and Piketty, T. (2015). *Carbon and Inequality: From Kyoto to Paris*. Paris: School of Economics.
Chancel, L., and Piketty, T. (2021). *Global Income Inequality, 1820–2020*. Paris: World Inequality Lab.
Chancel, L., Piketty, T., Saez, E., and Zucman, G. (2022). *World Inequality Report 2022*. Paris: World Inequality Lab.
Clouatre, D. (1992). The Concept of Class in French Culture Prior to the Revolution. In M. Cline Horowitz (ed), *Race, Gender, and Rank* (pp. 292–317). Rochester, NY: University of Rochester Press.
Crenshaw, K.W. (1989). Demarginalizing the Intersection of Race and Sex: A Black Feminist Critique of Antidiscrimination Doctrine. *Chicago Legal Forum*, 1989, 139–168.
Ganzeboom, H., Treiman, D., and Uitee, W. (1991). Comparative Intergenerational Stratification Research. *Annual Review of Sociology*, 17, 277–302.
Gethin, A., Martínez-Toledano, C., and Piketty, T. (2021). *Clivages Politiques et inégalités sociales*. Paris: EHESS, Gallimard, Seuil.
Harrington, M. (1962). *The Other America*. New York: Macmillan.
Korpi, W. (1983). *The Democratic Class Struggle*. London: Routledge & Kegan Paul.
Kuznets, S. (1955). Economic Growth and Inequality. *The American Economic Review*, 45(1), 1–28.
Marx, K. (1875/1969). Kritik des Gothaer Programs. In *Marx-Engels Werke*, vol. 19. Berlin: Dietz.
McPherson, C.B. (1962). *The Political Theory of Possessive Individualism*. Oxford: Clarendon Press.
Miliband, R. (1969). *The State in Capitalist Society*. London: Merlin Press.
Oesch, D. (2006). Coming to Grips With a Changing Class Structure. *International Sociology*, 21(2), 263–288.
Pew Research Center. www.pewresearch.org. Downloaded 8 November 2014.
Piketty, T. (2013). *Le capital au XXIesiècle*. Paris: Seuil.
Piketty, T. (2019). *Capital et idéologie*. Paris: Seuil
Poulantzas, N. (1968). *Pouvoir politique et classes sociales*. Paris: La Dévouverte.
Projekt Klassenanalyse (1973). *Materialien zur Klassenstruktur der BRD*. Berlin: VSA.
Rawls, J. (1971). *A Theory of Justice*. Cambridge, MA: Harvard University Press.
Ricardo, D. (1817/1971). *Principles of Political Economy and Taxation*. London: Penguin.
Rosanvallon, P. (2011). *La société des égaux*. Paris: Seuil.

Rousseau, J.-J. (1754/n.d.). *Discours sur l'origine de l'inégalité parmi les hommes, et si elle est autorisée par loi naturelle.* https://Gallica.BNF.fr/essentiels
Sen, A. (1992). *Inequality Examined.* Cambridge, MA: Harvard University Press.
Sen, A. (2009). *The Idea of Justice.* London: Penguin.
Therborn, G. (1978). *What Dies the Ruling Class Do When It Rules?* London: Verso.
Therborn, G. (1981). *Klasstrukturen I Sverige 1930–1980.* Lund: Zenit.
Therborn, G. (2013). *The Killing Fields of Inequality.* Cambridge: Polity.
Therborn, G. (2020). Dreams and Nightmares of the World's Middle Classes. *New Left Review*, 124, 63–87.
Tilly, C. (1998). *Durable Inequality.* Berkeley and Los Angeles: University of California Press.
Wallech, S. (1992). 'Class' Versus 'Rank': The Transformation of Eighteenth-Century English Social Terms and Theories of Production. In M. Cline Horowitz (ed), *Race, Gender, and Rank* (pp. 269–291). Rochester, NY: University of Rochester Press.
Weber, M. (1922/1964). *Wirschaft und Gesellschaft*, 2 vols. Köln: Kiepenheuer & Witsch.
World Economic Forum (2017). *Agenda in Focus: Fixing Inequality.* www.weforum.org>focus. Downloaded 8 November 2023.
Wright, E.O. (1979). *Class Structure and Income Determination.* New York: Academic Press.
Wright, E.O. (1985). *Classes.* London: Verso.
Wright, E.O. (1994). *Interrogating Inequality.* London: Verso.
Wright, E.O. (1997). *Class Counts.* Cambridge: Cambridge University Press.

2 Gender Inequalities

Progress and Challenges

Romane Frecheville-Faucon, Magali Jaoul-Grammare and Faustine Perrin

2.1 Introduction

Gender inequality refers to the unequal treatment, opportunities, and expectations imposed on individuals based on their gender, often resulting in the disadvantaged position of one gender (usually women) relative to the other (usually men). It encompasses various dimensions, including social, economic, political, and cultural disparities, which can manifest in different ways across societies and contexts. Gender inequality is one of the most pervasive forms of inequality and has been recognized as a significant challenge to human rights, social justice, and economic development. Despite considerable advancements in addressing gender inequalities throughout the twentieth and twenty-first centuries, various facets of contemporary society continue to perpetuate such disparities.

Extensive research has illuminated the pervasive discrimination experienced by women. Despite efforts to account for level of education and experience, studies consistently uncover a persistent wage gap between men and women (Blau and Kahn, 2017). The gender wage gap varies by country and industry but remains pervasive globally, with women earning on average 77 cents for every dollar earned by men (United Nations, 2022). Women are also more likely to be employed in low-wage, low-skilled jobs and are underrepresented in higher-paying fields such as science, technology, engineering, and mathematics (STEM) (Nimmesgern, 2016). Women also continue to be underrepresented in political leadership positions globally. According to the Inter-Parliamentary Union, women held only 26 percent of parliamentary seats globally in 2022 (World Bank, 2022). Throughout history, women have faced limited access to educational and training opportunities, impeding their ability to compete on equal footing in the job market. Nevertheless, studies indicate that higher levels of education among women contribute to the gradual reduction of the gender gap.

Despite progresses, gender disparities persist. A critical facet of gender inequalities lies in the division of labor within households. Traditional gender norms have burdened women with the majority of domestic work and caregiving responsibilities, constraining their full engagement in the workforce. Research actively explored the impact of policies such as parental leave and childcare subsidies on women's participation in the labor force (Jaumotte, 2004; Winkler, 2022; among others). Additionally, it investigated the evolving social norms surrounding gender roles and household duties. The issue of women's political representation and access to positions of power is a pressing concern in addressing gender inequality. Studies delving into the factors contributing to the underrepresentation of women have shown that gender policies (such as gender quotas) can boost women's representation and influence (e.g., Caul, 2001; Fernández and Valiente, 2021).

This chapter provides a comprehensive overview of gender inequalities in the twentieth and twenty-first centuries, examining the diverse dimensions that have profoundly impacted women's lives. Section 2.2 delves into the historical context of gender inequalities, with a particular focus on gender disparities in education. It highlights the remarkable progress made in advancing gender equality throughout the 20th century, including the establishment of crucial legal frameworks and policies. Section 2.3 acknowledges the persisting challenges and setbacks that continue to hinder progress, specifically regarding women's position in the labor market and their roles in the domestic economy. Section 2.4 explores the far-reaching consequences of gender inequalities on women when confronted with economic shocks. It sheds light on the adverse effects and the importance of addressing these disparities to ensure women's well-being and empowerment. Section 2.5 emphasizes the urgency of tackling gender inequality head-on, emphasizing the need for sustained advocacy, policy reform, and transformative social change. By addressing the persistent challenges faced by women in the 21st century, society can foster a more equitable future. Finally, Section 2.6 concludes the chapter by summarizing the key themes discussed throughout. It underscores the significance of understanding and addressing gender inequalities, ultimately highlighting the critical role of collective efforts in achieving a more just and inclusive society.

2.2 The Long History of Gender Inequalities

Historically, gender inequality has been deeply ingrained in social, political, and economic structures of societies (Perrin, 2013). Throughout much of human history, women have been relegated to subordinate roles in society, with limited opportunities for education, economic participation, and political representation. In many societies, women's legal rights have been severely limited.

2.2.1 Historical Context of Gender Inequalities

The feminist movement of the late nineteenth and early twentieth centuries challenged gender norms and fought for women's rights, including the right to vote, access to education and employment, and legal protections against discrimination. These efforts led to some progress toward gender equality in the following decades, including the establishment of legal frameworks and policies promoting gender equality.

Nonetheless, progress toward gender equality has been slow and uneven, and gender inequalities continue to persist in many aspects of society. Women still face significant barriers to accessing education, employment, and political representation, as well as pervasive gender-based discrimination. The historical legacy of gender inequality, combined with ongoing societal and cultural norms, continues to contribute to these disparities. Understanding the historical context of gender inequality is crucial for recognizing the persistence and complexity of this issue (e.g., Alesina et al., 2013; Giuliano, 2020; Perrin, 2022a) and for implementing effective policy reforms to promote gender equality and achieve sustainable development (United Nations, 2015).

The increasing exploration into the societal role of women has shattered persistent misconceptions regarding their historical employment, earnings, and overall economic contributions to both developed and developing economies. Recent research has significantly improved our understanding of how women have shaped long-term economic development. While women have always been part of the workforce, their societal status has not followed a linear trajectory; rather, it has evolved in tandem with the advancement of economies and societies (Merouani and Perrin, 2022).

In the realm of economic history, scholars delving into women's and gender-related issues primarily focused on how women's economic roles transformed during the industrialization era (Clark, 1920; Pinchbeck, 1930) and the subsequent impact on family economies (Tilly and Scott, 1989). A pivotal turning point occurred in the late 1980s, when Scott (1986) observed a significant surge in gender-oriented research within economic history. This surge not only enhanced our understanding of women's contributions to the economy but also shed new light on topics such as women's labor, wages, and their overall role in economic life. Economists and economic historians have further explored the influence of gender and women's economic activities on the trajectory of economic development (Boserup, 1970; Goldin, 1990), unveiling the vital significance of human capital as a key driver in the process (Diebolt and Perrin, 2013, 2019; Jaoul-Grammare and Perrin, 2017).[1]

The lack of quantitative indicators of gender equality in the past poses a challenge to our understanding of the historical dynamics of gender equality (Perrin, 2014, 2022b). Quantitative indicators play a crucial role in analyzing the extent of gender equality by providing measurable metrics to assess disparities and progress over time. The scarcity of data makes it difficult to establish comprehensive and accurate quantitative indicators that can effectively capture the complexities of gender equality in the past. In the absence of reliable quantitative data, researchers often rely on qualitative evidence, historical documents, surveys, and anthropological studies to gain insights into the experiences and conditions of women in different historical contexts. While these sources can provide valuable qualitative information, the absence of quantifiable data limits our ability to make precise comparisons, identify trends, and quantify the magnitude of gender inequalities across various periods. Efforts are being made to address this data gap and develop innovative methodologies to estimate and reconstruct historical indicators of gender (in)equality (Perrin, 2014, 2022b; Dilli et al., 2019; Szoltysek et al., 2017; Perrin et al., 2023; Hippe and Perrin, 2017).

Research indicates that gender equality has historically evolved alongside economic development. This intriguing relationship between gender equality and economic progress highlights the interconnectedness of social and economic factors in shaping societies. As economies transitioned from agrarian to industrial and subsequently to knowledge-based systems, significant transformations occurred in societal norms, values, and gender roles. During these transitions, women's roles and opportunities gradually expanded, driven by various factors such as advancements in technology, changes in labor demand, and evolving social attitudes (Merouani and Perrin, 2022). As economies diversified, new employment opportunities emerged beyond traditional gender-specific roles. Women began to enter sectors previously dominated by men, contributing to the overall economic growth and development of societies. Moreover, the expansion of education played a crucial role in promoting gender equality. With improved access to education, women gained knowledge and skills that empowered them to participate more actively in the workforce and take on roles traditionally reserved for men (Diebolt and Perrin, 2013, 2019). Education provided women with opportunities for economic self-sufficiency and upward mobility, leading to greater gender equality in various aspects of life.

It is important to note that the pace and extent of progress in achieving gender equality have varied across regions and time periods. Different societies have experienced different trajectories, influenced by cultural, political, and historical factors (Perrin, 2022a). However, the overarching trend suggests that as economies develop and become more inclusive, gender equality tends to improve.

2.2.2 Gender Inequalities in Education—Zoom on the French Case

Gender inequality is intricately linked to disparities in education and the acquisition of human capital. In France, gender equality at school, and the coeducation that goes with it, is the result of a long historical, institutional, and societal process (see Perrin, 2013).

2.2.2.1 Girls' Education in the Nineteenth Century

Until the end of the 19th century, girls' access to school only concerned the primary level; today, equality between girls and boys in school is enshrined in the Education Code: '*Schools, collèges, lycées and higher education establishments are responsible for transmitting and acquiring knowledge and working methods. They contribute to promoting gender diversity and equality between men and women, particularly in terms of guidance*' (Article L121–1 of the Education Code).[2] In spite of this, training courses and the associated professions remain largely gendered: '*Countries that would steer boys towards the humanities and girls towards engineering training have yet to be invented*' (Baudelot and Establet, 2001). However, since the 1990s, the fight against gender inequality in schools has become a political priority: '*Primary schools, lower and upper secondary schools and higher education must contribute to equality between girls and boys*' (Loi d'orientation de 1989). Since then, beyond the educational sector, gender equality has been at the heart of many reforms at the societal level.

In France, the beginning of the 19th century was marked by a notable lack of interest in girls' education, despite the demands of the French Revolution (Condorcet, 1792; Lakanal, 1793). The Civil Code of 1804 perpetuated the legal subordination of women, treating them as minors, criminals, or individuals with mental disorders, echoing the provisions of the *Coutume de Paris*. Napoleon's stance further reinforced this perspective, as he believed in 'raising believers, not reasoners' (Napoleon, 15 May 1807).[3] The disregard for girls' education is evident in the Enquiry conducted in 1833, which aimed to assess the state of primary schooling in France. Minister Guizot's instructions explicitly excluded girls from the survey, focusing solely on boys' and mixed schools. '*Only boys' schools and mixed schools will be visited. Within the latter, girls will not be counted*' (Guizot, 1834).

However, from the second half of the 19th century, subsequent governments gradually recognized the importance of girls' education. The Falloux Law of 1850 and the Duruy Law of 1867 mandated the establishment of girls' schools in municipalities with populations exceeding 800 and 500, respectively. The Bert Law of 1879 required each department to establish girls' teacher training colleges, and the Camille See Law of 1880 introduced coeducational *collèges* and *lycées* for girls, drawing inspiration from the American model. As early as 1870, Jules Ferry highlighted the significance of girls' education and the societal obstacles it faced, emphasizing the need for equal opportunities:

> To demand equal education for all classes is to do only half the work, only half of what is necessary, only half of what is due; I demand this equality, I demand it for both sexes. . . . The difficulty, the obstacle here is not in the expense, it is in the morals.
> (Jules Ferry, Conférence Populaire, 10 April 1870)

The Republican laws of 1881–1882 represented a significant advancement, as they abolished the distinction between girls and boys in education. Schooling became secular, free, and compulsory for all children aged 6 to 13, regardless of their gender. However, opposition, particularly from the Church, persisted: '*To give the same education to girls and boys is to confuse what nature, common sense, order, society and religion require to be distinguished*' (Monseigneur Donnet, Archbishop of Bordeaux, 1882). In 1886, the Goblet Law required municipalities with more than 500 inhabitants to have a girls' school or, with authorization, to replace it with a co-educational school. Higher education also witnessed a tradition of male exclusivity until the end of the Second Empire, denying women access to these institutions. While faculties gradually opened up to women in the provinces, the University of Paris remained resistant to their admission. Despite a decree in 1866 allowing women to attend university, the first woman's admission to the Faculty of Medicine in Paris required intervention from Empress Eugenie. Even in 1872, the Sorbonne continued to reject female students.

During the 20th century, various economic and societal factors contributed to the expansion of higher education opportunities for girls. These changes were accompanied by significant institutional reforms, such as the Haby Law of 1975, which promoted coeducation throughout the education system. These developments marked a substantial shift toward a more inclusive educational landscape in France (Jaoul-Grammare, 2018).

2.2.2.2 Twentieth Century—Turning Point in Gender Equality

The 1905 separation of the Church and State in France solidified the role of the State in education, particularly for girls. In 1919, the women's baccalaureate was established, and although the Bérard decree in 1924 granted girls the right to the same secondary education as boys, it was not until the 1930s that programs and schedules were unified. Mixed secondary education was introduced in the 1960s. The movement to open higher education to girls, initiated in the late 19th century, gained momentum with Marie Curie's Nobel Prize and was further amplified by the onset of World War I. Subsequently, numerous *Grandes écoles* gradually began admitting girls. The mixed *École Normale Supérieure* in Cachan was established in 1912, followed by the admission of women to the *École Centrale* six years later. In 1919, women gained access to the *École Supérieure d'Électricité* and the *École Supérieure de Chimie de Paris*. The *École Polytechnique Féminine* and *Haut Enseignement Commercial pour les Jeunes Filles* (HECJF) were founded in 1925 and played crucial roles in enabling young women to pursue higher education. However, it was not until the 1970s that women gained access to all *Grandes écoles* previously reserved for boys, such as *Polytechnique* in 1972, HEC in 1973, and ENS in 1981 after the merger of girls' and boys' ENS (Marry, 2003).

Alongside these institutional reforms, significant societal changes also contributed to the feminization of education and society. The abolition of legal incapacity in 1938, women's right to vote in 1944, freedom to work in 1965, the Neuwirth law on access to contraception from 1967 to 1972, and the Veil law in 1975 were all key milestones. With coeducation established across the education system, the 1980s witnessed an array of texts advocating for gender equality, extending beyond the school to society as a whole. Two parallel movements emerged: a political determination to establish gender parity in all domains and an aspiration to integrate women into scientific research by diversifying study choices for girls and boys. In 1984, interministerial agreements were signed, focusing on 'equality between girls and boys, women and men in the education system'. These agreements emphasized diversification of school choices, professional diversification, political parity, equal pay, and comprehensive education for equality. Concurrently, various actions were taken to encourage women's participation in scientific research. Advertising campaigns from the Ministry of Education between 1984 and 1992 aimed to eradicate gender stereotypes within professions. Additionally, research associations such as 'Women Engineers' (1982), 'Women and Mathematics' (1987), and 'Women and Science' (2000) were established, alongside awards like the L'Oréal-UNESCO Foundation Prize (1998) and the Irène Joliot-Curie Prize (2001). Partnerships such as the INTEGER Project[4] and the ERA-NET GENDER-NET Project[5] also aligned with the objectives of the Lisbon Strategy to reduce gender imbalances in scientific and technical fields.

Although there has been a reduction in inequalities over time, certain rigidities persisted. In 1833, girls comprised only one-third of primary school enrollments, a proportion that increased to 50 percent in 1881. While there were only two female baccalaureate graduates in 1896, their numbers equaled that of boys in the 1960s and are now in the majority. As of 2017, 84 percent of girls and 74 percent of boys possessed a baccalaureate qualification. The shift in higher education occurred in the early 1980s. However, girls continue to be underrepresented in science-related courses: in 2016, only 41 percent of final-year science students were girls, and in higher education, women accounted for 25 percent of basic science students, 29 percent of STAPS students, 28.5 percent of engineers, and 40 percent of doctors in scientific fields (Ministère de l'Éducation Nationale, Direction de l'évaluation, de la prospective et de la performance (DEPP), 2017).

The challenges in implementing reforms, despite numerous efforts to promote gender equality, are rooted in societal stereotypes (Leroy et al., 2013; Jaoul-Grammare, 2018). These stereotypes persist in the collective consciousness, associating certain professions and fields of study with specific genders (Figure 2.1). Consequently, engineering is often perceived as a male-dominated profession, while occupations such as social work and secretarial roles are seen as traditionally female (Guichard, 1992; Guichard et al., 1994a, 1994b; Wach, 1992). In the words of Marry (2003, p. 4), quoting Ferrand (1995): '*If the swallows of gender equality signal the arrival of spring, the full summer of equality has not yet arrived*'.

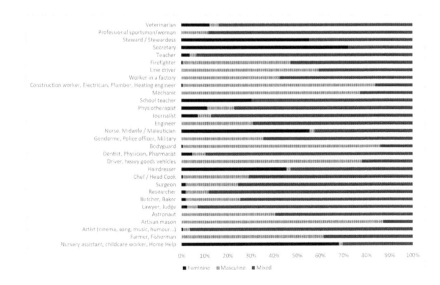

Figure 2.1 Gender perception of occupations

Source: Jaoul-Grammare (2023)

2.3 Contemporary Challenges in Gender Inequalities

Despite the catch-up of girls in education and the greater integration of women into the labor force, they continue to face disparities in comparison to men, in terms of both their position in the labor market and their roles in the domestic economy.

2.3.1 Unequal Position in Paid Activities

The persistent disparity in employment rates between men and women in Europe reveals a substantial gap of nearly 10 percentage points in 2019. While there has been an increase in female employment, accompanied by a decline in the female inactivity rate, women still exhibit a higher probability of being absent from the labor market, thereby augmenting the risk of precariousness.

Despite greater participation in the labor market and higher employment rates, women remain susceptible to precarious circumstances. As depicted in Figure 2.2, women are more inclined toward part-time employment, resulting in lower monthly wages. This trend persists due to a significant proportion of newly created jobs being part-time positions that predominantly favor women (Alper, 2019). For many women, part-time work continues to be a viable option for balancing family and professional responsibilities. Achieving a harmonious work–family equilibrium remains a challenge for women, who encounter greater inequalities related to parenthood compared to men,

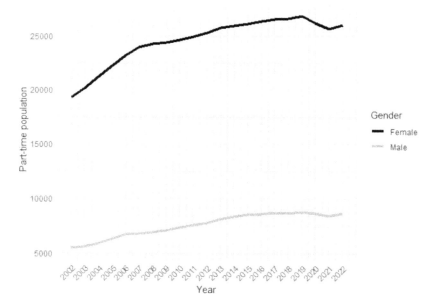

Figure 2.2 Part-time job in EU28, 2002–2022

Source: European Institute for Gender Equality

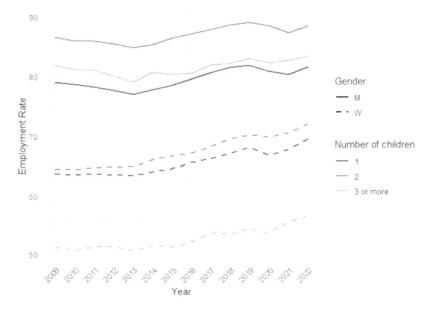

Figure 2.3 Employment by the number of children in EU28, 2009–2022

as fatherhood exerts minimal impact on their economic situation. Figure 2.3 showcases the disparities in employment rates between men and women based on the number of children. While the employment rates for both genders exhibit minimal variation among individuals with one or two children, a considerable decline in female employment rate becomes apparent for individuals with three or more children.

The progress achieved by women in the labor market serves as a positive indicator of their empowerment. Nevertheless, complete gender equality within the labor market has yet to be attained. Women still face lower employment rates, a higher likelihood of inactivity, and continued disparities associated with maternity. These factors undermine their economic situation and financial autonomy. Moreover, even when women are employed, their circumstances are not equivalent to those of men due to their disproportionate representation in precarious economic sectors, an outcome of occupational segregation.

2.3.2 Occupational Segregation

Occupational segregation refers to the unequal distribution of individuals across different economic sectors based on gender. The labor market is characterized by sectors that are predominantly occupied by men or women. In Europe, Bettio et al. (2009) find that more than a quarter of the employed population would need to change sectors in order to achieve gender equality in the distribution of men and women across economic sectors. However, there is significant variation among member countries, with a nearly ten-point gap between countries with the highest and lowest rates of segregation.

Reskin and Bielby (2005) emphasize that while economic factors may partially explain occupational segregation based on employer and worker preferences, sociology views it as a process primarily influenced by gender stereotypes and socialization. According to Seron et al. (2016), addressing the persistence of occupational segregation requires more than just economic incentives. For instance, they provide the example of engineering in the United States, where even when women choose to enter male-dominated sectors, they encounter barriers within the professional environment due to specific socialization processes.

However, Bettio et al. (2009) argue that while stereotypes play a significant role in occupational segregation, their impact may be overestimated. Other factors such as motherhood also contribute to the uneven distribution of men and women across sectors. The authors suggest that motherhood leads women to prioritize jobs and sectors with more flexible schedules, contributing to a form of 'resegregation'. Additionally, when excluding full-time workers, the level of segregation increases by 15 to 30 percentage points.

The field of study has also been considered as a factor influencing occupational segregation, but its importance remains mixed. Bettio et al. (2009) demonstrate that although Europe has witnessed a diversification of choices in higher education, potentially leading to a decrease in segregation, studies alone fail to fully explain the level of segregation in a country. They find that only 10 percent of jobs closely align with the fields of study pursued by workers. Moreover, the authors argue that women's choice to work in specific sectors can be explained by the influence of motherhood, as they tend to favor jobs and sectors with more flexible schedules. When excluding full-time workers, the level of segregation increases by 15 to 30 percentage points. Motherhood, care work, and women's employment are closely intertwined. This connection arises from the fact that the household economy, which includes caregiving and domestic work, heavily relies on women's contributions.

2.3.3 Burden of the Domestic Economy

The issue of domestic labor remains at the core of the battle against gender inequality, stemming from the division of labor based on sex. Men predominantly engage in paid work, while women shoulder the bulk of unpaid domestic production and caregiving responsibilities.

Despite some progress in the convergence of time allocation between women and men, unpaid work remains primarily carried out by women. The gap in the time devoted to childcare between women and men continues to be substantial (Figure 2.4). While changes in social norms contribute to this disparity (Fernandez and Sevilla Sanz, 2006; Voicu et al., 2009), institutions also play a crucial role in encouraging paternal engagement in childcare. Fox highlights that social policies aimed at promoting work–family balance predominantly focus on women. An example is the provision of paternity leave, which, in many countries, is either shorter than maternity leave or viewed as more of an individual choice (Fox et al., 2009). Nevertheless, studies suggest that paternity leave can stimulate men's involvement in care activities

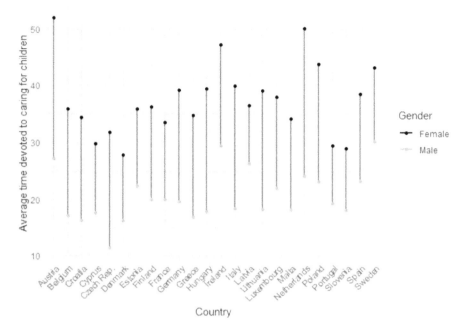

Figure 2.4 Average weekly hours spent in childcare, 2016

Source: European Institute for Gender Equality

Note: The list of countries includes Germany (DE), Denmark (DK), Spain (ES), Finland (FI), France (FR), Hungary (HU), Ireland (IE), Italy (IT), Poland (PL), Sweden (SE), Slovenia (SI), and the United Kingdom (UK).

(Anxo et al., 2007). Therefore, it represents a vital institutional lever for addressing inequalities in time allocation between women and men.

The disproportionate burden of care work negatively affects personal well-being and the availability of time for paid work, ultimately impacting women's financial independence (Humphries and Rubery, 1995). Unequal positions in the paid economy, occupational segregation, and the disproportionate responsibility of domestic work placed on women all impede women's empowerment, perpetuating an economic system where women and men do not experience equitable economic mechanisms. Despite women's increasing integration into the labor market, their positions do not align with those of men. Inequalities persist in both the labor market and the domestic sphere, maintaining the disparities between men and women.

2.4 Consequences of Gender Inequalities

Diverse economic positions result in disparate impacts of economic shocks on men and women. In this regard, both the 2008 financial crisis and the recent COVID-19 pandemic underscore the enduring presence of gender inequalities, exacerbating the economic circumstances of women who are already disproportionately vulnerable to the risk of poverty.

2.4.1 Gendered Impact of Economic Crises

The gendered impact of economic crises can be attributed to the uneven distribution of women and men across various sectors of activity. Périvier (2014) describes this impact difference through what she terms the '3 phases' of economic crises. During the initial phase, the economic situation experiences a negative shock that disproportionately affects sectors highly dependent on it, such as public works, construction, and manufacturing, which tend to be male-dominated sectors (Bettio et al., 2009; Métral and Stokkink, 2016). In the early stages of a crisis, the male unemployment rate dropped rapidly and exceeded that of women, marking a notable occurrence in Europe. On the other hand, women predominantly work in the public sector, which is less susceptible to economic fluctuations. This sets the stage for a second phase, characterized by the recovery of economic activity facilitated by the revival of sectors impacted by the crisis, supported by expansionary policies. Finally, Périvier (2014) describes the last phase as a period of austerity, primarily focused on controlling spending to rebalance strained national accounts resulting from the previous phase. It is in this final phase that the gendered impact of austerity measures manifests.

Controlling public spending, particularly the rate of its growth, often involves adjustments in public employment, public services, and social benefits. Theodoropoulou and Watt (2011) highlight these channels as common features of countries implementing budget cuts. One of the main measures to control public spending is reducing the overall public salary burden, achieved by factors such as not replacing retiring employees or reducing working hours. This reduction primarily affects sectors such as health, education, and social and cultural services, which are predominantly staffed by women (Périvier, 2014; Rubery, 2015). Cuts to public services and social benefits indirectly impact women's participation in economic activities. Such expenditures typically support the 'work–family' balance, a key factor influencing women's labor force participation. Himmelweit (2002) emphasizes the need to consider gender when assessing the impact of public expenditure, noting that activities and services no longer provided by the State are often absorbed by the domestic economy, predominantly shouldered by women. The increase in domestic workload has been identified by Rubery (2015) as a consequence of austerity policies. Women are consequently affected by a 'double penalty': on the one hand, they experience reduced employment opportunities and working hours due to restrictions in public employment; on the other hand, as users and beneficiaries of public services, they encounter difficulties in reconciling work and family responsibilities, leading to a higher prevalence of part-time work (Edgell and Duke, 1983).

The COVID-19 crisis had a distinct impact. While economic crises, such as the 2008 crisis, primarily affected men's employment, evidence suggests that women have experienced higher rates of unemployment during the COVID-19 pandemic (Carli, 2020). Unlike the 2008 crisis, which significantly impacted manufacturing and construction sectors, the service sectors (restaurants, hotels, tourism, culture, etc.), which are predominantly female-dominated, have been most affected. Reichelt et al. (2021) argue that women's higher exposure to the risk of unemployment can also be attributed to their higher representation in atypical employment.

Furthermore, the lockdown measures disrupted working conditions, with many individuals required to telecommute. Alon et al. (2020) demonstrate that men have greater access to jobs with telecommuting options, exposing women to a higher risk of job loss or reduced working hours.

In terms of the impact on the unpaid economy, several studies have examined the distribution of care activities within heterosexual couples. In England, both men and women increased their time spent with children, but the increase was more substantial for women. Using time-use surveys, Sevilla et al. (2020) demonstrate that employed women spent as much time with their children as their unemployed husbands, while unemployed mothers dedicated twice as much time to childcare as employed fathers. In cases where both parents were employed, mothers reduced their working hours and interrupted their paid work more frequently than men. Similar findings were reported for the United States (Carlson et al., 2022) and Germany (Reichelt et al., 2021), highlighting the shared patterns of childcare responsibilities and the reduction in women's working hours.

Both the 2008 crisis and the COVID-19 pandemic shed light on the persisting gender inequalities exacerbated by economic shocks. The impact of economic crises differs for men and women due to their unequal distribution across sectors and the gendered nature of policy responses. Understanding these dynamics is crucial for developing effective strategies to mitigate gender disparities and promote equitable economic recovery.

2.4.2 Women's Exposure to the Risk of Poverty

Persistent gender inequalities contribute to income disparities, encompassing wage inequality, unequal access to capital, and disparities in wealth accumulation. While the quantification of these inequalities varies across studies, valuable insights can be gleaned from the existing literature.

Horizontal occupational segregation emerges as a major factor driving this pay gap. Women are predominantly concentrated in sectors characterized by higher precariousness, such as sales, personal services, and restaurants (Mavrikiou and Angelovska, 2020). Despite ongoing desegregation efforts, a disparity in income growth persists between male-dominated and female-dominated sectors. For instance, Busch (2020) reveals that women's incomes in male-dominated or mixed sectors experience substantial growth, while incomes in female-dominated sectors remain stagnant, as observed in the case of Germany. In addition to the horizontal dimension of occupational segregation, a vertical dimension exists. It implies that even within the same sector, including female-dominated sectors, men have a higher likelihood of occupying positions with greater responsibility, leading to higher pay than women (Blackburn et al., 2001). In parallel to wage inequalities, disparities in wealth between men and women are also evident. Schneebaum et al. (2018) attribute these wealth inequalities to women's limited access to jobs or industries conducive to wealth accumulation. Consequently, men with greater capital hold economic power over women (Çağatay, 2003).

Lower employment rates, higher part-time employment rates, and income inequalities contribute to a higher poverty rate among women (Figure 2.5). The poverty rate is measured as the proportion of the population, encompassing both men and women, with an income below 60 percent of the median income. With the exception of Finland, the poverty rate for women exceeds that of men in the remaining countries examined. Several authors have argued that the conventional measurement method underestimates women's poverty (Corsi et al., 2016; Meulders and O'Dorchai, 2011). In social sciences, poverty is regarded as a phenomenon impacting households. Poverty statistics reflect the percentage of individuals belonging to households with disposable incomes below the poverty line. Meulders and O'Dorchai (2011) focus on 'individual poverty' or 'financial dependence' and reveal significantly higher rates than the traditionally accepted poverty rate, with differences of up to 30 percentage points. This phenomenon

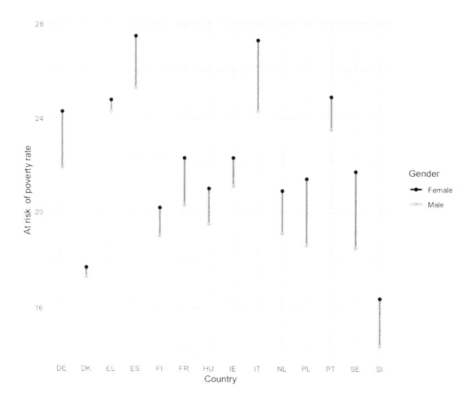

Figure 2.5 Men and women at risk poverty in 14 EU countries, 2020

Source: European Institute for Gender Equality

Note: The list of countries includes Germany (DE), Denmark (DK), Greece (EL), Spain (ES), Finland (FI), France (FR), Hungary (HU), Ireland (IE), Italy (IT), the Netherlands (NL), Poland (PL), Sweden (SE), Slovenia (SI), and the United Kingdom (UK).

predominantly affects women, as men's individual poverty rates align more closely with the standard poverty rate. Similar findings are reported by Corsi et al. (2016).

The individual approach highlights that studying women's poverty solely through the household lens captures only a fraction of the issue. It is imperative to delve deeper into income disparities between spouses. Hobson (1990) investigates this question by analyzing a dozen Western countries in the late 1970s or mid-1980s. Through her dependency value, she demonstrates that the contribution of spouses to household income varies from a difference of 40.6 percentage points in Sweden to 77 percentage points in Switzerland. Huber et al. (2009) find that, on average, countries with social-democratic welfare states exhibit lower income disparities between spouses in the mid-1990s, whereas Christian democratic countries demonstrate the highest income disparities.

Economics delves into the crucial aspect of women's independence by exploring the question of their economic autonomy in relation to their spouses. While this subject remains a matter of ongoing debate, it is important to note that defining women's economic independence solely within the framework of intra-household inequalities is a limited approach. This narrow perspective fails to acknowledge the independence of single women and neglects an assessment of their capacity to sustain themselves through their own income. Therefore, a comprehensive understanding of women's economic independence requires a broader examination that encompasses both married and single women, allowing for a more accurate evaluation of their self-sufficiency (Frecheville-Faucon, 2023). Recent studies focusing on the determinants of women's economic independence have shown that family policies not based on the male breadwinner model positively impact women's economic independence, highlighting the role of gender egalitarian welfare states (Alper, 2019).

2.5 Public Policies and Gender Inequalities

Despite the persistent challenges and obstacles, significant progress has been made toward achieving gender equality. This progress has been driven by legal frameworks, policies, and initiatives aimed at promoting gender equality.

2.5.1 *Welfare State and Women's Economic Emancipation*

While public employment is a driver for women's participation in the labor market, social spending also plays an important role, enabling work–life balance. Indeed, as the development of the welfare state has made it possible to support women's participation in the labor market, the decline in social policies observed in Western countries, and more particularly in Europe, raises questions about the role of the State in the women's emancipation. Public policies put in place after the 2008 crisis at the community level leave a mixed picture in terms of the fight against gender inequalities.

The traditional classification of welfare states, as proposed by Esping-Andersen (1990), highlights three categories based on the criterion of decommodification:

the liberal model, the social-democratic model, and the conservative-corporatist model. However, social protection cannot be solely determined by market forces or institutional frameworks. This classification overlooks the concept of 'demarketing' of labor, which is closely tied to the domestic economy. Orloff (1993) emphasizes that, historically, women have sought 'commodification' to achieve social and economic emancipation from men, but their access to the labor market has been strongly influenced by domestic work.

An alternative classification proposed by Lewis (1992) considers the interaction between the paid economy and the unpaid economy by focusing on the concept of 'defamilialization'. This concept refers to the extent to which care tasks are externalized from families and recognizes individuals as workers rather than solely defining them by their roles as spouses or mothers. Three models emerge from this perspective: (1) the 'male breadwinner' model, prevalent in liberal welfare states; (2) the 'parental' model, developed in countries like France, which provides social benefits for women as both workers and mothers or wives; and (3) the 'two breadwinner' model, observed in Scandinavian countries, which emphasizes the recognition and professionalization of care activities.

In the majority of European countries, social protection systems were designed to provide coverage for a salaried man and his family against life's risks. Consequently, they are often ill-suited to accommodate women as active participants in the labor force (Çağatay, 2003; Métral and Stokkink, 2016). The relationship between the welfare state and women's employment has sparked extensive debate in the social science literature. Does the welfare state promote women's empowerment, or does it perpetuate social norms that undermine gender equality? While the answer to this question is nuanced, it underscores the significant role of the welfare state in shaping women's activities.

One argument in favor of the State's involvement in women's emancipation is the transfer of care activities from the private sphere to the public sphere. Hernes (1984) demonstrates that as care activities become the responsibility of the State, women gain greater economic opportunities for their emancipation. Dahlerup (1987) supports this idea in the context of the Scandinavian-style welfare state, which provides services and employment opportunities that enhance women's independence. Similarly, Cavalcanti and Tavares (2003) shows that increased female labor force participation leads to the expansion of government size because women, upon entering the workforce, seek to delegate some family-related services to the State. However, Hernes (1987) questions this relationship between the welfare state and women's activities, raising the concern of whether women have truly achieved independence or if dependence has merely shifted from men to the State, which now guarantees women's economic activity. The author tends to support the latter proposition. Dauphin (2010) argues similarly, suggesting that the State has not eradicated the sexual division of labor. The role of 'woman-mother' persists, and policies promoting the 'work–family' reconciliation primarily target women.

The issue of women's dependence on the State and its public spending becomes particularly relevant in times of austerity. Périvier (2018) explores the consequences of austerity measures on the degree of decommodification and defamilialization within the welfare state. A retreat from corporatist models may disproportionately impact women due to income and career disparities. For instance, Bonnet et al. (2006) demonstrate that retirement pension inequalities between women and men in France hover around 40 percent, a gap that would widen further if only contribution-based benefits were considered, as women's retirement pensions primarily rely on survivor's pensions. Additionally, austerity measures lead to an increased labor market flexibility, which can disproportionately affect women, who are overrepresented in sectors vulnerable to market deregulation, such as sales and services (Périvier, 2018).

2.5.2 Public Policies for Gender Equality: The European Case

Gender mainstreaming is a paradigm that encompasses the design and analysis of public policies, with a strong emphasis on gender equality. It aims to be applied across all public policies and is built upon three key pillars. First, it involves implementing public policies that anticipate their impact on gender inequalities. This proactive approach ensures that policies are designed to address and prevent gender disparities from the outset. Second, gender mainstreaming utilizes structural tools to address the underlying causes of inequality. Rather than merely repairing or compensating for inequalities, the focus is on resolving them at their root and ensuring long-term change. Lastly, gender mainstreaming emphasizes the importance of avoiding the perpetuation of gender stereotypes through policy implementation, particularly in communication efforts.

In the late 1990s, the European Union adopted the gender mainstreaming approach following the 1995 Beijing Convention for Women. Consequently, objectives related to female employment emerged alongside the development of family policies aimed at facilitating women's professional careers. One crucial aspect of family policies is childcare expenditure, which has been extensively documented for its impact on women's economic activity. Jaumotte (2004) highlights the significance of childcare services and subsidies in fostering women's labor force participation. She examines the explanatory power of economic policies, particularly family policies and parental leave, and demonstrates that childcare subsidies play a decisive role in women's participation.

Esping-Andersen (2009) reinforces this idea by emphasizing that countries with robust social transfers, such as childcare services and parental leave, tend to have higher fertility rates and greater participation rates among mothers compared to countries where childcare responsibilities primarily rest with mothers themselves. Additionally, Erhel and Guergoat-Larivière (2013) investigate key variables influencing women's choice between full-time and part-time employment, focusing on the role of childcare and family policies. Their analysis, covering 24 European countries in 2005 and 2006, reveals a positive relationship between formal childcare availability and women's full-time employment, as well as a negative relationship with informal childcare.

To address the need for accessible childcare, the European Council established the Barcelona target in 2002, aiming for 90 percent of children between three years old and school age and 30 percent of children under three years old to be in childcare by 2010. While this target contributed to reducing childcare gaps, it appears that not all countries achieved the objective by 2018. It is important to note that the Barcelona target does not specify a minimum number of childcare hours, which can significantly influence the prevalence of part-time jobs for women. Nevertheless, this policy has led to a convergence of family policies within the European Union, with many countries choosing to invest in services and prioritize in-kind family benefits over cash benefits such as family allowances. Despite the efforts, EU policies have yielded mixed results. The policies, which emerged in the late 1990s, focused specifically on growth and employment. Women's employment was identified as an 'underutilized labor pool' (Jacquot, 2009) with the potential to boost growth and address broader issues such as population aging and the sustainability of social protection systems.

The Lisbon Strategy in 2000 exemplified this trend, setting a target of achieving a female employment rate of 60 percent by 2010 in each Member State, with an overall rate of 70 percent for the 15–24 age group. Gender mainstreaming was included as a condition for financing projects promoting employment within the European Social Fund, the community fund responsible for financing employment-related initiatives. However, these policies have limitations. Often, the measures implemented prioritize quantity of work rather than quality (Bettio et al., 2009; Périvier and Verdugo, 2018). As mentioned earlier, women's employment is primarily characterized by atypical jobs such as fixed-term contracts and part-time work. The objective of creating a more dynamic labor market appears to have taken precedence over promoting equality (Walby, 2004). The 2008 crisis marked a turning point in EU policies. Austerity measures were implemented without integrating the gender dimension, and the Europe 2020 strategy failed to adequately address the issue. The inclusion of gender in employment objectives was removed, and an overall employment rate of 75 percent became the sole target (Fagan and Rubery, 2018). Furthermore, Horizon 2020, which followed, seemed to depoliticize gender equality objectives in favor of economic ones (Vida, 2021).

The challenges in achieving gender equality remain substantial. The persistent inequalities have tangible consequences, particularly in terms of poverty and financial autonomy for women. While the state and social policies play crucial roles in women's emancipation, their effectiveness relies on a strong political will to implement and support these policies. Overall, addressing gender inequalities requires ongoing efforts and a comprehensive approach that encompasses all aspects of public policy, aiming not only to enable women's participation in the labor market but also to promote equal opportunities and eliminate gender stereotypes.

2.6 Conclusion

Efforts to address gender inequalities and promote equality have been ongoing throughout the past century. Despite the presence of legal frameworks and policies aimed at fostering gender equality, women continue to confront economic, political, social, and cultural barriers that hinder their full and equal participation in society. This chapter has explored the historical context of gender inequality, its various dimensions and manifestations, the advancements made toward gender equality, persistent challenges, and the significance of gender equality for sustainable development and social justice.

Gender equality is fundamental to achieving sustainable development. By empowering women and girls and ensuring their equal participation in the workforce and in decision-making processes, societies can unleash their full potential and reap the benefits of their talents and contributions. Ongoing research endeavors and interdisciplinary collaborations are crucial for improving our understanding of gender equality in different contexts. By combining quantitative and qualitative approaches, scholars strive to unravel the complexities of gender dynamics and shed light on the historical progression of gender equality.

Significant strides have been made in addressing gender inequalities across societies worldwide throughout the twentieth and twenty-first centuries. The expansion of women's rights, educational opportunities, and career advancements has played a pivotal role in reducing gender disparities. However, despite these positive developments, formidable obstacles remain that impede the achievement of complete gender equality. This chapter has shown that while gender inequalities have substantially decreased during these periods, there are persistent barriers that continue to hinder further progress. Various aspects of contemporary society contribute to perpetuate gender inequalities, manifesting in unequal pay, limited employment opportunities for women, discriminatory practices, and persistence of gender stereotypes.

Although the women's rights movement has made significant strides in the past, there are still numerous areas where women face disadvantages. Addressing gender inequality in the 21st century entails challenging traditional gender roles and stereotypes, promoting gender-neutral parenting and education, and establishing more equitable workplace policies. By collaborating and working together, society can strive toward a more equitable future for all. Continued efforts to advocate for gender equality, implement policy reforms, and foster broader social change will contribute to a more inclusive and equal society.

Notes

1 See Merouani and Perrin (2022) for a detailed survey of the literature.
2 « *Les écoles, les collèges, les lycées et les établissements d'enseignement supérieur sont chargés de transmettre et de faire acquérir connaissances et méthodes de travail. Ils contribuent à favoriser la mixité et l'égalité entre les hommes et les femmes, notamment en matière d'orientation* » (Article L121–1 du Code de l'éducation).
3 The only exception was the school created and reserved for the daughters of his generals: *La maison de la légion d'honneur d'Ecouen*.
4 Institutional Transformation for Effecting Gender Equality in Research aims at '*sustainable structural change in research and higher education institutions to improve professional equality between male and female researchers*'.
5 Project dedicated to the promotion of professional equality between women and men within research institutions and to the integration of the gender dimension in research content.

References

Alesina, A., Giuliano, P., and Nunn, N. (2013). On the Origins of Gender Roles: Women and the Plough. *Quarterly Journal of Economics*, 128, 469–530.

Alon, T., Doepke, M., Olmstead-Rumsey, J., and Tertilt, M. (2020). *The Impact of COVID-19 on Gender Equality* (NBER Working Paper No. 26947). Cambridge, MA: National Bureau of Economic Research.

Alper, K. (2019). *Income, Family and Women's Economic Independence* (LIS Working Paper Series No. 37). Luxembourg: Luxembourg Income Study (LIS).

Anxo, D., Fagan, C., Smith, M., Letablier, M.-T., Perraudin, C., et al. (2007). *Parental Leave in European Companies*. Luxembourg: Office for Official Publications of the European Communities.

Baudelot, C., and Establet, R. (2001). La scolarité des filles à l'échelle mondiale. In T. Blöss (ed), *La dialectique des rapports hommes-femmes*. Paris: PUF.

Bettio, F., Verashchagina, A., Mairhuber, I., and Kanjuo-Mrčela, A. (2009). *Gender Segregation in the Labour Market: Root Causes, Implications and Policy Responses in the EU*. Luxembourg: Publications Office of the European Union Luxembourg.

Blackburn, R.M., Brooks, B., and Jarman, J. (2001). The Vertical Dimension of Occupational Segregation. *Work, Employment and Society*, 15, 511–538.

Blau, F.D., and Kahn, L.M. (2017). The Gender Wage Gap: Extent, Trends, and Explanations. *Journal of Economic Literature*, 55(3), 789–865.

Bonnet, C., Buffeteau, S., Godefroy, P., and Tash, D. (2006). Effects of Pension Reforms on Gender Inequality in France. *Population*, 61(1), 41–70.

Boserup, E. (1970). *Woman's Role in Economic Development*. New York: St. Martin's Press.

Busch, F. (2020). Gender Segregation, Occupational Sorting, and Growth of Wage Disparities Between Women. *Demography*, 57, 1063–1088.

Çağatay, N. (2003). Gender Budgets and Beyond: Feminist Fiscal Policy in the Context of Globalisation. *Gender & Development*, 11, 15–24.

Carli, L.L. (2020). Women, Gender Equality and COVID-19. *Gender in Management: An International Journal*, 35, 647–655.

Carlson, D.L., Petts, R.J., and Pepin, J.R. (2022). Changes in US Parents' Domestic Labor during the Early Days of the COVID-19 Pandemic. *Sociological Inquiry*, 92(3), 1217–1244.

Caul, M. (2001). Political Parties and the Adoption of Candidate Gender Quotas: A Cross-National Analysis. *The Journal of Politics*, 63(4), 1214–1229.

Cavalcanti, T., and Tavares, J. (2003). Women Prefer Larger Governments: Female Labor Supply and Public Spending. *Economic Inquiry*, 49, 155–171.

Clark, A. (1920). *Working Life of Women in the Seventeenth Century*. New York: Harcourt, Brace & Howe.

Condorcet, N. (1792). *Rapport et projet de décret sur l'organisation générale de l'instruction publique*.

Corsi, M., Botti, F., and D'Ippoliti, C. (2016). The Gendered Nature of Poverty in the EU: Individualized Versus Collective Poverty Measures. *Feminist Economics*, 22, 82–100.

Dahlerup, D. (1987). Confusing Concepts—Confusing Reality: A Theoretical Discussion of the Patriarchal State. In *Women and the State: The Shifting Boundaries of Public and Private* (pp. 93–127). London: Routledge.

Dauphin, S. (2010). Action publique et rapports de genre. *Revue de l'OFCE*, 265–289.

Diebolt, C., and Perrin, F. (2013). From Stagnation to Sustained Growth: The Role of Female Empowerment. *American Economic Review*, 103(3), 545–549.

Diebolt, C., and Perrin, F. (2019). A Cliometric Model of Unified Growth. Gender Equality and Family Organization in the Long Run of History. In C. Diebolt, S. Carmichael, S. Dilli, A. Rijpma and C. Störmer (eds), *Cliometrics of the Family: Global Patterns and Their Impact on Diverging Development, Studies in Economic History*. Berlin: Editions Springer.

Dilli, S., Carmichael, S.G., and Rijpma, A. (2019). Introducing the Historical Gender Equality Index. *Feminist Economics*, 25(1), 31–57.

Edgell, S., and Duke, V. (1983). Gender and Social Policy: The Impact of the Public Expenditure Cuts and Reactions to Them. *Journal of Social Policy*, 12(3), 357–378.

Erhel, C., and Guergoat-Larivière, M. (2013). Labor Market Regimes, Family Policies, and Women's Behavior in the EU. *Feminist Economics*, 19, 76–109.

Esping-Andersen, G. (1990). *The Three Worlds of Welfare Capitalism*. Princeton, NJ: Princeton University Press.

Esping-Andersen, G. (2009). *Incomplete Revolution: Adapting Welfare States to Women's New Roles*. Cambridge: Polity.

Fagan, C., and Rubery, J. (2018). Advancing Gender Equality Through European Employment Policy: The Impact of the UK's EU Membership and the Risks of Brexit. *Social Policy and Society*, 17(3), 297–317.

Fernandez, C., and Sevilla Sanz, A. (2006). *Social Norms and Household Time Allocation* (IESE Research Papers D/648). Barcelona: IESE Business School.

Fernández, J.J., and Valiente, C. (2021). Gender Quotas and Public Demand for Increasing Women's Representation in Politics: An Analysis of 28 European Countries. *European Political Science Review*, 13(3), 351–370.

Ferrand, M. (1995). Les hirondelles de la mixité font-elles le printemps de l'égalité ? *Les Cahiers du Mage, Mixité des formations, mixité des professions*, 1, 33–35.

Fox, E., Pascall, G., and Warren, T. (2009). Work–Family Policies, Participation, and Practices: Fathers and Childcare in Europe. *Community, Work & Family*, 12(3), 313–326.

Frecheville-Faucon, R. (2023). *"Defamilializing" How Women's Economic Independence Is Measured* (Working Paper of BETA 2023-27), 21 p. Strasbourg: Bureau d'Economie Théorique et Appliquée, UDS.

Giuliano, P. (2020). *Gender and Culture* (IZA Working Paper, No 13607), 24 p. Bonn: Institute of Labor Economics (IZA).

Goldin, C. (1990). *Understanding the Gender Gap: An Economic History of American Women*. New York: Oxford University Press.

Guichard, J. (1992). School Failure and Representations of Self and Professions. *Orientation scolaire et professionnelle*, 2, 149–162.

Guichard, J., Devos, P., Bernard, H., Chevalier, G., Devaux, M., Faure, A., Jellab, M., and Vanesse, V. (1994a). Diversity and Similarity of Occupational Representations of Adolescents Enrolled in Different Training Courses. *L'Orientation scolaire et professionnelle*, 2(4), 409–437.

Guichard, J., Devos, P., Bernard, H., Chevalier, G., Devaux, M., Faure, A., Jellab, M., and Vanesse, V. (1994b). Habitus culturels des adolescents et schèmes représentatifs des professions. *L'Orientation scolaire et professionnelle*, 23(4), 439–464.

Guizot, F. (1834). *Rapport au Roi sur l'exécution de la loi du 28 juin 1833*. Paris: Paul Dupont.

Hernes, H.M. (1984). Women and the Advanced Welfare State—the Transition from Private to Public Dependence. In H. Holter (ed), *Patriarchy in a Welfare State*. Oslo: Universitetsforlaget.

Hernes, H.M., and Helga, M.H. (1987). *Welfare State and Woman Power: Essays in State Feminism*. Oxford: Oxford University Press.

Himmelweit, S. (2002). Making Visible the Hidden Economy: The Case for Gender-Impact Analysis of Economic Policy. *Feminist Economics*, 8(1), 49–70.

Hippe, R., and Perrin, F. (2017). Gender Equality in Human Capital and Fertility in the European Regions in the Past. *Investigaciones de Historia Economica—Economic History Research*, 13, 166–179.

Hobson, B. (1990). No Exit, No Voice: Women's Economic Dependency and the Welfare State. *Acta Sociologica*, 33(3), 235–250.

Huber, E., Stephens, J.D., Bradley, D., Moller, S., and Nielsen, F. (2009). The Politics of Women's Economic Independence. *Social Politics: International Studies in Gender, State & Society*, 16(1), 1–39.

Humphries, J., and Rubery, J. (1995). *The Economics of Equal Opportunities*. Massachusetts: Equal Opportunities Commission.

Jacquot, S. (2009). La fin d'une politique d'exception. *Revue française de science politique*, 59(2), 247–277.

Jaoul-Grammare, M. (2018). L'évolution des inégalités de genre dans l'enseignement supérieur entre 1998 et 2010. Une analyse de l'(in)efficacité des réformes politiques. *Education et Formations*, 96, 113–131.

Jaoul-Grammare, M. (2023). Gendered Professions, Prestigious Professions: When Stereotypes Condition Career Choices, *European Journal of Education*, 00, 1–26.

Jaoul-Grammare, M., and Perrin, F. (2017). A Gendered Approach of Economic and Demographic Interactions: Evidence from France. *Revue d'Économie Politique*, 127, 1083–1108.

Jaumotte, F. (2004). Labour Force Participation of Women: Empirical Evidence on the Role of Policy and Other Determinants in OECD Countries. *OECD Economic Studies*, 2003(1), 51–108.

Lakanal, J. (1793). *Projet d'éducation du peuple français, présenté à la Convention Nationale au nom du Comité d'Instruction Publique*.

Leroy, M., Biaggi, C., Debuchy, V., Duchêne, F., Gaubert-Macon, C., Jellab, A., Loeffel, L., and Rémy-Granger, D. (2013). *L'égalité entre filles et garçons dans les écoles et les établissements scolaires*. Rapport MEN-IGEN 2013–041. Paris: Ministère de l'Éducation Nationale – Inspection Générale de l'Éducation Nationale.

Lewis, J. (1992). Gender and the Development of Welfare Regimes. *Journal of European Social Policy*, 2(3), 159–173.

Marry, C. (2003). *Les paradoxes de la mixité filles-garçons à l'école. Perspectives internationales*. Rapport pour le PIREF et conférence au MEN. Paris: Programme Incitatif de Recherche sur l'Éducation et la Formation, Ministère de l'Éducation Nationale.

Mavrikiou, P.M., and Angelovska, J. (2020). The Impact of Sex Segregation by Economic Activity on the Gender Pay Gap Across Europe. *UTMS Journal of Economics*, 11(2), 129–142.

Merouani, Y., and Perrin, F. (2022). Gender and the Long-Run Development Process. A Survey of the Literature. *European Review of Economic History*, 26(4), 612–641.

Métral, A., and Stokkink, D. (2016). *Genre et crise économique. Un impact inégalitaire*. Bruselas: Pour la Solidarité. European Think & Do Tank.

Meulders, D., and O'Dorchai, S. (2011). Lorsque seul le ménage compte: Variations autour de la pauvreté des ménages et des individus en Europe. *Travail, genre et sociétés*, 26, 85–104.

Ministère de l'Éducation Nationale, Direction de l'évaluation, de la prospective et de la performance (DEPP). (2017). *Repères et références statistiques*. Paris: Ministère de l'Éducation Nationale.

Nimmesgern, H. (2016). Why Are Women Underrepresented in STEM Fields? *Chemistry—A European Journal*, 22(11), 3529–3530.

Orloff, A.S. (1993). Gender and the Social Rights of Citizenship: The Comparative Analysis of Gender Relations and Welfare States. *American Sociological Review*, 303–328.

Périvier, H. (2014). Men and Women During the Economic Crisis. *Revue de l'OFCE*, 41–84.

Périvier, H. (2018). Recession, Austerity and Gender: A Comparison of Eight European Labour Markets. *International Labour Review*, 157(1), 1–37.

Périvier, H., and Verdugo, G. (2018). La stratégie de l'Union européenne pour promouvoir l'égalité professionnelle est-elle efficace? *Revue de l'OFCE*, 158, 77–101.

Perrin, E. (2014). *On the Construction of a Historical Gender Gap Index. An Implementation on French Data* (Working Papers 05–14). Restinclières: Association Française de Cliométrie (AFC).

Perrin, F. (2013). *Gender Equality and Economic Growth in the Long Run: A Cliometric Analysis* (Doctoral dissertation, Université de Strasbourg and Scuola superiore Sant'Anna di studi universitari e di perfezionamento).

Perrin, F. (2022a). On the Origins of the Demographic Transition. Rethinking the European Marriage Pattern. *Cliometrica*, 16(3), 431–475.

Perrin, F. (2022b). Can the Historical Gender Gap Index Deepen Our Understanding of Economic Development? *Journal of Demographic Economics*, 88(3), 379–417.

Perrin, F., Karlsson, T., and Kok, J. (2023). The Historical Gender Gap Index. A Longitudinal and Spatial Assessment of Sweden, 1870–1990. *Journal of Economic History*, 83(4), 943–980.

Pinchbeck, I. (1930). *Women Workers and the Industrial Revolution, 1750–1850 (London School of Economics: Studies in Economic and Social History)*. London: George Routledge & Sons.

Reichelt, M., Makovi, K., and Sargsyan, A. (2021). The Impact of COVID-19 on Gender Inequality in the Labor Market and Gender-Role Attitudes. *European Societies*, 23, S228–S245.

Reskin, B.F., and Bielby, D.D. (2005). A Sociological Perspective on Gender and Career Outcomes. *Journal of Economic Perspectives*, 19(1), 71–86.

Rubery, J. (2015). Austerity and the Future for Gender Equality in Europe. *ILR Review*, 68(3), 715–741.

Schneebaum, A., Rehm, M., Mader, K., and Hollan, K. (2018). The Gender Wealth Gap Across European Countries. *Review of Income and Wealth*, 64, 295–331.

Scott, J.W. (1986). Gender: A Useful Category of Historical Analysis. *American Historical Review*, 91, 1053–1075.

Seron, C., Silbey, S.S., Cech, E., and Rubineau, B. (2016). Persistence Is Cultural: Professional Socialization and the Reproduction of Sex Segregation. *Work and Occupations*, 43(2), 178–214.

Sevilla, A., Phimister, A., Krutikova, S., Kraftman, L., Farquharson, C., Dias, M.C., Cattan, S., and Andrew, A. (2020). *How Are Mothers and Fathers Balancing Work and Family Under Lockdown?* London, United Kingdom: Institute for Fiscal Studies (IFS). https://doi.org/10.1920/BN.IFS.2020.BN0290

Szoltysek, M., Klüsener, S., Poniat, R., and Gruber, S. (2017). The Patriarchy Index: A New Measure of Gender and Generational Inequalities in the Past. *Cross-Cultural Research*, 51(3), 228–262.

Theodoropoulou, S., and Watt, A. (2011). *Withdrawal Symptoms: An Assessment of the Austerity Packages in Europe* (Working Paper 2011.02.). Brussels: European Trade Union Institute.

Tilly, L.A., and Scott, J.W. (1989). *Women, Work and Family*. London: Routledge.

United Nations. (2015). *Transforming Our World: The 2030 Agenda for Sustainable Development*. UN. https://sdgs.un.org/goals

United Nations. (2022). *Women in the Changing World of Work*. UN Women. www.oecd.org/gender

Vida, B. (2021). Policy Framing and Resistance: Gender Mainstreaming in Horizon 2020. *European Journal of Women's Studies*, 28(1), 26–41.

Voicu, M., Voicu, B., and Strapcova, K. (2009). Housework and Gender Inequality in European Countries. *European Sociological Review*, 25(3), 365–377.

Wach, M. (1992). Projets et représentations des études et des professions des élèves de troisième et de terminale en 1992. *L'Orientation scolaire et professionnelle*, 21(3), 297–339.

Walby, S. (2004). The European Union and Gender Equality: Emergent Varieties of Gender Regime. *Social Politics: International Studies in Gender, State & Society*, 11(1), 4–29.

Winkler, A.E. (2022). *Women's Labor Force Participation*. IZA World of Labor. ISSN 2054–9571. Institute of Labor Economics (IZA), Bonn.

World Bank. (2022). *Proportion of Seats Held by Women in National Parliaments*. The World Bank—Data. https://data.worldbank.org/indicator/SG.GEN.PARL.ZS

Part II
Inequalities in Income and Wealth

3 Piketty and the Distribution of Wealth

Jesper Roine

Economic inequality is typically studied in terms of *income inequality*. However, it is not common that income is measured in a way that fully captures the actual theoretical meaning of 'income'. This has, at least in my experience, caused some confusion in discussions about economic inequality and, in particular, the respective roles played by income inequality in relation to wealth inequality. If one reads the introduction to the *Canberra Group Handbook on Household Income Statistics*—the most comprehensive attempt at giving researchers guidance in terms of how to think about developing inequality statistics—income is introduced as referring to 'receipts, whether monetary or in kind, that are received at annual or more frequent intervals and are available for current consumption' (Canberra Group, 2011). This kind of definition emphasizes the *flow of income* over a time period, and this is often what is measured when we study 'income inequality' based on taxation of wages and capital income flows. However, further down in the *Canberra Handbook* introduction, it is also noted that 'the data should ideally be accompanied by some assessment of the change in the value of the household's net worth during the accounting period', that is, the change in the *wealth* of the household over the period. These two points are *both* crucial in determining the 'income' of a household in the economic sense, which emphasizes the change in consumption possibilities over a period.

According to classic definitions such as by Haig (1921), income is 'the money value of the net accretion to one's economic power between two points of time'. Simons (1938) defines income as 'the algebraic sum of (1) the market value of rights exercised in consumption and (2) the change in the value of the store of property rights between the beginning and end of the period in question'. The latter definition can be translated to 'consumption + the change in net worth'. Consumption must be paid for, and the only way of doing this is earning a flow of 'new money' (either from labor or from capital) or using part of one's stock of 'wealth'. If the flow of money exceeds consumption, this is by definition saved and adds to the wealth. If, on the other hand, consumption exceeds the flow of new income, this must be paid for by using previous savings or borrowing. Either way, this changes the net worth, or the wealth, of the individual.

Why this initial little excursion into the definitions of income? Simply to remind the reader of the underlying connection between income flows and changes in wealth as connected processes that *jointly* determine the income distribution over time. In relation to this chapter on Thomas Piketty and the role of *wealth* and its

DOI: 10.4324/9781003387114-6

distribution, it is important from the outset to understand that Piketty's main contribution does not lie in studying the wealth distribution per se (as opposed to the income distribution) but in insisting on economic inequality being determined by both flow and stock and showing, theoretically as well as empirically, why the distribution of wealth is important (and according to Piketty more important than previously recognized) for understanding long-run economic inequality.

3.1 Thomas Piketty's *Capital in the Twenty-First Century*

In the spring of 2014, Thomas Piketty became, if not a household name, at least a name recognized by most people who follow public discourse about economics and politics. The reason was the publication of his *Capital in the Twenty-First Century*, an almost 700-page book on the historical evolution of inequality in advanced economies that for weeks topped best-selling lists. Not the typical faith for 700-page academic works of any kind. The book stirred a lot of debate, mainly about Piketty's forward-looking discussion on 'Regulating Capital in the Twenty-First Century' (the title of the fourth section of the book, where he, among other things, argues for a global tax on capital) but also about his description of the inherent inequality dynamics of the economy. The debate was predictably divided with progressives and those to the left being widely favorable, while conservatives and those on the right were more often critical. But no one doubted the importance of the basic ideas and, in particular, the facts put forward in Piketty's book.[1]

So what exactly was it that was so new, and how should we understand this in relation to other discussions about economic inequality? And how has this come to impact current work on inequality questions? Later in the chapter, I will try to sketch answers to these questions by first looking back at the development of the inequality research focus leading up to the beginning of the project that forms the empirical base for Thomas Piketty's *Capital in the Twenty-First Century*—*Capital*, for short—then discuss some of the debates that followed and then describe some of the more recent work that continues advancing our understanding of the role of wealth in economic inequality. Many of the current debates about the proper reading of inequality data, in fact, hinge on some of the fundamental points made already in *Capital*.

3.2 Inequality Before Piketty and the 'Top Income' Literature

Most work on economic inequality in the decades before the late 1990s, when Piketty began the research that became the empirical backbone of his 2014 book, was concerned with the distribution of disposable incomes across households in the entire population, often with a particular focus on the lower part of the distribution. To arrive at measures of this requires detailed micro data based on large surveys or register data covering, if not the entire population, then at least representative samples, or large parts of the entire population.[2] Great improvements in data availability had made it possible to also adjust individual disposable incomes to household circumstances and to include and study the impacts on overall inequality from various government programs and other redistributive schemes. Data required for

Piketty and the Distribution of Wealth 61

these detailed studies were not commonly available in most countries prior to the 1970s or 1980s and very rarely prior to the 1960s.³ Furthermore, since collecting data was done differently across countries, comparability issues were large, and, also, inequalities were rarely decomposed into capital and labor income components. Even if great strides were taken to improve cross-country comparability, in particular through projects such as the Luxembourg Income Study (LIS), and attempts were made to compiling inequality data into panels such as the World Bank's World Income Inequality Database (WIID), it is fair to say that two key ingredients were missing in our inequality data: (1) the long-run development and (2) the relative role of capital income in relation to labor income.⁴

Both of these points are emphasized in the introductory chapter to the first of two volumes, edited by Thomas Piketty and Anthony Atkinson, on 'Top Incomes' published in 2007 and 2010 (Atkinson and Piketty, 2007, 2010). These volumes collect much of the work that would later become the empirical backbone of Piketty's influential book. As Piketty puts it in the introduction to the first volume:

> The primary motivation for this project was a general dissatisfaction with existing income distribution databases. [T]hey are not long-run and . . . they almost never offer any decomposition of income inequality into a labour income and capital income component. *This latter feature of existing data sets is unfortunate, because the economic mechanisms at work can be very different for the distribution of labour income (demand and supply of skills, labour market institutions, etc.) and the distribution of capital income (capital accumulation, credit constraints, estate taxation, etc.), so that it is fairly heroic to test for any of these mechanisms using such data.*
> (Piketty, 2007, p. 2)

The italics (added by me) insist on understanding economic inequality as the *joint outcome* of a process which involves a *flow* of income, coming from both labor—the distribution of which has one set of determinants—and from capital where the process depends on the underlying distribution of the *stock* of capital in society. This joint outcome based on both labor and capital is key here. This is, of course, not to suggest that this was an innovation by Thomas Piketty. This way of thinking about individual income dynamics as jointly determined by labor and capital incomes was developed by James Meade in the 1960s (Meade, 1964) and later repeatedly emphasized by, in particular, Anthony Atkinson (e.g., Atkinson, 1975, Atkinson and Harrison, 1978, Atkinson, 1981). As Atkinson (2007) explains:

> *In this framework, individual income, Yi, is decomposed into earned income, Wi, and capital income, the latter being the product of the rate of return ri and total (individual) wealth Ki. From this we can see the impact of macro variables such as factor shares, which already feature in the models of economic growth. But it goes beyond the earlier models in allowing for a distribution of wages and capital.*
> (Atkinson, 2007, p. 2)

Stiglitz (1969) later embeds this kind of process into a Solow (1956)—Swan (1956) growth model. But even if there were developments of models building on this, most of the empirical work on inequality did not emphasize the potential role of capital.[5] One can think of several reasons for this. One is that if individual savings and capital accumulation happen only because of consumption smoothing reasons, then capital over every person's lifetime simply mirrors individual earnings. If this were the case, one could argue that there is no separate reason to think about the distribution of capital in relation to inequality. It simply reflects differences in savings across the life cycle and whatever inequality is there is due to differences in earnings. Another, more empirically based point would be to note that incomes from capital form a relatively small fraction of total income for most people. If the focus is on inequality in the population at large—as it has been in much of the inequality literature—then capital income does not matter so much basically since only the rich have capital income. Both of these points have, as we will see, been raised in the discussions about the appropriate focus of inequality research following Piketty's *Capital*.

3.3 The Role of Capital in the Main Findings of the Top Income Literature

As mentioned earlier, much of the empirical work in *Capital* comes from what has become known as the 'top income project'. It was initiated by Thomas Piketty and Anthony Atkinson and built on Piketty's seminal contribution on long-run inequality in France, *Les hauts revenus en France au 20e siècle. Inégalités et redistribution, 1901–1998*, (Piketty, 2001). Almost simultaneously, Piketty, jointly with Emmanuel Saez, produced similar long-run top income series for the United States (Piketty and Saez, 2003); Atkinson (2004) did the same for the same for the UK; and in conference volumes based on presentations at both the European Economic Association and the American Economic Association (Piketty, 2005; Piketty and Saez, 2006), the ambition of producing long-run inequality series for as many countries as possible was formulated. The basic idea was to extend the methods used by Kuznets (1953) to generate inequality measures for as many countries and for as long a time span as data allows using a common methodology. This consists of using fiscal sources, in particular tax data, rather than household surveys. Income tax data typically extend back to the end of the 19th or the beginning of the 20th century for most Western countries. The data is often very detailed and allows for decomposing between labor income and capital income, and in some countries wealth was also taxed, so data on the wealth distribution is available separately.[6] A drawback, however, is that tax data, especially in the early periods, is typically limited to capturing only the top of the distribution due to the simple reason that most peoples' incomes fell below the tax threshold. Overtime coverage grows, but in most countries, it remains limited to the top decile for much of the 20th century. This creates challenges for arriving at comparable inequality measures. The standard way of proceeding is to define a top income group (those observed in the tax data) as a fraction of the full, potential tax population (if everyone would have filed a tax return), that is, the top x-percent. Their income (observed in the tax records) is then related to the total income, had all income been subject to taxation, arriving at an income share for the top x-percent of the population. Hence, the 'top income literature'.

It is worth emphasizing that the focus on top incomes was not key at the outset here. The primary aim of the project was to produce a long-run comparable series of inequality that looked at total income decomposed into labor and capital income, and the focus on top groups was mainly a consequence of data being limited to those with the highest incomes. However, it turned out that the focus on top groups gave rise to a number of important, previously overlooked, results. In particular, the concentration of capital incomes to the very top of the income distribution resulted in findings that became evident only when groups as small as the top-1 group (and sometimes even smaller groups) were treated separately.[7]

The most obvious new result from the top income project lies in the overall development of inequality over the 20th century. As the number of countries for which top income shares were estimated grew, a 'common trend' emerged.[8] This common trend can be described as a U-shaped development over time: declining top income shares over the first half of the century, a flattening-out or continued fall until around 1980, followed by an up-turn when top shares start to increase in many countries.[9] Figure 3.1 shows this development for 20 countries. Clearly, the point of this figure is not to show individual countries but rather to illustrate the overall trend (while at the same time showing the existing variation).

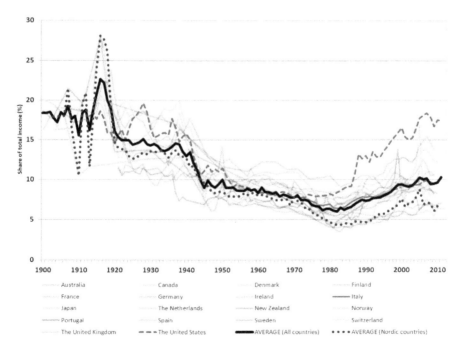

Figure 3.1 Top one income share in 20 countries 1870–2010. A U-shaped development over the 20th century due to fluctuations in capital (at least in the first half of the century)

64 *Jesper Roine*

This basic pattern of inequality development is in itself an important result and in a way what the project set out to do: create comparable empirical estimates of income inequality over the long run.[10] But there are other aspects of these series that are perhaps even more important, and they relate to the role played by capital incomes, and therefore indirectly to the underlying distribution of wealth. A first result has to do with the difference within the top decile group in terms of income composition (between wage and capital) and, consequently, the difference in income shares over time. Of course, income compositions vary across countries, but a common feature is that capital as a source of income is concentrated to the top of the distribution. A representative range across countries is one where, for the lower half of the top decile group (P90–95), wages make up some 70 to 95 percent of total income and capital around 30 to 5 percent, while in groups in the top 1 percent, the capital share is often way above 50 percent. This means that when something happens that affects the capital stock (or the capital income flows), the impact is much larger for the very top groups. This, it turns out, drives much of the development of inequality (as captured by the changes in the top decile income share). If one decomposes the top decile group into sub-groups and studies the P90–95 group, or even the P90–99 group, separately from the top 1 group, it becomes evident that much of the action in the top decile share is due to fluctuations in the top 1, which in turn are very influenced by capital incomes. Figure 3.2 illustrates this.

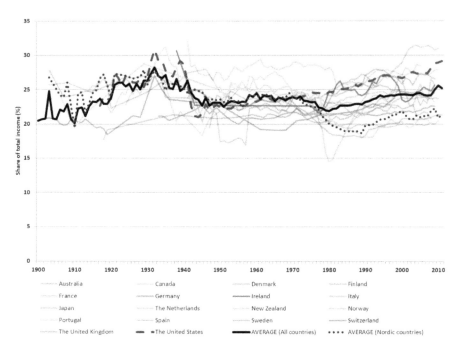

Figure 3.2 The income share of the P90–99 group, relatively flat over the 20th century due to capital incomes being less important than for the very top

This development is very marked especially when it comes to the fall of inequality in the first half of the 20th century. This is important in relation to previous thinking and, in particular, in relation to the conjecture that has become known as the Kuznets curve. When Kuznets sketched his idea in his 1954 presidential address to the AEA (Kuznets, 1955), he was clear on this being one out of several possible mechanisms but the Kuznets curve has still gained a special standing in thinking about how to explain the declining inequality over the path of development observed in Kuznets (1953).[11] The explanation is one of structural change where only a small fraction of the population initially gains access to the modern, more productive technology. This makes them earn higher incomes compared to those still in the less productive sector, thus increasing inequality at initial stages of development. Over time, however, as more and more individuals move into the new sector, inequality goes down. When the whole cycle is complete, the society has moved through a period of first increasing and later decreasing inequality—an inverse U-shape—to a new state where everyone earns higher incomes due to the productivity increase. Piketty's more careful study and decomposition showed that this was not what the data supported. The fall in inequality was instead a result more of episodes of sharp declines in capital incomes in connection with the wars and financial crises, while the top income earners' share of labor income remained relatively stable.[12]

The role of capital incomes in explaining the increasing income inequality after around 1980 is less straightforward. The main reason is the diverse developments across countries in the role of capital incomes in driving the increase. In the United States, in particular, but also in other Anglo-Saxon countries (as well as in China and India), much of the increase in top income shares, even in the very top groups, seems to be mostly related to increasing top wages. This is not the case in most European countries.[13]

The interpretation of the development of capital, both in the role of capital incomes and in the role of aggregate capital in relation to national income, has become one of the most contested issues in the debate that has followed the publication of Piketty's *Capital*.

3.4 The Role of Capital in *Capital*

Before going into the details of the debate about the role of capital (or wealth) in inequality over the past decades, let us summarize the main findings and arguments in Piketty's *Capital*. The book consists of 16 chapters organized into 4 main sections. The first section (chapters 1 and 2) contains some basic definitions and an overview of long-run economic growth. Here, it is made clear that all income is the result of production and that production in turn is a process that requires both capital and labor. This means that whatever is produced is also earned by either the laborers or the capital owners. Even if most definitions here are completely standard, it is worth noting that the definition of capital is not universally agreed upon. Piketty maintains that capital is best understood as the total market value of everything that is owned by either residents or governments of a given country.[14] This means that capital is a function of institutional arrangements concerning what can be owned (e.g. at times when individuals could be owned, slaves constituted capital). It also means that capital in Piketty's definition does not distinguish between 'productive' capital and 'wealth' as a mere store of value. This definition is important to note since it has bearing on some of the subsequent discussions about how to interpret the dynamics of capital and capital incomes. From the point of view of understanding capital in the production function, it may matter if capital has increased due to the capital stock of firms or due to private housing, for example. Piketty, however, maintains that distinctions between productive and unproductive capital are always bound to be arbitrary (many assets can be both a store of value and useful in the production process), and, in the presence of capital markets, it doesn't matter what form capital takes since it can always be converted between 'productive' and 'unproductive' based on its monetary value. Capital and wealth are therefore used interchangeably. Another important definition is introduced in this section, and this is what Piketty calls the *first law of capitalism*, namely that the share of national income received by capital owners, α, equals the rate of return to capital, r, times the capital/income ratio, $K/Y = \beta$. This 'law' is simply a definition but one that is useful for Piketty's discussion about how individual income distribution dynamics are affected by the overall balance between capital and income.

The second part (chapters 3–6) studies the aggregate dynamics of the capital/income ratio, β. This is shown to have been high in England and France in the 19th century, after which it falls substantially during the first half of the 20th century, mainly due to wars, crises and policy shifts. In recent decades it has recovered, but at the same time, it has changed in composition from being almost entirely dominated by land in the 19th century to now being dominated by housing and financial assets. The US capital/income ratio on the other hand is found to be more stable. In this part of the book, Piketty also formulates what he calls his *second law of capitalism*. This is a formula which aims at capturing what determines the capital income ratio in the long run. Piketty maintains that β, that is, the K/Y ratio, is determined by the savings to economic growth ratio s/g. Intuitively, K is replaced by savings, s, while national income grows by Y. *If* the savings rate s and the growth rate g remain at some average levels over time, the ratio s/g will approach K/Y in the long run. This is an important *if* that has been criticized and we will return to this later in the chapter.

Together, the two simple 'laws of capitalism' illustrate Piketty's main message and also the main reason for why the capital aspect of income dynamics is central to his work. If we combine the two expressions and assume that the rate of return to capital, r, remains permanently above the growth rate of the economy g, then the share of income to capital, α, increases by definition. This inequality, $r > g$, is the relationship Piketty wants to emphasize. We can note that this would, of course, not matter if everyone had equal stakes in capital. But if capital is concentrated (which we know it to be), the dynamic also has a positive feedback loop. Unless capital owners consume all they earn, they can save even more, which is as long as $r > g$

gives an even higher return compared to those who get their income from labor income that grows by g.

In the third part of the book (chapters 7 to 12), Piketty moves on to study the individual income distribution. This process consists of the individual labor income distribution and the individual distribution of wealth which, in turn, determine the distribution of capital income. In addition, since capital has the property that it can be owned, it can also be inherited. This makes the question: What is the share of all capital that is inherited over time? important (this is the topic of Chapter 11). Just as the capital share of all income can be expressed as α, the share of inherited wealth can be expressed as β (the capital/income ratio) times the mortality rate in the population, times the average wealth of those who die. The expression tells us that inheritance may not necessarily play any role regardless of the role of capital in the economy. If those who die have no wealth left, that is, if all savings are consumed over each person's lifetime, no capital will be inherited. But if this is not the case, inheritance may play a role, and indeed, all other things being equal, inheritance becomes larger with an increasing β. Piketty's calculations of the inheritance share of income in France indicates that the role of inheritance was large in the 19th century, fell in the first half of the 20th century and has now increased again. This indicates what should perhaps not be surprising; as the role of capital increases so does the role of inheritance.[15]

In the final part of the book (chapters 13–16), Piketty discusses various aspects of policy to deal with what he has described as inherent inequality dynamics in the economy. Most attention has been given here to the proposals to tax (net) wealth at a global level, a policy which Piketty admits is perhaps not feasible but should still be considered, given its many benefits. In particular, he emphasizes that without any tax on wealth itself, it is close to impossible to see how the true income of very wealthy individuals can be taxed at anything close to the same level as the labor incomes of individuals with much lower incomes. The reason is simple; in a world where the return on capital is r, the income of a very wealthy person is likely to be much larger than what is seen in tax returns when only labor and capital income (flows) are taxed. This is provided that income is defined including the change in net worth as suggested by Haig (1921) and Simons (1938). Piketty even gives an explicit example to illustrate his point (in chapter 15). An individual with a fortune of ten billion euros earning a 5 percent yields an income of 500 million euros per year. But it is unlikely that the person declares anything close to this in income. The taxed income is more likely to be something like five million euros. Whatever the tax on this amount, it means that the person earns 495 million euros tax free. This is the problem with modern tax systems without a tax on wealth according to Piketty. The actual tax paid by the very rich is very low in relation to actual economic income.

This final point brings us back to the initial point made in the beginning of this chapter; income, properly defined, is the sum of the flow of income, based on work as well as in the form of capital income, *plus the net change of the value of the individual capital stock*. Piketty does not ignore the distribution of labor in which income plays an important role, nor the fact that increasing wage inequality is behind much of what has happened to inequality in the United States in the past decades. But he does insist that economic inequality is composed of several different processes where the distribution of labor incomes is affected by things such as supply and demand of different skills and institutional aspects of the labor market, while capital and the distribution of capital is affected by things such as capital accumulation, credit constraints and estate taxation. This is what Piketty emphasized as the key contribution already in the beginning of the top income project (quoted earlier), and bringing both empirics and a theoretical framework capturing the dynamics of these joint processes together is the great achievement of *Capital in the Twenty-First Century*.

3.5 The Debates After *Capital*

As mentioned in the beginning of the chapter, Piketty's book was met with mostly praise and admiration but also with some criticism. The critique can broadly be categorized into those emphasizing what they see as flaws in Piketty's theoretical framework and those who have issues with the interpretation of the data and in particular the view on capital.[16] Of course, these points are sometimes connected, but it may still be useful to discuss them separately.[17] In addition, another point of view was that there may be important issues, such as capital dynamics, that primarily concern the top 1 percent group, but for the large majority—the 'other 99 percent' as David Autor puts it in an overview article—other mechanisms are more important.[18]

A first set of objections had to do with the theory and the interpretation of the equations. First about whether the so-called 'Laws of Capitalism' are anything of the sort, and second, to what extent $r > g$ can be seen as an explanation of inequality. Regarding the 'laws', many point out that they are not really 'explanations' of anything. The 'First Law' on the capital share of income being equal to the rate of return to capital times the capital/income ratio is nothing but a definition, while the second—the Harrod–Domar equation known in the theory of economic growth since at least the 1940s—has more promise in the sense that it does not hold under all circumstances and could as such be proven to be incorrect, but only if we somehow impose further restrictions on the variables (Ray, 2014). Looking just at the equation $\beta = K/Y = s/g$, and then assuming, for example, that if g falls (as Piketty finds likely it will in the future) while s stays the same, this will lead to an increased capital/income ratio, K/Y. But as for example, Krusell and Smith (2015) point out it seems unlikely that s would remain unchanged if g goes down. If g goes to zero, all income would need to be invested just to maintain the capital stock K which seems very unlikely to happen. Another point is that even if K/Y would go up, it is not obvious that the capital share of income goes up. Combining the two laws gives that the income share that goes to capital $\alpha = r \times s/g$. But if g falls causing the capital stock to grow, it also seems likely that the rate of return, r, falls. The question is by how much? This depends on the elasticity of supply. Under the common assumption of a Cobb–Douglas production function, the effect on r from an increasing capital stock is exactly offset by a decrease in the rate of return to this capital stock. In this case, the income share of capital is constant regardless of what happens to K/Y.[19]

All of these points are (of course) known to Piketty, and he does seem unconcerned with addressing them in terms of developing any of his equations further. Reading *Capital* one can note that he in several passages mentions all of these possibilities and basically concludes that there are many determinants of savings and interest rate etcetera. He simply views the equations as convenient when making different thought experiments about different possible outcomes. Some of these he finds more plausible than others based on historical data which is the basis for his 'predictions' about the future dynamics. But it is admittedly difficult to view this use of the equations as a model in the traditional sense.

Similarly, many have also pointed out that $r > g$ is not, in itself, a novel inequality, nor is it necessarily a reason for spiraling increasing inequality. It is a well-established result in standard growth theory that $r > g$ is required for the economy to be dynamically efficient. If $r < g$, everyone (every generation) could be made better off by reducing savings. There are also many ways in which $r > g$ holds without this leading to increasing inequality (e.g. Acemoglu and Robinson, 2015). The $r > g$ assumption that is really driving the increasing inequality is that the rich, and in particular the very rich, can save larger shares of their income (and, without capital taxes, it is also possible to save in the form of 'retained earnings' making the advantage of the rich even larger).[20]

In the end, many of the discussions about the 'model' in Piketty's *Capital* have not really led to any new insights. It remains the case that Piketty acknowledges most of the points—indeed many of them are already mentioned in his text—but he does not feel compelled to develop any alternative framework simply because he does not think that there exists a 'true' model of the economy. He seems to view his equations as relationships that have economic meaning but where the exact mechanisms behind individual decisions that yield the economy-wide savings rates and interest rates and growth rates are affected by many things which cannot be pinned down in ways that would satisfy those who criticize his framework.

Another part of the critique, however, has moved the academic literature forward in more interesting ways. This has to do with the definition of capital and how it relates to the individual distribution of wealth and in the end income from that wealth. An important dimension of this debate has to do with the *composition* of wealth. This affects both some of the theory predictions and the interpretation of how capital translates to individual inequality. A key result (also stated by Piketty) is that a large part of the recent increase in K/Y, the capital/income ratio, is due to housing. Housing is typically not seen as part of 'productive capital' so it matters for discussions relating to how capital enters the production function (Bonnet et al., 2014). It also matters for the distribution of wealth. Owner-occupied housing is much more widely spread in the population compared to ownership of 'productive capital'. If this component of wealth increases relatively more, this could even have an equalizing effect on the distribution of wealth. The same could be said for the stock of pension savings, which has also grown in importance (Waldenström, 2021).

Fundamentally, many parts of how to think about capital and its distribution and consequently the distribution of income in society have to do with delimitations among the household sector, the corporate sector and government. The perspective, laid out already in the introduction of *Capital*, is deceptively simple. Everything that can be owned and traded is finally owned by a physical person, and all activities that take place that produce economic value end up as income somewhere. This means that all income flows and all ownership of wealth can be distributed across individuals in society. This is in essence what the so-called DINA project aims to do. DINA stands for Distributional National Accounts and can be thought of as an attempt at distribution of everything in the economy across all individuals. However, an important obstacle in practice is that between individual households and the macroaggregates of income and wealth stand firms and government. In many countries, government provides many services that would otherwise have to come from individual incomes so the value of these should somehow be allocated to individuals if we want the distribution of income as consumption possibilities. Similarly, government pensions schemes act as substitutes for individual savings for retirement, so public pension funds are also assets that should be allocated across individuals. Both of these points are likely to equalize the distribution of income and wealth. By how much depends on how they are treated and what assumptions are made. But on the other hand, there are funds held by corporations—in some cases—closely held corporations owned by single (or few) individuals. How should we think about these assets, and how should we value them in the absence of market prices? These are some of the questions that have been much debated in recent years especially in the United States. Estimates by Saez and Zucman (2016) on wealth inequality based on capitalized income tax data and estimates on income inequality based on DINA for the United States in Piketty et al. (2018) show substantial and increased inequality, much driven by capital income. These have in turn been challenged by Smith et al. (2019) who argue that labor income is more prevalent in the top groups. Smith et al. (2023) argue that the share of top wealth is only about half of that found by Saez and Zucman (2016). Auten and Splinter (2023) argue that differences in the treatment of incomes over time, and in particular how they appear on tax returns, lower inequality substantially. When looking at their top 1 percent income share after tax, this has hardly increased at all. Saez and Zucman (2020) have, in turn, responded to these 'revisions' of their previous results and maintain that the quantitative results of sharply increasing income and wealth inequality remain even after addressing the points raised.

In addition to questions about the proper attribution of different incomes and how to think about wealth in firms and the role of government, there is, of course, also the question of how much wealth and income tax evasion and avoidance there is, and how this affects our measures of inequality. Starting with the work by Gabriel Zucman (Zucman, 2012), a lot of progress has been made in improving our knowledge of these questions (see, e.g., Alstadsæter et al., 2019 and reference therein).

In the end, the role of capital and its impact on economic inequality remain a contested issue. But it has become a central one. This was not the case before Thomas Piketty, who, in the late 1990s, embarked on the work that first led to the top income project and later led to the publication of *Capital* and after that the creation of the World Inequality Database (WID) and work on Distributional National Accounts. All of these efforts have shifted the research on economic inequality in fundamental ways for a long time to come.

Notes

1 Examples include Krugman (2014), Milanovic (2014), Lindert (2014), Solow (2014) and Summers (2014).
2 The focus on the overall distribution and the focus on the lower half had several implications in relation to the top of the distribution. First it was not common to have measures of the development of the very top, such as the top 1 percent group (and certainly not smaller top groups). The relation between 'the rich' and 'the poor' was captured by measures such decile ratios such as P90/P10 or, at best, P95/P5. Second, the fact that surveys often were the source meant that the top was not well represented, and especially for smaller samples, top-coding data was important since 'accidentally' getting a 'super-rich' person or household disturbed the representativeness of the sample. In this sense, the top of the distribution was not just absent but often seen as a problem for arriving at a representative picture of 'most people'.
3 See section 7.1 in Roine and Waldenström (2015) for an overview of how inequality research has developed leading up to the so-called top income literature.
4 For a critical assessment of the inequality data compilations at the time see, for example, Atkinson and Brandolini (2001), and for a critical appraisal of using such measures in cross-country regressions to study the inequality-growth question, see for example, Banerjee and Duflo (2003).
5 Much of this theoretical work is summarized in Piketty (2000).
6 This renewed interest in the long run and the reevaluation of historical sources also led to new studies on the historical trends in the wealth distribution (e.g., Kopczuk and Saez, 2004; Dell et al., 2007; Piketty et al., 2006; Roine and Waldenström, 2009).
7 Again, it is not the case that the importance of top groups was completely overlooked in previous work. Atkinson and Harrison (1978), for example, note the importance of top groups especially when studying the distribution of wealth.
8 Whether or not the trend is similar across countries depends on perspective. In particular, the rise of inequality in many countries has been debated (e.g., an op-ed by Allan Meltzer in *WSJ* (9 March 2012) emphasized the common trend suggesting that inequality trends can best be understood as due to common global economic forces. This was criticized by e.g. Paul Krugman in the *NY Times* (10 March 2012) and others who instead emphasized the large differences in developments across countries especially after 1980. We will come back to this debate later in the chapter).
9 Roine and Waldenström (2015) give an overview of the main results.
10 Roine et al. (2009) give an early illustration of how the data can be used to empirically study questions of the determinants of inequality over time.
11 As Kuznets remarks in his conclusion, his presentation is 'perhaps 5 per cent empirical information and 95 per cent speculation, *some of it possibly tainted by wishful thinking*' (my emphasis). This point is perhaps more important than what is usually acknowledged. Piketty (2014) notes that Kuznets in his 1953 study is aware that much of the decrease in inequality in the United States between 1913 and 1948 is 'accidental' and due to large shocks rather than any automatic process. Still, Kuznets (and many of his readers!) choose to emphasize a more optimistic view according to which structural change and economic growth that follows initially may cause inequality, but that if given time, the 'fruits of economic growth' will be shared broadly by all (p. 14, Piketty, 2014).
12 See, for example, Chapter 8 in Piketty (2014). Figures 8.1 and 8.2 show the pattern very clearly for France, but similar results are found in other countries as well.
13 See, e.g., Chapter 9 in Piketty (2014). Figures 9.2 and 9.3 show the contrast between Anglo-Saxon countries and Continental Europe.
14 Piketty defines capital as 'the total market value of everything owned by the residents and government of a given country at a given point in time, provided that it can be traded on some market' (p. 48).

15 It should, however, be noted that welfare state arrangements may influence how the role of inheritance is transmitted into inequality in a number of ways discussed in Ohlsson et al. (2020). If the welfare state provides insurance for many things that individuals would otherwise save for, especially old age care, this will lower motives to save privately and thereby lower individually transmitted wealth. The same is true for collective pension systems. This illustrates why the composition of private wealth is important for how we should think about the extent to which the growth of wealth translates to an increased inheritance of wealth.
16 There were also some discussions about the empirical estimates (e.g., Auerbach and Hassett, 2015) as well as criticism of the policy suggestions, but I will not discuss these points separately here.
17 For those interested in delving deeper into these debates, the AEA symposium on *Capital*, which includes critical comments from Auerbach and Hassett (2015), Weil (2015) and Mankiw (2015) as well as a reply from Piketty (2015), is a good starting point. The collected volume *After Piketty* (2017), edited by Heather Boushey, Bradford DeLong and Marshall Stienbaum contains 21 chapters on different dimensions of the debate that point not only to needed clarifications and alternative interpretations but also to future questions that need addressing.
18 In a special issue of *Science* devoted to inequality, Piketty and Saez (2014) made one contribution focusing on the long run and the role of wealth. Another contribution by David Autor (2014) emphasized the role of education in explaining the rise of earnings inequality. In the abstract he writes: 'The singular focus of public debate on the "top 1 percent" of households overlooks the component of earnings inequality that is arguably most consequential for "the other 99 percent" of citizens'.
19 This is due to the elasticity of substitution being equal to 1 in the C–D production function. If the elasticity of substitution is above 1 (which it so far does not seem to be empirically), the capital income share would grow. This kind of technological development would be one where 'robots' can replace labor in all tasks. In this kind of world, income distribution depends on the ownership of the 'robots' (Freeman, 2014).
20 This point is made by, for example, Ray (2014).

References

Acemoglu, D., and Robinson, J.A. (2015). The Rise and Decline of General Laws of Capitalism. *Journal of Economic Perspectives*, 29(1), 3–28.
Alstadsæter, A., Johannesen, N., and Zucman, G. (2019). Tax Evasion and Inequality. *American Economic Review*, 109(6), 2073–2103.
Atkinson, A.B. (1975). *The Economics of Inequality*. Oxford: Clarendon Press.
Atkinson, A.B. (ed) (1981). *Income, Wealth and Inequality*. Oxford: Oxford University Press.
Atkinson, A.B. (2004). Top Incomes in the U.K. Over the Twentieth Century. *Journal of the Royal Statistical Society*, 168(2), 325–343.
Atkinson, A.B. (2007). Measuring Top Incomes: Methodological Issues. In A.B. Atkinson and T. Piketty (eds), *Top Incomes Over the Twentieth Century: A Contrast Between European and English-Speaking Countries*. Oxford: Oxford University Press.
Atkinson, A.B., and Brandolini, A. (2001). Promise and Pitfalls in the Use of 'Secondary' Data-Sets: Income Inequality in OECD Countries as a Case Study. *Journal of Economic Literature*, 39(3), 771–799.
Atkinson, A.B., and Harrison, A. (1978). *The Distribution of Personal Wealth in Britain*. Cambridge: Cambridge University Press.
Atkinson, A.B., and Piketty, T. (eds) (2007). *Top Incomes Over the Twentieth Century: A Contrast Between European and English-Speaking Countries*. Oxford: Oxford University Press.
Atkinson, A.B., and Piketty, T. (eds) (2010). *Top Incomes: A Global Perspective*, vol. II. Oxford: Oxford University Press.

Auerbach, A.J., and Hassett, K. (2015). Capital Taxation in the Twenty-First Century. *American Economic Review*, 105(5), 38–42.
Auten, G., and Splinter, D. (2023). Income Inequality in the United States: Using Tax Data to Measure Long-term Trends. *Journal of Political Economy*, Forthcoming.
Autor, D. (2014). Skills, Education, and the Rise of Earnings Inequality among the 'Other 99 percent'. *Science*, 344(6186), 843–851.
Banerjee, A., and Duflo, E. (2003). Inequality and Growth: What Can the Data Say. *Journal of Economic Growth*, 8(3), 267–299.
Bonnet, O., Bono, P.-H., Chapelle, G., and Wasmer, E. (2014). Does Housing Capital Contribute to Inequality? A Comment on Thomas Piketty's Capital in the 21st Century. *Sciences Po Economics Discussion Papers 2014–07*. Paris: Sciences Po Department of Economics.
Boushey, H., DeLong, J.B., and Steinbaum, M. (eds) (2017). *After Piketty—The Agenda for Economics and Inequality*. Cambridge, MA: Harvard University Press.
Canberra Group (2011). Expert Group on Household Income Statistics. In *Handbook on Household Income Statistics*. Geneva: United Nations Economic Commission for Europe.
Dell, F., Piketty, T., and Saez, E. (2007). Income and Wealth Concentration in Switzerland Over the Twentieth Century. In A.B. Atkinson and T. Piketty (eds), *Top Incomes Over the Twentieth Century: A Contrast Between European and English-Speaking Countries*. Oxford: Oxford University Press.
Freeman, R. (2014). Who Owns the Robots Rules the World. *IZA World of Labor*, 2014, 5.
Haig, R.M. (1921). *The Concept of Income—Economic and Legal Aspects. The Federal Income Tax*. New York: Columbia University Press, pp. 1–28.
Kopczuk, W., and Saez, E. (2004). Top Wealth Shares in the United States, 1916-2000: Evidence from Estate Tax Returns. *National Tax Journal*, 57(2), 445–487.
Krugman, P (2014). Why We're in a New Gilded Age. *New York Review of Books*. 8 May. www.nybooks.com/articles/archives/2014/may/08/thomas-piketty-newgilded-age/. Downloaded 27 November 2023.
Krusell, P., and Smith, A.A. (2015). Is Piketty's 'Second Law of Capitalism' Fundamental? *Journal of Political Economy*, 123(4), 725–748.
Kuznets, S. (1953). *Shares of Upper Income Groups in Income and Savings*. New York: National Bureau of Economic Research.
Kuznets, S. (1955). Economic Growth and Income Inequality. *American Economic Review*, 45(1), 1–28.
Lindert, P.H. (2014). *Making the Most of Capital in the 21st Century* (Working Paper Series No. 20232). New York: National Bureau of Economic Research.
Mankiw, G. (2015). Yes, r > g. So What? *American Economic Review*, 105(5), 43–47.
Meade, J.E. (1964). *Efficiency, Equality and the Ownership of Property*. London: George Allen and Unwin.
Milanovic, B. (2014). The Return of 'Patrimonial Capitalism': A Review of Thomas Piketty's Capital in the Twenty-First Century. *Journal of Economic Literature*, 52(2), 519–534.
Ohlsson, H., Roine, J., and Waldenström, D. (2020). Inherited Wealth Over the Path of Development: Sweden, 1810–2016. *Journal of the European Economic Association*, 18(3), 1123–1157.
Piketty, T. (2000). Theories of Persistent Inequality and Intergenerational Mobility. In A.B. Atkinson and F. Bourguignon (eds), *Handbook of Income Distribution*, vol. 1. Amsterdam: North-Holland.
Piketty, T. (2001). *Les hauts revenus en France au 20ème siècle*. Paris: Grasset.
Piketty, T. (2005). Top Income Shares in the Long Run: An Overview. *Journal of the European Economic Association*, 3(2–3), 1–11.
Piketty, T. (2007). Top Incomes Over the Twentieth Century: A Summary of Main Findings. In A.B. Atkinson and T. Piketty (eds), *Top Incomes Over the Twentieth Century: A*

Contrast Between European and English-Speaking Countries. Oxford: Oxford University Press.

Piketty, T. (2014). *Capital in the Twenty-First Century*. Cambridge, MA: Belknap of Harvard University Press.

Piketty, T., Postel-Vinay, G., and Rosenthal, J.-L. (2006). Wealth Concentration in a Developing Economy: Paris and France, 1807–1994. *American Economic Review*, 96(1), 236–256.

Piketty, T., and Saez, E. (2003). Income Inequality in the United States, 1913–1998. *Quarterly Journal of Economics*, 118(1), 1–39.

Piketty, T., and Saez, E. (2006). The Evolution of Top Incomes: A Historical and International Perspective. *American Economic Review*, 96(2), 200–205.

Piketty, T., and Saez, E. (2014). Inequality in the Long Run. *Science*, 344(6186), 852–861.

Piketty, T., Saez, E., and Zucman, G. (2018). Distributional National Accounts: Methods and Estimates for the United States. *Quarterly Journal of Economics*, 133(2), 553–609.

Piketty, T., and Zucman, G. (2015). Wealth and Inheritance in the Long Run. In A.B. Atkinson and F. Bourguignon (eds), *Handbook of Income Distribution*, vol. 2B. Amsterdam: North-Holland.

Ray, D. (2014). *Nit-Piketty: A Comment on Thomas Piketty's Capital in the Twenty First Century*. www.econ.nyu.edu/user/debraj/. Downloaded 26 November 2023.

Roine, J., Vlachos, J., and Waldenström, D. (2009). The Long-Run Determinants of Inequality: What Can We Learn From Top Income Data? *Journal of Public Economics*, 93(7–8), 974–988.

Roine, J., and Waldenström, D. (2009). Wealth Concentration Over the Path of Development: Sweden, 1873–2006. *Scandinavian Journal of Economics*, 111(1), 151–187.

Roine, J., and Waldenström, D. (2015). Long-Run Trends in the Distribution of Income and Wealth. In A.B. Atkinson and F. Bourguignon (eds), *Handbook of Income Distribution*, vol. 2A. Amsterdam: North-Holland.

Saez, E., and Zucman, G. (2016). Wealth Inequality in the United States Since 1913: Evidence from Capitalized Income Tax Data. *Quarterly Journal of Economics*, 131(2), 45, 519–578.

Saez, E., and Zucman, G. (2020). Trends in US Income and Wealth Inequality: Revising After the Revisionists. (NBER Working Paper No. 27921). Cambridge, MA: National Bureau of Economic Research.

Simons, H. (1938). *Personal Income Taxation: The Definition of Income as a Problem of Fiscal Policy*. Chicago: University of Chicago Press.

Smith, M., Yagan, D., Zidar, O., and Zwick, E. (2019). Capitalists in the Twenty-First Century. *Quarterly Journal of Economics*, 134(4), 1675–1745.

Smith, M., Zidar, O., and Zwick, E. (2023). Top Wealth in America: New Estimates and Heterogeneous Returns. *Quarterly Journal of Economics*, 138(1), 515–573.

Solow, R. (1956). A Contribution to the Theory of Economic Growth. *Quarterly Journal of Economics*, 70(1), 65–94.

Solow, R. (2014). Thomas Piketty Is Right. *The New Republic*, 22 April.

Stiglitz, J.E. (1969). Distribution of Income and Wealth Among Individuals. *Econometrica*, 37(3), 382–397.

Summers, L.H. (2014). The Inequality Puzzle: Piketty Book Review. *Democracy: A Journal of Ideas*, 32, Spring.

Swan, T. (1956). Capital Accumulation and Economic Growth. *Economic Record*, 2(32), 334–361.

Waldenström, D. (2021). *Wealth and History: An Update* (CEPR Discussion Paper 16631) London: Centre for Economic Policy Research.

Weil, D. (2015). Capital and Wealth in the Twenty-First Century. *American Economic Review*, 93(7), 34–37.

Zucman, G. (2012). The Missing Wealth of Nations, Are Europe and the U.S. Net Debtors or Net Creditors? *Quarterly Journal of Economics*, 128(3), 1321–1364.

4 J.K. Galbraith and Inequality
From Confidence to Misanthropy

Benny Carlson

To write an essay on John Kenneth Galbraith (1908–2006), even if only on one aspect of his extensive activity, is a challenge. He is after all one of the most famous and widely read economists of the 20th century. At the same time, it is a pleasure to approach his writings due to the originality of his views and the wit of his wordings.

Anyone interested in the life and work of Galbraith should start out with Richard Parker's monumental biography, which amply demonstrates all the economic and political issues on which Galbraith had definite opinions over the years:

> [M]ajor reductions in military spending; greater international cooperation for economic development and political freedom; welfare reform aimed at poverty reduction, including a guaranteed annual income; increases in the minimum wage; democratic trade unions; environmentalism; racial equality, including affirmative action; feminism and gender equality; major federal aid to education; urban reform; campaign finance reform; aid to and support of the arts; farm price supports; limits on financial speculation; progressivity in taxation, including sharp limits on windfall profits and executive compensation; increased public regulation of certain concentrated industries such as transportation, finance, utilities, weapons and pharmaceuticals; and publicly financed health care.
>
> (Parker, 2005, p. 303)

At the end of the biography, Parker (2005, p. 639) notes that the late Galbraith 'hammered especially hard on income and wealth inequality'. However, as we shall see, inequality was not always at the top of his agenda.

Born on a farm in Canada (he started out as an agricultural economist) and becoming professor of economics at Harvard for 25 years, Galbraith had an outstanding career in academic and public life.[1] He wrote some 40 books, of which more than seven million copies were sold during his lifetime, and 1,100 articles. 'His distinctive voice and imagination added a lengthy list of memorable phrases to economic argument and the English language—"the affluent society," "the conventional wisdom," "countervailing power," to name only a few' (Parker, 2005, p. 6).

DOI: 10.4324/9781003387114-7

76 *Benny Carlson*

Galbraith frequently questioned 'the conventional wisdom' and moved against the stream in economics and politics. Two economists were of particular importance to him: Thorstein Veblen[2] and John Maynard Keynes. Galbraith spent a year (1937) at the University of Cambridge, where he 'quickly became a full-fledged Keynesian' and adopted Keynes as a role model in two ways: 'as an engaged and politically purposive intellectual' and through 'a clear preference for expressing economics arguments in English rather than in mathematical models or equations' (Parker, 2005, pp. 96–98). He also, perhaps somewhat surprisingly, held Adam Smith in great esteem.[3]

Galbraith was thus a combination of institutionalist and Keynesian. He ceaselessly accused mainstream (neoclassical) economists and textbooks, taking perfect competition as a point of departure, of being out of tune with reality.[4] He was critical of the belief that markets can solve most problems by themselves and was a supporter of a strong welfare state, leaning toward Social Democracy of a Scandinavian brand. He was thus 'a progressive whom the old free marketeers regarded as dangerous' (Shlaes, 2019, p. 40). Parker (2005, p. 133) pinpoints his position: 'The market has value, but so does the state when it acts in democratic interest. This is the core of the Galbraithian approach to economics'. 'Galbraith was a champion of social democracy . . . but he was not an enemy of capitalism', writes Jeff Madrick (2017, pp. ix–x) and adds that the political and economic development during Galbraith's later years was frustrating to him: 'Once he was among the most cited economists in the world, but as he continued to defend a robust welfare state, the evolving mainstream profession moved in the other direction'. Moving against the mainstream in theory as well as in policy recommendations meant that Galbraith became a somewhat 'lone figure at Harvard and did not produce academic followers' (Rutherford, 2011, p. 339).

Some economists might have found Galbraith dangerous. However, some just dismissed his writings as having little to do with serious economic research. One of the most well-known Swedish economists from the 1960s and onwards, Assar Lindbeck, may be cited as an example. He concluded that Galbraith's mode of working was 'impressionistic, not to say fictional, and not scientifically analytical' and that his mode of depiction was sweeping and typical of 'people who long ago lost touch with the scientific frontier within their discipline' (Lindbeck, 1968, pp. 202, 206).

Galbraith's particular style has already been mentioned. Andrea Williams (2001, p. x), editor of *The Essential Galbraith*, paints his style in the following words: 'sardonic humor, felicitous phrasing, reasoned argument in reasonable words or, as he would say, clarity of thought reflected in clarity of prose'.

4.1 The Way Forward

In view of Galbraith's enormous productivity, it would be suicidal to dive headlong into his writings in search for his views on economic inequality. I will therefore focus on three of his most famous books in which he dealt with inequality, one from his earlier, one from his midterm and one from his later production: *The*

Affluent Society (1958), *Economics and the Public Purpose* (1974) and *The Culture of Contentment* (1992); the first issue of *The Affluent Society* can furthermore be compared to the last revised edition from 1999.[5] I will limit myself to displaying his views on economic inequality in Western, industrialized nations, primarily the United States, not on inequality between rich and poor countries or within poor countries, nor race or gender inequality.[6] I will quote him generously since his particular style may easily be lost when rewritten.

4.2 Early Days

In his first bestseller, *American Capitalism* (1952), Galbraith launched the concept of 'countervailing power'. The idea was that as competition subsided and private power in the form of giant corporations increased, countervailing forces arose in the shape of trade unions in the labor market and retail businesses (in the United States) or consumer cooperatives (in Scandinavia) in the commodity market. This can perhaps be seen as an equality issue as it means that economic power becomes more equally distributed between different interest groups.

Inequality was no hot issue after the world war, not even among Keynesians:

> Mainstream Keynesians after World War II would focus on full-employment growth, and mostly ignore the structure or income and wealth inequality, simply preferring to believe, as President Kennedy put it, that 'a rising tide lifts all boats.' Galbraith would not, because he believed that the structure of inequality itself directly gave shape to different levels of aggregate income, and thus implied very different government remedies for achieving optimal economic performance. He most famously revisited this argument during the Kennedy administration's debates over how to spur economic growth, arguing . . . that targeted deficit spending should be chosen over across-the-board tax cuts because of its distributive, along with its efficiency, effects.
>
> (Parker, 2005, p. 99)

Galbraith was one of few economists highlighting poverty and inequality, not least in *The Affluent Society*, and in 1964, Lyndon Johnson appointed him to the White House task force charged with formulating policies for the Office of Economic Opportunity, a key player in the war on poverty. Galbraith, unlike many other liberals, 'always maintained a sharp distinction between the specific problem of poverty and the much larger issue of economic inequality' (Parker, 2005, p. 482).

4.3 The Affluent Society

In the 1950s, Galbraith set out to write a book on poverty. However, he turned the idea around and wrote a book on *The Affluent Society*. Years later, in view of remaining poverty, he pondered whether he should have written a companion volume, *The Non-Affluent Society*.

The Affluent Society became Galbraith's entry ticket to the public hall of fame. 'The book spent nearly a year on *New York Times* bestseller list—unheard of for a book about economics—and the title itself swiftly gained a permanent place in the English language' (Parker, 2005, p. 311). Sales at home and abroad soon passed the million mark.

In the case of *The Affluent Society*, which includes a chapter on inequality, one can compare the first 1958 edition with his last revised 1999 edition to see how Galbraith's views had changed over the years. In the introduction to the 40th anniversary edition, Galbraith (1999, p. viii) notes that although economic life had become more secure over the years, 'I would now, however, more strongly emphasize, and especially as to the United States, the inequality in income and that it is getting worse—that the poor remain poor and the command of income by those in the top income brackets is increasing egregiously'.

Galbraith (1958, p. 3) states the purpose of his book as follows: 'The first task is to see the way our economic attitudes are rooted in the poverty, inequality and economic peril of the past. Then the partial and implicit accommodation to affluence is examined'.

According to Galbraith, people's minds were stuck in ideas from a time when poverty and inequality were permanent and inevitable conditions of life. People's thinking reflected 'the conventional wisdom', a concept similar to paradigm. Galbraith (1958, pp. 25, 27) strove back in time to pinpoint these old ideas. He started out with the classical economists: Adam Smith 'had little hope that the distribution between merchants, manufacturers and landlords on the one hand, and the working masses on the other, would be such as much to benefit the latter'. And 'With Ricardo and Malthus, the notion of privation and great inequality became a basic premise'. With the marginal productivity theory, it was assumed that capital and labor are compensated at a rate corresponding to their marginal products. Still, there was uneasiness about some facets of inequality.

> The inheritance of wealth was a special source of discomfort. Perhaps one could justify riches as the reward for the skill, diligence, foresight and cunning of the original creator. None of this justified its high fortuitous devolution on the individual who happened to be his son.
>
> (Galbraith, 1958, p. 39)

The American context was somewhat different. Wealth grew like nowhere else, but at the same time Social Darwinist ideas, preached by for example William Graham Sumner, had a strong footing.

> Here, if anywhere, the ordinary man had a chance. Perhaps he did, but he also had to face the fact that all economic life was a mortal struggle. He might win but he might also lose, and for him to accept the full consequences of loss—hunger, privation and death—was a social necessity. Poverty and insecurity thus became inherent in the economic life of even the most favored country. So, of course, did inequality, and this was firmly sanctified by the fact that

those who enjoyed it were better. If observation suggested that economic life might be less severe in the United States, Social Darwinism emphasized the contrary.

(Galbraith, 1958, p. 62)

In his chapter on inequality, Galbraith (1958, p. 78) returns to the central tradition of economics, focused on efficiency and competition: 'The competent entrepreneur and worker were automatically rewarded. The rest, as automatically, were punished for their incompetence and sloth'. If people were poor, their only hope, according to social radicals, lay in redistribution of wealth and income. The conservative rejoinder was that redistribution would take from a man what was rightfully his and that tampering with the system would make the lot worse for everyone, including the poor, by reducing the will to work, save and invest: 'in the conventional wisdom the defense of inequality does rest primarily on its functional role as an incentive and as a source of capital' (Galbraith, 1958, p. 80).

Galbraith (ibid.) illustrates the conventional wisdom with a quote from an address before the National Association of Manufacturers in 1954, according to which egalitarianism 'destroys ambition, penalizes success, discourages investment to create new jobs, and may well turn a nation of risk-taking entrepreneurs into a nation of softies'. Galbraith's (1958, p. 81) counter-arguments are that not many businessmen would concede that they were holding back due to insufficient pecuniary incentive, that the rich man's saving 'is the residual after luxurious consumption' and that there are empirical examples to quote: Norway, one of the most egalitarian countries, had one of the highest rates of capital formation and economic growth.

Now, the paradox according to Galbraith (1958, p. 82) is this. On the one hand, '[n]o other question in economic policy is ever so important as the effect of a measure on the distribution of income'. On the other hand, 'few things are more evident in modern social history than the decline of interest in inequality as an economic issue'.

In the first edition of his book, Galbraith (1958, p. 83) concludes that after World War II, no attempt had been made to make the tax more progressive and hence society more egalitarian. At the same time, conservatives had 'not been able to mount any major attack on the tax itself'. In the last revised edition, Galbraith's (1999, p. 70) conclusion is, not surprisingly, that 'the income tax in the years since World War II has greatly regressed as an instrument for income redistribution'. In the first edition, he cites figures showing that in 1955, the tenth of the US population with the lowest incomes received (after taxes) 1 percent of the total money income, whereas the tenth with the highest income received 27 percent of the total. In the last edition, the corresponding figures for 1970 were 2 and 27 percent, respectively. Why he quoted such old figures is a mystery. He just notes that 'In the years since, the share going to the very rich has much increased'.

In the first edition, Galbraith (1958, p. 85) hits a positive note: 'While taxes have restrained the concentration of income at the top, full employment and upward pressure on wages have increased well-being at the bottom'. In the last edition, this paragraph is gone. Both editions include a sentence saying that 'to comment on the wealth of the wealthy, and certainly to propose that it be reduced, has come to be considered bad taste' (Galbraith, 1958, p. 87, 1999, p. 71). In the first edition, he figures this could change if the rich became richer and the rest stationary. This is what has happened, but to complain about it still seems to be in bad taste.

Being rich has, according to Galbraith, three basic benefits: power, possession of things and esteem. Over time, these returns to wealth had been circumscribed. The power and prestige of the US government increased, trade unions appeared and the professional manager took power over corporations from the rich man. (One can note that this was written before the tycoons of Facebook, Amazon and the like entered the scene.)

In the old days, the rich liked to show off: 'The great houses, the great yachts, the great balls, the stables, and the jewel-encrusted bosoms were all used to identify the individual as having a claim to the honors of wealth', writes Galbraith (1958, p. 91) and continues: 'Such display is now passé'. There were reasons for this change of mind: fear of expropriation or, during the Great Depression, even revolution. 'Purely ostentatious outlays, especially on dwellings, yachts, and females, were believed likely to incite the masses to violence'. Furthermore, the display of wealth was deemed vulgar and lost much of its function as more people became rich.[7] 'Lush expenditure could be afforded by so many that it ceased to be useful as a mark of distinction' (Galbraith, 1958, p. 92). At the same time, meritocratic competition had reduced hostility towards the rich, even though they had a head start: 'Nothing could operate more effectively to dry up the supply of individuals who otherwise would make an attack on inequality a career' (Galbraith, 1958, p. 94).

At the end of the inequality chapter, Galbraith turns to the issue of growth versus redistribution. He concludes that increased production is an alternative to redistribution. This was understandable. 'It is the increase in output in recent decades, not the redistribution of income, which has brought the great material increase in the well-being of the average man' (Galbraith, 1958, p. 96). Even liberals had come to accept this fact, and the pursuit of economic growth had 'become deeply embedded in the conventional wisdom of the American left' (Galbraith, 1958, p. 97). There was even a belief that growth could eliminate poverty. Galbraith (1958, p. 97) adds that '[t]his latter, in fact, is suspect' and forty years later (1999, p. 79) that '[t]his latter is untrue'. There would always remain a self-perpetuating margin of poverty at the base of the income pyramid. However, the inequality issue was not at the forefront. 'The oldest and most agitated of social issues, if not resolved, is at least largely in abeyance, and the disputants have concentrated their attention, instead, on the goal of increased productivity' (Galbraith, 1958, p. 97).

In other chapters, Galbraith wrote on economic security, poverty and other issues related to inequality. One strategy for those opposed to reduced inequality was to undermine the faith in government services:

> The payment for publicly produced services has long been linked to the problem of inequality. By having the rich pay more, the services were provided and at the same time the goal of greater equality was advanced. This community

of objectives has never appealed to those being equalized. Not unnaturally, some part of their opposition has been directed to the public services themselves. By attacking these, they could attack the leveling tendencies of taxation. This has helped to keep alive the notion that the public services for which they pay are inherently inferior to privately produced goods.
(Galbraith, 1958, p. 136)

Galbraith to the contrary regarded many private goods as inferior—or rather less necessary—compared to public services. One of his most well-known arguments is that private production creates its own demand through massive advertising. 'A man who is hungry need never be told of his need for food' (Galbraith, 1958, p. 158). The primary function of production was no longer, according to Galbraith, to supply goods for consumers but rather to supply income security for workers. He wished for a 'social balance' between the supply of privately produced goods and services and those of the state. The good news was that government revenues grew automatically with the growth of the economy. The bad news was that a large proportion of the federal revenues were earmarked for military purposes.

What, then, were the most vital public services needed? Unemployment compensation was one. In the 1958 edition, Galbraith was concerned that a compensation level close to the wage would add inflationary pressure and argued that the level should vary with unemployment—high unemployment, high level, low unemployment, low level—and be provided by states. In the 1999 edition, he urged that the compensation be close to the wage and nationalized. In the case of people difficult to employ, he (in the 1999 edition) found Milton Friedman's idea of a negative income tax interesting.

Galbraith discerned a conflict between the goals of equality and social balance. 'All this—schools, hospitals, even the scientific research on which increased production depends—must wait while we debate the ancient and unresolvable question of whether the rich are too rich' (Galbraith, 1958, p. 313).

> The only hope—and in the nature of things it rests primarily with liberals—is to separate the issue of equality from that of social balance. The second is by far the more important question. The fact that a tacit truce exists on the issue of inequality is proof of its comparative lack of social urgency. In the past the liberal politician has encountered the conservative proposal for reduction in top bracket income taxes with the proposal that relief be confined to the lower brackets. And he has insisted that any necessary tax increase be carried more than proportionately by the higher income brackets. The result has been to make him a co-conspirator with the conservative in reducing taxes, whatever the cost in social balance; and his insistence on making taxes an instrument of greater equality has made it difficult or impossible to increase them.
> (Galbraith, 1958, p. 314)

For the same reason, Galbraith (1958, p. 315) favored the sales tax: 'The community is affluent in privately produced goods. It is poor in public services. The obvious solution is to tax the former to provide the latter—by making private goods more expensive, public goods are made more abundant'. Public goods and services were needed to reduce poverty. In the 1999 edition, Galbraith added an afterword, and in its last paragraph he pleaded the cause of the poor—'let us put elimination of poverty in the affluent society strongly, even centrally, on the social and political agenda' (Galbraith, 1999, p. 263).

4.4 The AEA Agenda

In his second-most well-known book (after *The Affluent Society*), *The New Industrial State* (1967), Galbraith investigated the world of large corporations and their management, the 'technostructure', not the world of inequality and poverty:

> There are many poor people left in the industrial countries, and notably in the United States. The fact that they are not the central theme of this treatise should not be taken as proof either of ignorance of their existence or indifference to their fate. But the poor, by any applicable tests, are outside the industrial system.
> (Galbraith, second edition, 1971, p. 320)

A basic argument in the book was that that the state and the large corporations would merge and that planning must replace the market. In that way, the planning systems of US capitalism and Soviet communism would converge.

A few years later, when Galbraith became president of the American Economic Association (AEA), he put inequality on top of the agenda at the association's meeting in December 1972.

> This might have been seen as a personal mea culpa, since many people thought the subject had been minor to Galbraith's writing. But in truth that charge better applied to the economics profession as a whole. Between the end of World War II and 1964, when LBJ's War on Poverty began, of the nearly 800 articles in the *American Economic Review* only three dealt with poverty or inequality in the United States.
> (Parker, 2005, p. 481)

In his presidential address to the AEA, Galbraith took aim at the neoclassical view of a competitive market complemented with some exceptions (monopoly, oligopoly). He could understand that economists stuck to this theory, fearing that 'we shall lose the filter by which scholars are separated from charlatans and windbags;' however, there was 'more danger in remaining with a world that is not real' (Galbraith, 2001, pp. 143–144). In reality, as he saw it, the economy was split in two. On the one hand, there was the corporate sector, the planning system, offering its (unionized) employees good working conditions. On the other hand, there was the entrepreneurial sector, the market system, offering poor conditions. It was not easy to move from the latter to the former. Inequality was thus not any longer produced by the market but by the division between the corporations (controlling their markets) and the smaller businesses (controlled by the market) and the difficulty for people to move from the latter to the former. 'There is, accordingly, a continuing source of inequality between the two parts of the economy derived from the occluded movement between them' (Galbraith, 2001, p. 129).[8]

4.5 Economics and the Public Purpose

In *The New Industrial State*, Galbraith had focused on 'the world of the large corporation', arguing that 'it is more deeply characteristic of the modern industrial scene than the dog laundry or the small manufacturer with a big idea', thus more or less dismissing the rest of the economy (Galbraith, 1971, p. 398). In his next major work, *Economics and the Public Purpose* (1974), he wished to broaden his view to encompass the whole economic system and focus more on economic inequality. He now made great efforts to frame in detail his idea of an economy split in two: on the one hand, the market system and small businesses, disciplined by market and state, aiming to maximize their profits; on the other hand, the planning system and large corporations, able to control market and state, aiming to stabilize their profits and maximize their growth. In the market system, entrepreneurs and workers were prepared to reduce their income in order to remain in business. This was a major source of inequality.

> That the market system survives, at least in part, because of its ability to reduce the reward of its participants leads on to an obvious and ominous conclusion. It is that there is a presumption of inequality as between different parts of the economic system. The convenient social virtue adds to this presumption by helping people to persuade themselves that they should accept a lesser return—that some part of their compensation lies in their social virtue.[9]
> (Galbraith, 1974, p. 77)

This was not a temporary but rather a constant state of affairs:

> In the market system managers and workers continue to supply products and services at levels of remuneration that are below those for comparable talent in the planning system. And this is a durable condition. It follows that equality is not the tendency between the planning and markets systems: the basic tendency is to inequality. . . . The relationship between the planning and the market systems, their unequal rate of development, the exploitation of the second by the first, the resulting inequality in return are central features of the modern economy.
> (Galbraith, 1974, p. 132)

Neoclassical economists, who did not share Galbraith's view of an economy split in two, expected this inequality to be reduced since people could move up the payment ladder. Galbraith, on the contrary, figured that the inequality would be ever worse as people who could not find employment in the planning system would become entrepreneurs in the market system and use their comparative 'advantage' of self-exploitation.[10] 'It means that the broadly equalizing assumption of neoclassical economics must be rejected; instead, in the absence of energetic reform, the tendency of the economy is to one comparatively affluent, one comparatively impoverished working force' (Galbraith, 1974, p. 203).

The idea that people are rewarded according to their contribution to production did not, as previously mentioned, find sympathy with Galbraith. Remuneration depends on tradition and people's position in the pyramid of power. Galbraith (1974, pp. 203–204) noted the obvious that 'those who have the least pleasant jobs get the least' and 'The higher in the executive hierarchy, the greater, in general, the avowed enjoyment in work and the greater the pay'.

Galbraith's reform agenda more or less turns on its head the normal antagonism between socialist planners and market advocates. It starts with 'steps to reduce the inequality between the planning and the market systems—to improve the bargaining power of the market system and reduce its exploration by the planning system'. This, Galbraith (1974, p. 222) exclaims: 'is here called The New Socialism'! Next on the agenda were efforts to make the planning system serve, not define, the public interest.

Reform presupposed critical thinking to break the planning system's hold over people's minds. 'This means the elimination of all distinction between useful and unuseful fields of learning' (Galbraith, 1974, p. 227), fight against producer persuasion (advertising) and the disclosure of public policies serving the planning system.

Galbraith (1974, p, 229) compared the capitalist and the Soviet planning systems. While their ends were similar, their means were different. In the Soviet system, critical thinking was suppressed. In the capitalist system, it was 'either ignored or stigmatized as eccentric, unscientific, lacking in scholarly precision or otherwise unworthy'. Nonetheless, the fight against the capitalist planning system should not aim for suppression:

> The remedy is not illiberal suppression of the techniques for compelling belief but a truly liberal resistance to such belief. One does not suppress neoclassical economics; one shows its tendentious functions and seeks to provide a substitute. One does not prohibit advertising; one resists its persuasion. One does not legislate against science and engineering; one sees their eminence in relation to the arts as the contrivance of the planning system.
> (Galbraith, 1974, pp. 229–230)

Galbraith (1974, p. 231) believed that such critical thinking was gaining ground and cited polls showing loss of confidence in leaders of industry, banking, education, science, advertising and military: 'All these developments suggest', he thought, 'a healthy trend'. When Galbraith wrote these words, critical thinking was leaning to the left. Had he lived to see that lack of confidence in traditional leaders might lean in quite another direction, he would probably have been less amused.

The role of government was at the core of Galbraith's (1974, p. 242) agenda: 'The government is a major part of the problem; it is also central to the remedy'.

Through its symbiotic relationship with the planning system, it contributed to unequal income distribution and poor distribution of public resources. Thus, there must be an effort to free government from corporate domination; the public interest must be separated from the planning interest.

To overcome the inequality between the planning and market systems, Galbraith proposed a battery of measures to increase the bargaining power of the participants in the market system and thereby their income:

> The key pillars are: organization by small businessmen and the self-employed to allow of some approach to parity of bargaining with the planning system; a far more vigorous use of the minimum wage; and strong support to trade union organization in those areas where, in the past, it has been least encouraged and where it is most needed. But adding strongly to the bargaining power these steps provide is the institution of an alternative income at generous levels.
>
> (Galbraith, 1974, p. 263)

This alternative income, what today is called universal basic income, was supposed to be modestly below earnings in the planning system. This solution, Galbraith (1974, p. 263) well understood, would mean that some people would prefer not to work and that some services would disappear, but this did not bother him: 'This should be viewed not as a loss but as a modest advance in the general state of civilization'. 'It accepts that some work and pay are worse than unemployment' (Galbraith, 1974, p. 311).

Galbraith also took aim at income inequality within the planning system. The head of General Motors earned 50 times more than a worker at the floor. A reduction of this gap would cause no problem. There was no lack of executive talent, and '[t]o be an executive would still be far better than fitting bolts on the shop floor' (Galbraith, 1974, p. 265).

Some parts of the economy—housing, health care and transportation—were underdeveloped in the United States and should, according to Galbraith, come under public ownership like in most parts of Western Europe. Galbraith (1974, p. 283) was sure that socialism was the melody of the future. 'Circumstances, it is evident, are not kind to those who see themselves as the guardians of the market economy, the enemies of socialism'. Circumstances, not ideology, would determine the way forward.

The final step in Galbraith's reform agenda concerned fiscal policy, monetary policy and controls. Insufficient investment or excessive wage demands could trigger downward or upward cumulative spirals. The means to increase stability and equality was 'a large and stable flow of public expenditures' and 'a strongly progressive tax structure' (Galbraith, 1974, p. 305). The use of expenditures and taxes should work systematically in one direction: 'If demand is excessive, the *generally* appropriate procedure will be to increase taxes. . . . If demand is deficient, the generally proper procedure will be to increase public expenditure'. Galbraith's critics of course understood where this was heading, and he (1974, pp. 307–308) readily 'confessed': 'It will be suggested—and by some trumpeted—that the policy here proposed means, over time, an upward drift in taxation. This is so'.

The use of monetary policy, on the other hand, should be reduced since it favored those in the planning system against those in the market system. Interest rates should be low and stable. Control of the volume of lending should be exercised through tax and expenditure policy. Finally, wages and prices in the planning system should be regulated. They should not be frozen but controlled in a way that increased stability and reduced inequality. Wage increases should be confined to average productivity gains, and wage controls should aim at narrowing wage differentials. 'There should be a strong and positive effort to narrow the present gap between worker and executive' (Galbraith, 1974, p. 314). Galbraith (1974, p. 316) ends his book with a *grande finale* which in retrospect sounds somewhat naïve:

> Fortunately the rules that reflect the public interest are rather simple. If public expenditures are increasingly for public purposes, if taxes are increasingly progressive, if monetary policy is passive, if expansion of demand is accomplished by increased public expenditure and contraction of demand by increased taxes, if wage increases are kept in accordance with productivity gains, if increased equality is a major consideration in making wage adjustments and if price increases are allowed only in response to hardship resulting from the evening-up of wages and the absence of productivity gains—then an essential public management is being achieved.

4.6 The Culture of Contentment

In the 1970s, Galbraith radiated confidence. Things would surely move in the direction he hoped for. Very soon, however, things moved in a very different direction. Consequently, in *The Culture of Contentment* from 1992, Galbraith's sarcasm flowed. 'It was easy to detect in the book a harsh note of dismay at the results of twelve years of the most conservative national leadership since the 1920s', writes Parker (2005, p. 623). In the foreword to a new edition, Jeff Madrick (2017, pp. x–xi), journalist and author of books in a Galbraithian spirit, similarly characterized the book as 'an indictment of economic policies under Presidents Ronald Reagan and George H.W. Bush' and concluded that Galbraith's thinking 'stood courageously in direct contrast to the antigovernment, allegedly scientific consensus that by 1992 leaned decidedly toward laissez-faire governance'.

According to the updated figures Galbraith presented, the average after-tax annual income of those in the upper 20 percent of the income distribution had increased from 73,700 (constant) dollars in 1981 to 92,000 in 1990 whereas the income of the average manufacturing worker had declined. 12.8 percent of the population lived below the poverty line at the end of the 1980s, and the top 1 percent controlled 13.5 percent of all income before taxes. At the same time, government support and subsidy for the poor were seen as 'seriously suspect as to need and effectiveness of administration and because of their adverse effect on morals and working morale'. Government support for the comparative well-to-do, like social security pensions and banking deposit insurance, was another thing. 'The comparatively affluent can withstand the adverse moral effect of being subsidized and supported by the government; not so the poor' (Galbraith, 2017, p. 12).

The economically and socially fortunate were now a majority, not of all citizens but of those who voted. These formed 'the Contended Majority' or 'the Culture of Contentment' (Galbraith, 2017, pp. 12–13). Even though he was very critical of the political development in the United States, Galbraith (2017, p. 15) had to admit that it reflected the preferences of this 'majority': 'In defense of Ronald Reagan and George Bush as Presidents, it must be said and emphasized that both were, or are, faithful representatives of the constituency that elected them'.

The contended majority was suspicious of government expenditure with some exceptions: 'Social expenditure favorable to the fortunate, financial rescue, military spending and, of course, interest payments [on government loans]' (Galbraith, 2017, p. 20).

> What remains—expenditure for welfare, low-cost housing, health care for those otherwise unprotected, public education[11] and the diverse needs of the great urban slums—is what is now viewed as the burden of government. It is uniquely that which serves the interests of those outside the contended electoral majority; it is, and inescapably, what serves the poor.
>
> (Galbraith, 2017, pp. 20–21)

Instead of government action to bolster the poor, the prevailing idea was that tax reductions for the rich would benefit the poor. Galbraith (2017, p. 22) phrased this idea as 'the doctrine that if the horse is fed amply with oats, some will pass through to the road for the sparrows'.

Galbraith figured there was no ambition to eliminate poverty because of the need for a 'functional underclass' (comparable to Marx's industrial reserve army). In his 1958 book, he had dismissed the idea that people are rewarded according to their contributions to the economy, and he had not changed his mind:

> It is a basic but rarely articulated feature of the modern economic system that the highest pay is given for the work that is most prestigious and most agreeable. This is at the opposite extreme from those occupations that are inherently invidious, those that place the individual direct under the command of another, as in the case of the doorman or the household servant, and those involving a vast range of tasks—street cleaning, garbage collection, janitorial services, elevator operation[12]—that have an obtrusive connotation of social inferiority.
>
> (Galbraith, 2017, p. 26)

In the 1990s, the maxim that economic growth will lift all boats was widespread. In this maxim, Galbraith (2017, p. 30) did not put much faith. Social mobility did not match the need for a functional underclass: 'the normal upward movement that was for long the solvent for discontent has been arrested. The underclass has become a semi-permanent rather than a generational phenomenon'. He was surprised that the underclass in the major cities did not react with more violence and found the explanation in the fact that parts of it (immigrants, blacks from the South) had escaped from even worse conditions.

In *The Affluent Society*, taxation and public services had been Galbraith's number one priority, a priority which could be jeopardized by too much focus on equality. In *The Culture of Contentment* (2017, p. 33), he concluded that 'the only modestly fortunate' abstained from urging higher taxes on the very rich. 'There is at work here a companionate acceptance of inequality in order to protect against the common enemy, which is higher taxes on all'. The fortunate did not want to pay for public support of the functional underclass, and what followed was a resistance to all taxation. This was no surprise.

> The fortunate pay, the less fortunate receive. The fortunate have political voice, the less fortunate do not. It would be an exercise in improbably charitable attitude were the fortunate to respond warmly to expenditures that are for the benefit of others. So government with all its costs is pictured as a functionless burden, which for the fortunate, to a considerable extent, it is. Accordingly, it and the sustaining taxes must be kept to a minimum; otherwise, the liberty of the individual will be impaired.
> (Galbraith, 2017, p. 36)

In order not to arouse 'moral disquiet' over the disparity between affluent and poor people, the argument had been developed that government is 'inefficient, incompetent, in motivated assault on private well-being and, above all, a burden' (Galbraith, 2017, p. 37).

Politicians like Reagan and Bush Sr, who cut taxes and welfare spending, had thus, in Galbraith's (2017, p. 39) bitter words, 'been reacting faithfully to the will of their constituency', thus 'been faithful to democratic principle'.[13]

Inequality gaps were widening. In 1980, CEOs of the 300 largest American companies had incomes 29 times that of the average manufacturing worker; in 1990, their incomes were 93 times greater. Galbraith (2917, p. 47) had no difficulty seeing through the arguments legitimizing such figures: anyone borrowing a minor sum was seen as 'a person of average intelligence', but the one who managed to borrow a very large sum was seen as a 'financial genius'. The corporate executive, the top bureaucrat, was celebrated as the entrepreneurial hero once portrayed by Joseph Schumpeter.

Galbraith took aim at some of the conservative scholars who had reaped fame in the 1980s, like Arthur Laffer and Charles Murray. He did not think 'that anyone of sober mentality took Professor Laffer's curve and conclusions seriously', and with Murray's *Losing Ground* (1984), 'the doctrinal base of the age of contentment was complete'—'the rich needed the spur of more money, the poor the spur of their own poverty' (Galbraith, 2017, pp. 81, 83–84).

Summing up his argument, Galbraith once more nominated progressive taxation and public expenditure as the only remedies for inequality and poverty.

> The only effective design for diminishing the income inequality inherent in capitalism is the progressive income tax. Nothing in the age of contentment has contributed so strongly to income inequality as the reduction of taxes on the rich; nothing, as has been said, so contributes to social tranquility as some screams of anguish from the very affluent. That taxes should now be used to reduce inequality is, however, clearly outside the realm of comfortable thought.
>
> (Galbraith, 2017, p. 139)

Public action was needed but dependent on higher taxes:

> Life in the great cities could be improved, and only will be improved by public action—by better schools with better-paid teachers, by strong, well-financed welfare services, by counseling on drug addiction, by employment training, by public investment in the housing that in no industrial country is provided for the poor by private enterprise, by adequately supported health care, recreational facilities, libraries and police. The question once again, much accommodating rhetoric to the contrary, is not what can be done but what will be paid.
>
> (Galbraith, 2017, p. 140)

However, not much would happen unless the age of contentment came to an end. Galbraith (2017, p. 122) could imagine this being accomplished by any of three possible shock scenarios: 'widespread economic disaster, adverse military action that is associated with international misadventure, and eruption of an angry underclass'. Decades later, all three scenarios have, to some extent, played out: the Great Recession after the 2008 financial crash, the US military debacles in Iraq and Afghanistan and the Black Lives Matter revolt. Not surprisingly, these events have not had any effects favoring economic equality or the poor. Rather, large segments of the middle and working classes have sided with the superrich in anger over taxes, 'socialist' public services (health care), immigrants, racial minorities and poor people. The age of contentment was replaced by the disgruntled age of Trump, and voter suppression has been employed to keep the previously contended majority in power.

4.7 Concluding Remarks

In *The Affluent Society* (1958), Galbraith focused on 'the conventional wisdom', ideas rooted in 19th-century classical, neoclassical and Social Darwinist thinking, which cemented the perception that inequality is inevitable and/or necessary for economic growth. Before modern growth set in, inequality and poverty were seen as natural conditions of life. After modern growth set in, they were seen as whips and carrots needed to keep the economy going. As people are being rewarded according to their contributions, the thrifty would climb the ladder, and the lazy fall into the abyss. The fact that institutions, inherited distribution of economic and political power, habit and sheer prejudice to a large extent decide who will be losers and winners was not taken into consideration, particularly not by conservative pundits. Eventually, as the majority of people reached a decent living standard, those left behind were more or less forgotten.

In the first edition of the book, Galbraith noted that no steps had been taken after World War II (WWII) to make the income distribution more equal by way of progressive income taxation. In the 40th anniversary edition, he could just confirm that the reduced taxes on the rich had increased inequality. He readily admitted (in the early as well as in the late edition) that economic growth, not redistribution, explained the increased material well-being of the ordinary man. However, there would always be a margin of poor people. A rising tide on the market ocean would not lift all boats—some would be left in the mud. These boats must be made seaworthy through state intervention. This was to Galbraith of 1958 the top priority. There must be 'social balance' between goods produced by the private sector and services produced by the public sector. Discussions about the overarching and long-term—even 'ancient and unresolvable'—issue of economic inequality to some extent hampered ambitions to solve the more immediate issue of reducing poverty.

There was, as Galbraith asserted in his 1972 AEA address, an income inequality produced by the split of the economy into big corporations, dominating their markets and paying good and steady wages, and small businesses, at the mercy of the market and generating less good and reliable income, particularly since it was very difficult for people to move from the latter to the former. Only five years earlier, in *The New Industrial State*, he had been fully focused on the world of big corporations and mentioned the rest of the economy in terms such as 'dog laundries'. This left the impression that the modern corporation was the future and small businesses the past. Now he looked at the whole economic system and adjusted his views.

In *Economics and the Public Purpose* (1974), Galbraith elaborated his theme of a split between big corporations (the planning system) and small businesses (the market system) and launched an ambitious reform agenda, 'The New Socialism'. People's eyes must be opened—critical thinking encouraged, belief in the Establishment undermined. Government must be divorced from its symbiotic marriage with big corporations and focus on support to small businesses, the self-employed and their workers with minimum wages and universal basic income. Housing, health care and transportation must be public sector commitments. Taxes and public expenditure must be increased, monetary policy limited to keeping interest rates low and wage and price controls imposed to achieve economic stability and equality.[14]

Whether Galbraith's view of the dual economy is as relevant today as it perhaps was half a century or more ago is hard to say. Some giant industrial corporations have lost much steam, but new digital giants have arisen. Their power over people is greater and more subtle compared to the old ones. Old corporate slogans like

'Juicy fruit, a packet full of sunshine' seem just silly compared to the new giants' manipulation of people's minds through algorithms.

In the mid-1970s, Galbraith seemed confident about the economic and political travel direction and in a self-assured mode launched a maximalist reform agenda. However, irrespective of whether it was circumstances or ideology that reigned, things took a very different turn from the one he had imagined. Socialist ideas did not gain terrain (at least not outside of universities), taxes were lowered and made less progressive, monetary policy became the main stabilizing tool, wage and price controls were scrapped and income inequality increased. Galbraith referred to CEOs in the United States earning 29 times the average worker in 1980. In 2018, according to news reports, CEOs earned 278 times more than workers (*New York Times*, 2020). The gap had widened tenfold!

When Galbraith wrote *The Culture of Contentment* (1992), his account of the Reagan–Bush era, these trends were obvious. The rich became richer, and wages for workers stagnated. However, Reagan and Bush were hardly to blame. They had executed the will of the contented majority of voters who showed up at the polls. The only way to reduce income inequality was through progressive income tax. This way was blocked since 'the only modestly fortunate' were allied with the rich in their resistance against higher taxes. The conventional wisdom was that lower taxes for the rich would somehow trickle down to benefit the poor. As Galbraith phrased this process: 'if the horse is fed amply with oats, some will pass through to the road for the sparrows'.

Galbraith concluded that the will to equip the state with tools to raise boats from the bottom was weaker than ever. There was a need for a 'functional underclass', and the opposition to increased taxes focused on painting public sector activities as inefficient and wasteful compared to private sector activities. He regarded some conservatives (like Charles Murray) as mere cynics: the rich needed the spur of more money, the poor the spur of their poverty.

Galbraith was now in a misanthropic mood and believed that only economic and military failures could tilt the development in a new direction. These kinds of events generally weaken people's trust in politicians and government. Galbraith had long before played with the idea of sowing mistrust in 'the Establishment'. He had been playing with fire. What he apparently did not consider seriously enough is that widespread discontentment and upheaval rarely favor economic stability and equality. Parts of the underclass may revolt, but the formerly complacent majority will hardly be in the mood to show increased generosity toward the poor but rather to degenerate into populist—mostly right-wing—fury: 'drain the swamp'. The result: loot and shoot! At least, this is what has happed in the United States.

Notes

1 He was 'tsar' of consumer price controls during World War II; advisor and speech-writer to three American Presidents (Harry Truman, John F. Kennedy and Lyndon Johnson) and to several Democratic presidential candidates (Adlai Stevenson, Eugene McCarthy, Robert Kennedy, George McGovern); ambassador to India, 1961–1963; president of the American Economic Association in 1972; author and narrator in the BBC TV series 'The Age of Uncertainty', aired all over the world in the late 1970s.

2 Galbraith (2001, p. 221) regarded Veblen as 'a genius—the most penetrating, original and uninhibited source of social thought in his time'; his writings were 'sardonic, laconic and filled with brilliant insights'. Galbraith to some extent identified with Veblen. They both descended from hardworking farmers of non-British descent (Veblen was Norwegian, Galbraith Scottish), and they both saw themselves as outsiders with more insights than insiders, even when they had become famous. When Galbraith (2001, p. 216) wrote of Veblen's university colleagues, he probably had his own in mind:

> A man like Veblen creates great problems for such people. They cherish the established view and rejoice in the favor of the Establishment. Anyone who does not share their values is a threat to their position and, worse still, to their self-esteem, for he makes them seem sycophantic and routine, which, of course, they are.

3 However, when in 1973 Galbraith gave an address, the world was quite different from Smith's. 'Smith is not a prophet for our time, but ... he was magnificently in touch with his own time'. See Galbraith (2001, p. 166). Galbraith's view of Marx was somewhat similar: not a contemporary prophet.

4 'The neoclassical system owes much to tradition—it is not implausible as a description of a society that once existed' is one of Galbraith's (1974, p. 27) laconisms.

5 Urszula Zagóra-Jonszta (2020) compares Galbraith's view of income inequality with Milton Friedman's. Except for *The Affluent Society*, she uses Polish translations of writings by Galbraith.

6 Galbraith devoted considerable attention to the latter issues. *The Nature of Mass Poverty* (1979) is concerned with less developed countries. 'My concern is with the poverty in those communities, rural in practice, where almost everyone is poor—where, if there is wealth or affluence, it is the exceptional fortune of the few' (Galbraith, 1979, p. 2). *Economics and the Public Purpose* (1974) includes two chapters (iv and xxiii) on the household and women as a 'crypto-servant class'.

7 Galbraith's views of the well-to-do were inspired by Veblen's *Theory of the Leisure Class*, which he classified as:

> [T]he most comprehensive ever written, on snobbery and social pretense. Some of it has application only to American society at the end of the nineteenth century—at the height of the gilded age of American capitalism. More is wonderfully relevant to modern affluence.
>
> Galbraith (2001, p. 212)

8 The last quotation is from a speech Galbraith gave in 1976 when he received the Veblen-Commons Award from the Association for Evolutionary Economics.

9 Social virtue was yet another of Galbraith's catch phrases, similar to conventional wisdom, reflecting the idea that someone is doing some kind of sacrifice for the larger community or rather for the well-to-do section of the community.

10 This scenario could be extended to a global level with the planning system dominating in developed countries and the market system dominating in underdeveloped countries. This, according to Galbraith, was the face of modern imperialism.

11 Galbraith did not view education primarily as the way of getting people into the labor market and up the economic ladder but rather as a way to improve people's critical thinking and, as Gruchy (1972, p. 155) puts it, to refine their wants into 'the higher, non-commercial dimensions of life'. Galbraith was good at poking fun of commercial intrusions into these higher dimensions, as for example when he in a lecture/article on 'Economics and the Quality of Life' wrote that 'good theater and good music require the protection of a mood; they cannot be successfully juxtaposed to rhymed jingles on behalf of a laxative' (Galbraith, 2001, p. 104).

12 One may wonder if there were any elevator operators left at the beginning of the 1990s. Anyway, anyone doubting that remuneration is, to a large extent, a reflection of social standing rather than of productivity may compare tips accruing to a waitress serving

dozens of customers at a regular diner to a waitress serving a few noble couples at a finer restaurant.
13 Ronald Reagan, elected US president in 1980, was known for his humorous remarks. Galbraith was not amused. When Reagan's presidency ended, Galbraith pinned the following legacy in the *New York Times*: 'In recent years, the rich have not been working because they had too little money, and the poor have not been working because they had too much' (Quoted from Parker, 2005, p. 577).
14 The similarities between Galbraith and his ten years older Swedish colleague Gunnar Myrdal (1898–1987) are all too obvious. Both had institutionalist and Keynesian leanings, both were reformist socialists and favored a long-term growing public sector armed with public enterprises, planning capacity, high and progressive taxes, a broad supply of services and low and stable interest rates. Myrdal (1944) even wrote an essay on 'high taxes and low interest rates'.

References

Galbraith, J.K. (1956 [1952]). *American Capitalism: The Concept of Countervailing Power*. Boston: Houghton Mifflin Company.
Galbraith, J.K. (1958). *The Affluent Society*. Boston: Houghton Mifflin Company.
Galbraith, J.K. (1971 [1967]). *The New Industrial State*. Boston: Houghton Mifflin Company.
Galbraith, J.K. (1974). *Economics and the Public Purpose*. London: André Deutsch.
Galbraith, J.K. (1979). *The Nature of Mass Poverty*. Cambridge, MA and London: Harvard University Press.
Galbraith, J.K. (1999). *The Affluent Society*. London: Penguin Books.
Galbraith, J.K. (2001). *The Essential Galbraith*. Boston and New York: Houghton Mifflin Company.
Galbraith, J.K. (2017 [1992]). *The Culture of Contentment*. Princeton and Oxford: Princeton University Press.
Gruchy, A.G. (1972). *Contemporary Economic Thought: The Contribution of Neo-Institutional Economics*. Clifton, NJ: Augustus M. Kelley Publishers.
Lindbeck, A. (1968). Galbraith—skönlitterär angripare av industristaten. *Svensk Sparbankstidskrift*, 52(4), 201–206.
Madrick, J. (2017). Foreword. In J.K. Galbraith (ed), *The Culture of Contentment* (pp. ix–xxiii). Princeton, NJ and Oxford: Princeton University Press.
Myrdal, G. (1944). Höga skatter och låga räntor. In *Studier i ekonomi och historia tillägnade Eli Heckscher på 65-årsdagen den 24 november 1944* (pp. 160–169). Uppsala: Almqvist & Wiksell Boktryckeri AB.
New York Times (2020). The Jobs We Need. 24 June.
Parker, R. (2005). *John Kenneth Galbraith: His Life, His Politics, His Economics*. Chicago: The University of Chicago Press.
Rutherford, M. (2011). *The Institutionalist Movement in American Economics: Science and Social Control*. Cambridge: Cambridge University Press.
Shlaes, A. (2019). *Great Society: A New History*. New York: HarperCollins.
Williams, A.D. (2001). Introduction. In J.K. Galbraith (ed), *The Essential Galbraith* (pp. ix–x). Boston and New York: Houghton Mifflin Company.
Zagóra-Jonszta, U. (2020). The Problem of Income Inequality in the View of John Kenneth Galbraith and Milton Friedman. *Social Inequalities and Economic Growth*, 62(2), 7–17.

5 Atkinson on Inequality

Arne Bigsten

Anthony Atkinson was born in 1944 and began his academic studies at Cambridge University in 1963. After a year of mathematics, he transferred to economics. Atkinson has said that he decided to become an economist after reading *The Poor and the Poorest* on UK poverty and working with deprived children in Hamburg (Atkinson, 2019, p. 1). In 1967, he went for a year to MIT in the United States, where he was the research assistant to Robert Solow. He then returned to Cambridge, England, where he had obtained a fellowship and a lectureship. In 1971, he became professor at the University of Essex. Then he held chairs at the University College, London; London School of Economics and Oxford University until his death in 2017. Alongside his work as a teacher and researcher, he was very actively engaged in economic societies and committees. He was president of the Econometric Society, the Royal Economic Society, the European Economic Association and the International Economic Association. He also founded the *Journal of Public Economics*. He was the editor of the journal for 25 years and made it the leading field journal in public economics.

Throughout his career, Atkinson was concerned about the contribution of economics to the development of society. He devoted most of his academic life to work on inequality and to thinking about public policy and ways of reducing inequality and poverty. Atkinson (2014) argued forcefully against economists who think that that economics should not be concerned about the distributional implications of policy measures.

Atkinson's contribution to the analysis of inequality is massive. His early work focused on theory, but soon his focus shifted towards empirical work. He applied public economics tools to analyse economic policy choices. Atkinson moral principles were unchanged over his career, while he regarded his views about economics 'as tentative and open to revisions as (he) learned more and acquired more evidence' (Atkinson, 2014, p. x).

Jenkins (2017, p. 1151) says that Atkinson's work 'brought the analysis of distributional issues back to a central position in economics' and that 'the modern analysis of economic inequality started with his 1970 *Journal of Economic Theory* paper'. Atkinson has contributed over a broad spectrum, and we will touch upon the major dimensions. However, our primary focus will be on his work on income distribution policies and the welfare state.

The outline of the rest of the chapter is as follows. In Section 5.1, we look at Atkinson's take on conceptual issues such as what inequality is, why it matters and how it should be studied. In Section 5.2, we look at his seminal contribution to the issue of measurement of inequality (Atkinson, 1970). In Section 5.3, we look at his work on the evolution of inequality during the last century, as well as the recent evolution of poverty. Section 5.4 is about his work on the evolution of global inequality and poverty. In Section 5.5, we summarize Atkinson's views on the causes of inequality, in particular his thinking about theory. Section 5.6 is the key part of this chapter, since this is where we discuss policies that he thinks should be used to reduce inequality as well as the role of the welfare state in doing so. In Section 5.7, we look briefly at his thoughts about foreign aid as a tool for global equalization and poverty reduction. Finally, in Section 5.8, we discuss his views on what is possible to achieve in terms of enhanced equality and the future of the welfare state. We also provide some concluding remarks on the importance of Atkinson's work.

5.1 Conceptual Issues

In his address to the Royal Economic Society in 1997, entitled 'Bringing Income Distribution in From the Cold', Atkinson (1997) argued that the subject of income inequality had been marginalised within economics for much of the 20th century, while he thought it should have been central to the subject. On this issue, he quarrelled with for example Lucas, who argued that economic growth is much more important than income distribution. Atkinson disagreed with Lucas for two reasons. First, he emphasised that the distribution of current total income does matter for individuals and that equality contributes to a more cohesive society and a greater sense of shared interests. Second, he argued that total production is affected by the distribution.

Atkinson's book *Inequality: What Can Be Done?* (2015) is in a way the culmination of his life's work on the issue of inequality. In the book (as well as elsewhere), Atkinson argued that there are both intrinsic and instrumental reasons to be concerned about inequality. The intrinsic reason is about justice. The instrumental reasons for concern about inequality are, for example, that it leads to lack of social cohesion, increased crime, bad health and other social problems (Atkinson, 2015). See also Piketty (2015).

There is also an ongoing debate as to whether one should focus on the inequality of opportunity or on the inequality of outcomes. Some argue that one should only be concerned with the former, while Atkinson argued that outcome as an indicator of standard of living also matters. Furthermore, it influences the inequality of opportunity of the next generation.

When studying inequality, you must specify inequality of what, and inequality among whom. On the first aspect, you can look at either consumption or income. Consumption measures the use of resources, that is, it measures the standard or well-being. Income measures the flow of resources, that is, the opportunity to reach a certain level of welfare. It measures potential spending power. A long chapter on his book *Measuring Poverty around the World* (Atkinson, 2019, Chapter 3) discusses all the variations and complications one needs to consider, and there are numerous.

With income, we mean the sum of all receipts (monetary or in kind), but we mostly ignore things such as imputed rent from own housing, value of public services and change in asset values. These factors should, in principle, be included to give a full measure of income, but we often lack relevant data. The answer to the question about inequality among whom is that it mostly concerns individuals or households (standardized with the help of equivalence scales). In this case, we focus on inequality measured vertically (rich vs. poor), but one could also look at inequality horizontally, that is by gender, location, ethnic group, etc. Finally, one could also go beyond cross sections and introduce a time dimension in the analysis. Atkinson was interested in both how inequality is related across generations (Atkinson, 1981) and the life cycle variation of incomes (Atkinson, 1971; Atkinson et al., 1992).

Some analysts argue that we should be focusing on poverty and not be so concerned about inequality, but Atkinson thought that inequality is a central issue. Still, he pointed out that there is a relationship between inequality and poverty and that high inequality is correlated with high poverty rates (Atkinson, 2015, p. 25). Assume that by poverty, we mean lack of resources. A crucial choice is whether to use consumption or income as our indicator of poverty. Consumption, which measures the use of resources, is typically used when it comes to poverty studies. The issue of poverty is in a sense an aspect of inequality focusing on the bottom part of the distribution. We will therefore discuss this issue as well, although this chapter is focused on inequality.

5.2 The Measurement of Inequality

Once you have formulated your question, you must meet the challenge of measuring the extent of inequality. Atkinson made a huge contribution to this issue with his 1970 paper on the measurement of inequality. Finally, you need good data to be able to do the empirical analyses. Atkinson also contributed to and discussed data collection issues a lot (Atkinson, 2019).

In his seminal paper from 1970 in the *Journal of Economic Theory*, Atkinson presented a new inequality measure, which has become known as the *Atkinson index*. The index is based on a social welfare function, since 'underlying any such measure is some concept of social welfare' (Atkinson, 1970, p. 244). He uses a social welfare function with convenient properties, such as additive individuals, concavity of income and a constant elasticity of marginal utility of income. Atkinson introduced 'the concept of equally distributed equivalent level of income, or the level of income per head which if equally distributed would give the same level of social welfare as the present distribution' (Atkinson, 1970, p. 250). The index therefore gives the share of current income, which could be sacrificed without lowering aggregate welfare, if there is perfect equality.

The index formula has a coefficient, which is used to weigh incomes. The coefficient is measuring the level of 'inequality aversion', that is, it determines which weight you put on incomes at various levels. The lower the coefficient is, the more sensitive the index is to changes in the lower part of the distribution, and vice versa. The index can be seen as a normative measure. If the inequality aversion parameter is 0, that is, there is no aversion to inequality, then welfare increases equally irrespective of if an income increase goes to a rich or a poor individual. If, on the other hand, inequality aversion is high, it matters a lot who gets an income increase. If the aversion goes to infinity, it is only what happens to the income of the poorest individual that matters for social welfare. The index then goes towards one. The index thus can vary between 0 and 1, and it measures how much welfare can be increased if the society moves from the existing distribution to perfect equality.

The chapter has profoundly affected the way social scientists think about and analyse inequality. Jenkins (2017, p. 1155) says in his review of Atkinson's work that the chapter made three contributions. The first one was that it was a theoretical contribution by 'emphasizing the welfare economic foundations of inequality measurement'. Atkinson showed that some concept of social welfare or normative notion underlies any measure of inequality. Later, Atkinson noted, 'The analysis is quite consistent with a variety of views about principles of economic justice' (Atkinson, 1983, p. 5). He showed that different indices are differently sensitive to changes at different levels of income.

The second contribution was that Atkinson devised a way of checking 'whether two distributions could be ordered in terms of their inequality according to *all* standard inequality indices'.

Third, he provided a new class of inequality measures in which different attitudes to equality preferences were explicitly incorporated via one (inequality aversion) parameter. Atkinson introduced the concept of equally distributed equivalent level of income, which is 'the level of income per head which if equally distributed would give the same level of social welfare as the present distribution' (Atkinson, 1970, p. 250).

The article had a massive impact on subsequent theoretical and empirical work on inequality. Jenkins (2017) identifies four main fields of research that build on the work of Atkinson. They are concerned with the nature of the social welfare function, social welfare comparisons, policy comparisons and multidimensional comparisons. The last one of those starts from the realization that well-being depends not on money income alone, and there is presently a lot of work on this topic. Atkinson and Bourguignon (1982) proved a set of dominance results for multidimensional comparisons. In a later paper, Atkinson and Bourguignon (1987) proved yet another set of dominance results, where differences in needs are considered.

Atkinson and Bourguignon edited three massive volumes of the *Handbook of Income Distribution* (2000, 2015a, 2015b), the size of which is an indication about the rapid increase of research on income distributional issues. The fact that Piketty's (2014) book on capital in the 21st century became an international bestseller is another indication of this.

5.3 The Evolution of Inequality and Poverty

In Chapter 2 of his 2015 book on inequality, Atkinson reviews historical data on changes in inequality. He notes that Piketty (2014) has pointed out that inequality in the Western countries declined between 1914 and1945, and that this was caused by the chaos of the Wars as well as economic and social shocks. However, soon after World War II, earnings inequality increased in the United States, but still there was not an accompanying increase in household inequality up until 1980. The increase of household inequality was held back by the influx of women into the labour market and the increase in government transfers. Therefore, the Gini coefficient of the United States was about the same in 1980 as it was in the late 1940s. Since then, it has increased substantially.

During the same period (until 1980), inequality fell in Europe. Atkinson (2015, p. 75) says that this decline was due to 'the welfare state and the expansion of transfers, the rising share of wages, the reduced concentration of personal wealth, and reduced dispersion of earnings as a result of government intervention and collective bargaining'. Thus, there were a set of factors driving this process. Atkinson was sceptical against uni-causal explanations of economic outcomes, and inequality is certainly determined through a complex process involving all parts of the economy.

The inequality of market incomes continued to increase in the 1980s and onwards, but the contribution of transfers and taxation now moved in the opposite direction. This meant that overall inequality started to increase.

> In the immediate post-war decades, the welfare state was ahead in the race to keep up with widening inequality of market incomes, but since the 1980s it has failed to do so—often as a result of explicit policy decisions to cut back on benefits and on coverage.
> (Atkinson, 2015, pp. 67–68)

Post-war equalization was due to not only redistribution but also capital income becoming less unequal. Top Ten's wealth share fell from 1950 to 1980—due to the share of housing going up. But from the 1980s, 'the trend to less wealth concentration ended' (Atkinson, 2015, p. 72). There was in Western societies what Atkinson (2015, p. 17) referred to as the Inequality Turn.

Atkinson notes that the pattern has looked different in Latin America in the 2000s, where there has been some equalization. This has been due to increases in minimum wages, government cash transfer programmes and conditional cash transfer programmes.

Today income inequality is higher than it was in 1980 in most of the Organisation for Economic Co-operation and Development (OECD) countries. The largest increases have been in the United States and the United Kingdom, while the increases in continental Europe have been smaller. Atkinson (2015, p. 81) wonders at the end of his review of distributional changes whether the world has changed, and whether this affects the design of policies for equality. His answer is a tentative yes. We will return to this later in the chapter.

Atkinson (2019, p. 1) thinks that it is important to investigate the extent and nature of poverty to spur action and design efficient policy. In the *Inequality* book, Atkinson looks at measures of world poverty. Much of the book is devoted to a comparison of the estimates of international organizations with those of national ones. Third, he looks at issues related to causes and correlates of poverty.

There are instrumental and intrinsic reasons to be concerned with poverty of countries other than your own. The intrinsic argument depends on there being at least some empathy for one's fellow citizens. Atkinson thinks that it is realistic to assume that there is less sympathy for citizens of other countries than for those of one's own, but it should be greater than zero to motivate action for citizens in other countries.

For example, the World Bank uses consumption as a welfare indicator. It measures the standard that has been achieved by individuals or households. Purchasing power comparisons are necessary for us to be able to compare standards across countries. The current extreme poverty line is set at 1.90 dollar per day in PPP USD of 2011, which was calculated as the average of 15 national poverty lines.

Extreme poverty has declined globally in recent decades (at least until the pandemic), and it has increasingly been concentrated to Africa. There is also some poverty in the rich countries, but it is seldom extreme in the sense that it is measured in developing countries. In the rich countries, there are people characterized as poor, but then the concept is typically some percentage, say 60 percent, of the median income in the country. Therefore, one may think of the 'Poverty Problem' in rich countries more as an inequality problem.

In recent years, there has been increasing focus on multidimensional poverty. This follows quite naturally from the capabilities (Sen, 2009) or rights approaches. The policy question is what one should do when a household fails to reach a certain number of minimum levels on a set of indicators. One could look at the results individually on a dashboard of indicators or on a number weighing indicators together to get one indicator value. Ravallion (2016, pp. 279–280) describes the latter as a mashup index. He thinks that there is too much arbitrariness possible in the weighing of the components and that their policy-relevance in any case may be limited.

5.4 Global Inequality and Global Poverty

So far, we have focused on inequality within a nation, but one could of course also look at global inequality, that is inequality among the citizens of the world. Atkinson was also interested in this issue.

During last century, there was a period up until about 1980, when inequality within (at least Western) countries declined, at the same time as inequality between countries increased. This process was then reversed. The time pattern of inequality among countries can thus be described as an inverted U-curve, where latterly there has been convergence.

The fall in global inequality indices is strongly affected, when large countries like China and India grow relative to the richer countries. Still, although the gap between countries is falling in relative terms, it is still increasing in absolute terms in many instances. Not all developing countries have grown like China and India!

Together with Piketty and Saez, Atkinson started the trend of research on top income shares. The novelty was that they managed to use previously unused tax data to derive long time series. Atkinson and Piketty (2007, 2010) made cross-national studies (see also Atkinson, 2011). They showed, among other things, that the English-speaking countries had a pattern different than the rest of the OECD countries. Already in Atkinson (1995), he showed that there were large variations among OECD countries in terms of income distribution. In this book, he also discussed the pros and cons of a basic income policy. He did not reach a conclusion but at least sought to provide the basis for political decision-making on this topic.

Atkinson also contributed early papers on the distribution of wealth (Atkinson and Harrison, 1978), earnings mobility (Atkinson and Micklewright, 1992) and intergenerational mobility of income (Atkinson et al., 1983).

Atkinson (2019, p. 1) argued that poverty is one of the great challenges of the world at present, alongside climate change. In his last book (published posthumously), Atkinson (2019) discusses global poverty and the Sustainable Development Goals (SDGs). He thinks that the work on empirical poverty measurement at the World Banks started in the 1970s by Hollis Chenery has been a remarkable achievement. It has been challenging to get good global poverty estimates, but better data and consumer price indices have made it easier to make cross-country comparisons. At the heart of SDGs lies concern for global poverty. The construction and spread of estimates of global poverty have played a key role in raising public concern about the evolution of poverty in the world.

The key SDG goal is the one on poverty, which says that poverty in all its dimensions shall be eradicated by 2030. This means that both regular income poverty and non-monetary poverty should be eliminated by 2030. This is not likely to happen, of course!

Since SDGs are global, one needs a global measure of poverty. However, the World Bank approach is not sufficient according to Atkinson. Instead, he proposes (as he did previously with Bourguignon) a combination of an absolute and a relative poverty line to be used when you measure poverty in both rich and poor countries. The poorest countries would be evaluated according to the absolute poverty line, but after a point, this poverty line would slope upwards at some rate (he tries 30 percent and 50 percent slopes). The curve slopes upward when the mean consumption is three and a third of the poverty line applied at the bottom of the distribution. Computed in this way, there will be more 'poor' people in the world. The way that Atkinson does it for 2013 gives an estimate of 26.1 percent poor in the world at 30 percent slope and 31.1 percent when the slope is 50 percent.

Atkinson (2019, p. 215) ends his (incomplete) book on the measurement of poverty by the conclusion that our knowledge about poverty around the world is imperfect, but he thinks that 'we know enough to act'. The failure to act cannot be attributed to lack of information, he says.

5.5 Causes of Inequality

Atkinson devoted much of his career trying to understand the causes of inequality. In doing so, he looked at historical experiences and on what has driven inequality change in different periods. He looked, of course, at the reasons for the recent increase in inequality in Western countries (the Inequality Turn) and points to the forces of technological change and globalisation as well as the changing role of the welfare state. In Chapter 3 of his book on inequality (Atkinson, 2015), he also lists the growth of financial services, changing pay norms, reduced role of trade unions and scaling back of the redistributive tax-and-transfer policy as causes.

In the rest of the chapter, he reviews the economics of inequality. Since there is no unified theory of inequality, he touches upon a variety of approaches that can help us understand the evolution of inequality. Much work on income distribution is based on the standard static and competitive framework (Atkinson and Bourguignon, 2000, Chapter 1). In this model, the income distribution is determined by the distribution of endowments, wealth and technological factors. This model is the starting point of many analyses of inequality. It can be extended by the incorporation of factor accumulation into a dynamic general equilibrium model, which can explain changes over time in inequality. Depending on what capital market imperfections you allow for, you can get a variety of results. Piketty (2014), of course, discussed the implications of capital accumulation for inequality at length.

Atkinson goes beyond the classical model and puts a lot of emphasis on the work of Tinbergen (1975) who describes the development in the labour market as a race between the increased demand for educated workers and the expansion of the educated population. Changes in the wage premium for the skilled, relative to the wage of the unskilled, depend on what happens to supply and demand of the two categories of workers. These changes may, in turn, be driven by globalisation and technological change.

The globalisation story (at least in a Heckscher–Ohlin model with perfect competition) is that globalisation leads to further specialisation, which in the rich countries would mean a shift towards high-tech goods requiring skilled labour. This would mean that the latter's wage premium increases and so does the inequality between skilled and unskilled workers.

In addition, technological progress also may change the demand for different types of labour. It is not self-evident that it increases demand for skilled labour, since that requires that the elasticity of substitution is greater than 1. Nevertheless, the evidence seems to suggest that the elasticity is greater than 1, so increased inequality seems likely. The evidence also shows that top incomes (of presumably well-educated workers) have increased faster than incomes further down the scale.

Atkinson often emphasised that the labour market is a social institution. This means that it is not supply and demand alone that determine wages. For example there may be trade unions and collective bargaining seeking to change the wage structure in favour of the lower paid workers. In recent years, there has been a decline in union power, which may have contributed to a widening of the wage distribution.

The determination of earnings in modern-day market economies is highly complex. Recent models have incorporated various selection mechanisms, and they may include unobservability of effort and agency problems. These new models may explain, for example, why earnings differ between identical individuals, but it is difficult to combine different stories into an agreed-upon full model that can explain earnings distribution. He also notes that many important markets in modern economies are characterized by monopolistic competition, where firms have a certain price-setting power. This also influences the wages they pay, with consequences for inequality.

Atkinson notes that the share of profits has risen recently, and this leads to increased inequality among households. Although many individuals own their house and a share of some investment fund, the capital ownership is highly unequal. Therefore, an increased capital share is a force for increased inequality.

Atkinson (2015, p. 110) sums up his review as follows: 'Experience suggests that a fall in inequality has come about through a combination of reduced inequality of market incomes and more effective redistribution'.

5.6 Policies to Reduce Inequality

Throughout his career, Atkinson produced major studies on policies that could help reduce inequality. Examples of such works are *Public Economics in Action* (Atkinson, 1995), *The Economic Consequences of Rolling Back the Welfare State* (1999) and *Public Economics in an Age of Austerity* (Atkinson, 2014).

Much of Atkinson's research concerned taxation and the welfare state. Early on, he looked at normative issues such as how best to design a tax to raise a certain revenue (Atkinson and Stiglitz, 1972, 1976). The extensive work on public economics by Atkinson and Stiglitz (1980) was drawn together in what was to become the standard textbook in the field, *Lectures in Public Economics*. In the book, they list various reasons as to why economies may fail to reach a Pareto-efficient resource allocation, for example income distribution issues, missing markets, imperfect competition, externalities, incomplete information, public goods and others. Because of such market failures, they argued that there is room for government interventions to improve outcomes.

Atkinson worked a lot on issues of policy design in the welfare state and on what could be done to reduce poverty and reduce inequality (Atkinson, 1969). He worked on all kinds of policy issues such as pensions, unemployment benefits, several types of taxes, family benefits and wealth and wealth taxes (Atkinson, 1972, 1983, 1989, 1995). He contributed a lot to the development of tax-benefit microsimulation models, which are now widely used (Atkinson and Sutherland, 1988).

While many economists analysed the potentially negative incentive effects of the welfare state, Atkinson thought that it could have a positive role to play through 'income replacement (social insurance) and income maintenance and poverty alleviation' (Atkinson and Micklewright, 1991; Atkinson, 1999). He also wrote about the link between macroeconomic policy and inequality in connection with the austerity programmes during the financial crisis (Atkinson, 2014). The last book that he published before his death was on what political and social institutions could do to reduce inequalities (Atkinson, 2015). This book in a sense summarized his take on this issue, and we will discuss it extensively here.

When it comes to thinking about how one should try to steer society, he agrees with Amartya Sen. They both think that we should be concerned with whether what we do advances or retreats justice and not look for transcendental optimality. This stance also characterises his last book on policy for equality, Atkinson (2015, p. 302), where he wrote, 'I do not believe that rising inequality is inevitable!' He did not think that it was impossible to change income distribution but that it was rather a matter of political will. The book is a final statement from Atkinson on where he thinks we should take our societies and how. Atkinson is clearly a dedicated defender of the welfare state, which has been under pressure during the years of liberal backlash. Thus, the book is about what policymakers should do now, but he points out that it is not only governments that make a difference. Also, the choices of consumers matter.

The bulk of Atkinson's book consists of proposals for action against inequality. He presents 15 proposals as a package to deal with the problem. His programme for equality draws a lot on the research that he did over his career. He thinks that the 21st century will be different in terms of the nature of the labour market and in the globalisation of the economy, and he tries to consider those changes when de draws up his proposals.

Atkinson presented his proposals under five different headings. His first theme is *technological change and countervailing power*. His *Proposal 1* there is that policymakers should be concerned about the direction of technological change and consider its distributional consequences.

He further argues that consumers and employees have too little power relative to producers. To deal with this problem, he suggests that there should be better legal protection of trade unions. He furthermore suggests that broader social objectives could be embodied in firms by legislation, taxation, legal liability in civil courts and ethical codes.

Competition policy also has distributional implications. It should be used to control the behaviour of firms with monopoly or monopolistic power. This leads to his *Proposal 2*, which says that public policy should aim at a proper balance of power among stakeholders, via competition policy, legal framework for trade unions and social and economic councils.

His second theme is *employment and pay in the future*. Here, he notes that the period from the end of World War II to the mid-1970s was a period of low unemployment, but then unemployment went up to levels not unlike those of the mid-war period.

He thinks that employment is very important for society (Atkinson, 2015, p. 139). He writes, 'employment is the principal route for individuals and their families to escape poverty and for societies to lower the level of inequality'. Moreover, he thinks that work is a merit good that give employees a sense of belonging and value.

When discussing the issue of unemployment, he identifies one change in the structure of our economies, which he thinks will have major implications for the future and for policymaking. He thinks that the nature of employment is changing. Now, more people have a portfolio of activities rather than one fixed full-time job. More people have part-time and unpaid internship. This has implications for the design of social protection as well as for the goal of full employment.

He notes when discussing this that before the industrial revolution, people had a mix of part-time employment and self-employment (Atkinson, 2015, p. 134). Then the concepts of unemployment and retirement had little meaning. We are now moving back towards such a system of non-standard work. He argues that we must change our definition of unemployment. It should be measured in a way that is compatible with the 21st-century labour market.

This leads up to his *Proposal 3*, which demands that the government should adapt an explicit target of employment and underpin this ambition by offering guaranteed public employment at the minimum wage.

Guaranteed employment is certainly a radical proposal! Atkinson thinks that individuals seeking the benefit and meeting the qualifications should be guaranteed a position for a minimum number of hours per week and paid the minimum wage, working for a public body or an approved non-profit organisation. Failure to apply should have no effects for benefit receipts. The scheme would be for those with a long-term attachment to the labour market—nationals and non-nationals. He does not want to use citizenship as a criterion for inclusion, since that would lead to financing of people not living in the country. Nor does he want to make it possible to migrate from abroad to get access. Non-citizens must have been in the country and been attached to the labour market before they can demand the favour. Atkinson thinks that the programme will have an impact on the workers. It would change the relationship of the individual with the economy and be a clear signal of inclusion. He notes, however, that the effect on inequality is unclear.

He also writes about ethical pay policies and wants to see an economy-wide approach to earnings determination.

This leads to *Proposal 4*, which suggests a statutory minimum wage set as a living wage plus a code of practice of pay above the minimum wage. He thinks that the government should use the state's market power to influence firms. There should be a broad national conversation about wage structure.

The third theme is *capital shared*, where Atkinson discusses ways of making the ownership of capital more equal.

His *Proposal 5* is that the government should offer, via national savings bonds, a guaranteed positive real interest rate on savings, with a maximum holding per person. This is not a very radical proposal.

Proposal 6, on the other hand, is radical. Here, he suggests that there should be a capital endowment paid to everyone at adulthood (say at 18 years of age), scaled according to the number of years in the country. This would give young people a more even start in life.

Atkinson's *Proposal 7* is the creation of a sovereign wealth fund. A public investment authority should be created operating a fund with the aim of building up the net worth of the state by holding investment in companies and in property.

His fourth theme is *progressive taxation*, where Atkinson has a long list of proposals. He wants to see the restoration of taxation that is more progressive. He notes that the social objective of taxation goes beyond the objective of revenue maximization. It is also about fairness.

Atkinson's *Proposal 8* is a top marginal tax rate of 65 percent and a broadening of the tax base.

He furthermore suggests, in his *Proposal 9*, that the government should introduce a personal income tax on earned income discount, limited to the first band of earnings.

Proposal 10 is about taxing wealth transfers. Atkinson suggests that receipt of inheritance and gifts inter vivo should be taxed under a progressive lifetime capital receipts tax. The receipts of this should be allocated to the payment of a minimum inheritance for all.

Proposal 11 is about the taxation of owner-occupied housing. There should be a proportional or progressive property tax based on property assessments.

He would also like to see an annual wealth tax. Much of people's wealth is not from savings but from price increases on for example houses or asset revaluations. However, wealth taxes are hard to collect unless there is international action. Therefore, there should be a global tax and a minimum tax on corporations (related to the turnover in the country). The multinational companies certainly benefit from local infrastructure, and they should pay. The OECD is discussing this issue now, so there is a chance of progress here.

Atkinson notes that there are some problems with current systems of inheritance taxation. As said already, he proposes a shift to a lifetime capital receipt tax on inheritance and gifts, which he thinks would be much more acceptable. However, he proposes quite high rates of taxation on the wealth that is inherited (and not worked for). He also proposes a proportional (or progressive) tax on occupied housing property in contrast to the regressive tax that has recently been put in place in both England and Sweden. He also argues for an annual wealth tax—especially since inequality now is much higher than 40 years ago. Savings of households have played a small role in explaining wealth increase in recent decades. They are rather due to asset revaluations.

Atkinson's fifth theme is *social security for all*. He believes that the welfare state has a key role in reducing inequality. It ensures a minimum level of resources for citizens; the recent scaling down of social protection, which has increased inequality, upsets Atkinson. He talks about one key measure, namely the restoration of benefit levels.

Atkinson is concerned about the effects of having means-tested benefits. First, they give high marginal tax rates, which blunt the incentives to move out of poverty. Second, not everyone who is entitled claims the benefits. Therefore, there are both incentive effects and intrinsic fairness considerations in favour of benefits for all.

Atkinson notes that child benefits have a key role to play, since there are generally high returns to early childhood programmes. He views the child benefit as a basic income for children. His *Proposal 12* is that child benefits should be paid at a substantial rate. He also thinks that this income should be taxed like general income, which would give it some degree of focus on the poorer groups.

His *Proposal 13* concerns the introduction of a basic income for adults. This should be the same for everyone, possibly with adjustments for age or sickness/

disability. The idea is that it would replace all existing social transfers. However, he does not think that we could take this step immediately. Instead, he thinks that there should first be a system that complements the existing social transfer system, which lifts everyone up to the level of the basic income. He also notes that there must be a qualifying condition in terms of making a social contribution. It should be paid on the criterion of participation, not citizenship. He also discusses the possibility of taking a first step (on the EU level) of establishing a basic income for children.

The alternative to basic income or participation income is a renewed system of social insurance. His *Proposal 14* is about (1) the restoration of social insurance programmes to their previous role and (2) the adaptation to the labour market of the 21st century. Atkinson is concerned about the changes in the structure of the labour market and what this will imply for the welfare system. He wants to see an increase of the benefit coverage of the unemployment insurance. It needs to accommodate to slivers of time. Atkinson suggests that everyone should have a Minimum Pension Guarantee. He suggests a system where the state tops up pensions to a certain minimum level.

His *Proposal 15* is about international solidarity. He suggests that one should give 1 percent of gross national income (GNI) in foreign aid. Atkinson is not convinced that we should only aim for 1 percent of GNI. We discuss this dimension later in the chapter.

In the final part of his 2015 book, he discusses the arguments against his proposed policies for increased equality. He looks at three dimensions of the critique. They are that there is a growth-equity trade-off, that globalisation prevents action and that we cannot afford income distribution policies.

Atkinson (2015, Chapter 9) first discusses at length the standard objection to redistribution, namely that there is a growth-equity trade-off. He has a couple of arguments against this reason for not caring about equality. First, he notes that this is not a knockdown argument. Even if there is a trade-off, it may well be welfare enhancing to seek to increase equality. His second argument is that in certain areas, equity and efficiency may point in the same direction.

Atkinson discusses at length those markets in our economies, which are characterized by imperfect competition and unemployment, and there is a major place for institutions. In this world, we must compare second-best situations. Atkinson points out that there are many situations, where there may be complementarity between equity and efficiency. Reasons for this includes that there may be more than one possible market outcome, and there may be efficiency wages.

> In defence of his proposed package, he makes the following remark: Shifting away from means tested benefits may eliminate elements of the poverty trap; strengthening social insurance may increase labour market attachment; the capital endowment may allow young people to set up their own businesses; the provision of a guaranteed rate of return on savings, may reduce uncertainty about people's incomes in retirement.
>
> (Atkinson, 2015, p. 258)

He also notes that there is no clear correlation between inequality and growth across countries. Therefore, it is hard to draw general conclusions about the equity-efficiency trade-off. What we really want to know is how different instruments, such as taxes and redistribution, affect growth. There has been increasing support for these views in the recent empirical literature. For example, recent work by Berg et al. (2018) shows that there is often a positive relation between equality and growth. They also find that redistribution is beneficial for growth if it is not very extensive.

The second objection is that globalisation prevents action. Here, he argues that it is true that the welfare state requires tax revenue, but that experience shows us that the welfare state can be maintained in the globalized world. One argument for this is that the welfare state was first developed during the previous period of globalisation in the late 19th century. Second, he argues that countries still have a lot of control over their destiny. National governments are still the primary source of policymaking. Third, he notes that international cooperation on for example taxation is possible.

On the third objection which is about affordability, he argues that we clearly can afford the welfare state. The question is whether we want to have it, and Atkinson clearly is a staunch supporter of it.

One of Atkinson's collaborators, Piketty (2020), has taken the discussions of the importance and role inequality further. Piketty argues that it is the struggle for equality and education that drives economic development and human progress. Like Atkinson, he believes that ideological and political factors are key determinants of inequality. Like Atkinson, he favours what he calls a social-democratic society (or a welfare state). Also, such states were unable to hold back the inequality increases, which started around 1980. According to Piketty, it was replaced by hypercapitalism, driven by globalisation and the latest information technology. Piketty discusses how one could bring inequality down again. His political agenda resembles Atkinson's in many ways, but it goes further and is more radical than Atkinson's pragmatic agenda. The debates about inequality-related policies continues anyway, and Atkinson's work and collaborations have been an especially important input into this discussion.

5.7 Foreign Aid

Atkinson discusses the case for development aid. It can be either an ethical case or given for the instrumental reasons that aid can have beneficial consequences such as reducing the migration pressure, increasing political stability or reducing the risk of terrorist attacks. Atkinson (2004, 2009; Atkinson et al., 2012) worked on how to increase external finance for developing countries and on the role of the MDGs.

As we saw earlier, Atkinson also included one proposal on foreign aid in his list of measures suggested in his *Inequality* book (Atkinson, 2015). He notes that the total cost of bringing everyone up to the poverty line at the time of writing would only be some 110 billion dollars. Therefore, the elimination of extreme poverty is not financially impossible. Atkinson admits that the effectiveness of aid is an issue, but he still thinks that some will reach the needy. He thinks that aid works if at least some part of it trickles down to the poor.

The aid critic Deaton (2013, p. 312) asks, 'Who put us in charge?' This question applies to both reasons, says Atkinson. Aid is not only about generating growth, but it also aims to deal with the current plight of the poor and the fragility of their circumstances (Atkinson, 2015, p. 234). There are many outcomes, which should be counted irrespective of their impact on growth. Atkinson thinks that one could argue that we have a liability to make sure that everyone reaches a global minimum standard. He thinks we should consider merit goods such as basic health and primary education, which can be seen both as fundamental human rights and as fundamental to the development process.

So, should we be concerned about global poverty or global welfare? It all boils down to a moral judgement, and here we can take various positions. In standard welfare economics, we normally think of welfare within a 'society', by which we mean a nation. However, one could in principle think of the world as our 'society' and apply the same welfare function on the world population. Atkinson (2019, Chapter 10 and elsewhere) argues that it is unrealistic to assume wide acceptance for such a broad all-inclusive definition of a society with which we are concerned. People are typically more willing to share with and take care of people within their own nation. However, normally we would not totally ignore the fate of the rest of humankind but have some solidarity also with non-nationals. Therefore, Atkinson assumes that we care to some extent also for non-nationals, but less so than for nationals. Thus, this solidarity lies somewhere between no solidarity at all and complete solidarity. Atkinson thinks that a realistic description of our situation is that we are willing to help non-nationals—but to a limited degree. Therefore, he recommends that we give aid, possibly more than the 1 percent that has been talked about and which was until recently the official goal of Sweden.

5.8   Conclusions

Atkinson's interest in the inequality issue was due to his desire for a good and fair society. His ambition was to influence policy and to help making societies better. He clearly saw the welfare state as the basic ingredient of such a society—at least in the situation that we are in at present. Atkinson's policy advice has always been formulated as interventions, which can improve the situation we are in, while he has never pointed out what the optimal society or the utopian end station would be. He did not think that this was useful.

What did Atkinson think about the way forward? He says that there has been an Inequality Turn since 1980 and argues that we should aim to reduce inequality again. This needs to be done to secure not only equality of opportunities but also a functioning democracy. 'The present levels of inequality are intrinsically inconsistent with the conception of a good society!' (Atkinson, 2015, p. 301).

Atkinson has contributed enormously to our empirical knowledge about the distribution of income, earnings and wealth as well as policies to reduce inequality. He has worked on these topics very carefully with attention to the quality of available data. Until the very end of his career, Atkinson felt that we 'need to place distributional analysis at the heart of the analysis' (Atkinson, 2015, p. 301).

Atkinson had a quality that has become less prominent among economists of today, namely the view that the key role of economics is to illuminate workable solutions of social problems. He had an enormous impact on both the profession and public policymakers. Overall, he was certainly one of the most impressive and important economists of his time—without having received the 'Nobel Prize' in economics.

References

Atkinson, A.B. (1969). *Poverty in Britain and the Reform of Social Security*. Cambridge: Cambridge University Press.
Atkinson, A.B. (1970). On the Measurement of Inequality. *Journal of Economic Theory*, 2(3), 244–263.
Atkinson, A.B. (1971). The Distribution of Wealth and the Individual Life-Cycle. *Oxford Economic Papers*, New Series, 23(2), 239–254.
Atkinson, A.B. (1972). *Unequal Shares: Wealth in Britain*. London: Allen Lane, The Penguin Press.
Atkinson, A.B. (1981). On Intergenerational Income Mobility in Britain. *Journal of Post Keynesian Economics*, 3(2), 194–218.
Atkinson, A.B. (1983). *Social Justice and Public Policy*. London: Harvester-Wheatsheaf.
Atkinson, A.B. (1989). *Poverty and Social Security*. London: Harvester-Wheatsheaf.
Atkinson, A.B. (1995). *Public Economics in Action: The Basic Income/Flat Tax Proposal*. Oxford: Oxford University Press.
Atkinson, A.B. (1997). Bringing Income Distribution in from the Cold. *Economic Journal*, 107(441), 297–321.
Atkinson, A.B. (1999). *The Economic Consequences of Rolling Back the Welfare State*. Cambridge, MA: MIT Press.
Atkinson, A.B. (ed) (2004). *New Sources of Development Finance*. Oxford: Oxford University Press.
Atkinson, A.B. (2009). Giving Overseas and Public Policy. *Journal of Public Economics*, 93(5–6), 647–653.
Atkinson, A.B. (2011). The Restoration of Welfare Economics. *American Economic Review, Papers and Proceedings*, 101(3), 157–161.
Atkinson, A.B. (2014). *Public Economics in an Age of Austerity*. London: Routledge.
Atkinson, A.B. (2015). *Inequality: What Can Be Done?* Cambridge, MA and London: Harvard University Press.
Atkinson, A.B. (2019). *Measuring Poverty Around the World*. Princeton, NJ: Princeton University Press.
Atkinson, A.B., Backus, P., Micklewright, J., Pharoah, C., and Schnepf, S. (2012). Charitable Giving for Overseas Development: UK Trends Over a Quarter Century. *Journal of the Royal Statistical Society, Series A*, 175(1), 167–190.
Atkinson, A.B., and Bourguignon, F. (1982). The Comparison of Multi-Dimensional Distributions of Economic Status. *Review of Economic Studies*, 49(2), 183–201.
Atkinson, A.B., and Bourguignon, F. (1987). Income Distribution and Differences in Needs. Chapter 12 in G.R. Feiwel (ed), *Arrow and the Foundations of the Theory of Economic Policy*. New York: Macmillan.
Atkinson, A.B., and Bourguignon, F. (2000). Introduction: Income Distribution and Economics. In A.B. Atkinson and F. Bourguignon (eds), *Handbook of Income Distribution*, vol. 1. Amsterdam: Elsevier North-Holland.

Atkinson, A.B., and Bourguignon, F. (2015a). *Handbook of Income Distribution*, vol. 2a. Amsterdam: Elsevier North-Holland.
Atkinson, A.B., and Bourguignon, F. (2015b). *Handbook of Income Distribution*, vol. 2b. Amsterdam: Elsevier North-Holland.
Atkinson, A.B., Bourguignon, F., and Morrison, C. (1992). *Empirical Studies of Earnings Mobility. Fundamentals of Pure and Applied Economics*, vol. 52. Chur, CH: Harwood Academic Publishers.
Atkinson, A.B., and Harrison, A. (1978). *Distribution of Personal Wealth in Britain*. Cambridge: Cambridge University Press.
Atkinson, A.B., Maynard, A.K., and Trinder, C.G. (1983). *Parents and Children: Incomes in Two Generations*. London: Heinemann.
Atkinson, A.B., and Micklewright, J. (1991). Unemployment Compensation and Labour Market Transitions. *Journal of Economic Literature*, 29(4), 1679–1727.
Atkinson, A.B., and Micklewright, J. (1992). *Economic Transformation in Eastern Europe and the Distribution of Income*. Cambridge: Cambridge University Press.
Atkinson, A.B., and Piketty, T. (eds) (2007). *Top Incomes Over the Twentieth Century: A Contrast Between European and English-Speaking Countries*. Oxford: Oxford University Press.
Atkinson, A.B., and Piketty, T. (eds) (2010). *Top Incomes: A Global Perspective*. Oxford: Oxford University Press.
Atkinson, A.B., and Stiglitz, J.E. (1972). The Structure of Indirect Taxation and Economic Efficiency. *Journal of Public Economics*, 1(1), 97–119.
Atkinson, A.B., and Stiglitz, J.E. (1976). The Design of Tax Structure: Direct Versus Indirect Taxation. *Journal of Public Economics*, 6(1–2), 55–75.
Atkinson, A.B., and Stiglitz, J.E. (1980). *Lectures on Public Economics*. Maidenhead: McGraw-Hill.
Atkinson, A.B., and Sutherland, H. (eds) (1988). *Tax-Benefit Models. STICERD Occasional Paper*. London: London School of Economics.
Berg, J.D., Ostry, C.D., Tsangarides, C.G., and Yakhshilikov, Y. (2018). Redistribution, Inequality, and Growth: New Evidence. *Journal of Economic Growth*, 23, 259–305.
Deaton, A. (2013). *The Great Escape: Health, Wealth, and the Origins of Inequality*. Princeton NJ and Oxford: Princeton University Press.
Jenkins, S.P. (2017). Anthony B. Atkinson (1944–). In R. Cord (eds), *The Palgrave Companion to Cambridge Economics* (pp. 1151–1174). London: Palgrave Macmillan.
Piketty, T. (2014). *Capital in the Twenty-First Century*. Cambridge, MA, and London: The Belknap Press of Harvard University Press.
Piketty, T. (2015). Putting Distribution Back at the Center of Economics: Reflections on Capital in the Twenty-First Century. *Journal of Economic Perspectives*, 29(1), 67–88.
Piketty, T. (2020). *Capital and Ideology*. Cambridge, MA: The Belknap Press of Harvard University Press.
Ravallion, M. (2016). *The Economics of Poverty: History, Measurement, and Policy*. Oxford: Oxford University Press.
Sen, A. (2009). *The Idea of Justice*. London: Allen Lane.
Tinbergen, J. (1975). *Income Distribution: Analysis and Policies*. Amsterdam: North-Holland.

Part III
Discrimination, Plunder, and Inequalities

6 Discrimination as a Determinant of Economic Inequality

Ali Ahmed, Mats Lundahl and Eskil Wadensjö

The purpose of the present essay is to illustrate the usefulness of economics as a tool for the analysis of the effects of discrimination. Economics is not a unified science (nor is, for that matter, that of physics), which means that we will point to and apply different approaches. The essay consists of two well-known historical cases of racial discrimination: the South African apartheid system and the unfair treatment of blacks in the United States plus a survey of some contemporary cases of ethnic discrimination. The cases have been chosen because they have been subject to very different analytical approaches: a mainly mainstream, neoclassical one—orthodox if you want—in the former case and a heterodox, holistic one in a classic analysis of the second one.

Our first case, racial discrimination in South Africa, lends itself excellently to disaggregated multisectoral neoclassical general equilibrium analysis—for two reasons. The relevant sectors and the different production factors that they employ are easy to identify. By the same token, the approach allows us to identify the winners and losers from the different discriminatory policies.

Our second case, Gunnar Myrdal's analysis of the racial issue in the United States during the early 1940s, presents a more grandiose—holistic—approach, a dynamic and interdisciplinary extension of the traditional general equilibrium approach. The purpose of his analysis was to get away from what he considered to be an obsession with static equilibrium situations and approaches based exclusively on economics. Myrdal was convinced that there was no such thing as a purely economic, social or political problem. For him, there were only problems, and the only way of analyzing them was to use an approach that took all the relevant variables—regardless of category—into account. Several other theories of discrimination which bear on the US experience have been developed. Among them, those based on preferences, monopsony, and statistical discrimination are most in focus. Also discussed and evaluated are policies against discrimination, for example, affirmative action.

In the final section, we turn our attention to modern examples of institutionalized and systemic discrimination and oppression, highlighting the continued relevance of the discussed theories for addressing current social issues. This is crucial, as it dispels the notion that apartheid in South Africa and racial disparities in the United States are merely historical concerns. By examining contemporary instances of institutionalized and systemic discrimination, we emphasize the

DOI: 10.4324/9781003387114-10

persistent significance and need of the analysis and discussion presented in the first parts of this essay. These modern cases not only reflect the complexities seen in historical contexts but also validate and expand upon existing theories. This last section is, therefore, a vital link between past and present, showing that discrimination, in its various forms, remains an urgent and widespread issue. It also underscores the necessity for well-informed and proactive policy measures to effectively combat discrimination, drawing from historical insights and current realities.

6.1 Racial Discrimination in South Africa

In 1948, the National Party won the parliamentary elections in South Africa. It would rule the country until 1994. The main issue in the elections had been the segregation—apartheid—of Africans from whites. Racial discrimination was, however, not new in South Africa. It had begun with the first landing of the Dutch in the Cape area in 1652. Broadly speaking, three phases of it may be distinguished (Lundahl, 1982). During the first one, which extended from that year until the discovery of diamonds in Kimberley in 1867 and gold on the Witwatersrand in 1886, the main issue was land. In order to expand their animal husbandry, the Europeans systematically deprived the Africans of their land, especially after *Die Groot Trek*, which began in the mid-1830s. The Boers expanded northwards in a fan-shaped pattern and founded the republics of Transvaal and the Orange Free State.

The process may be analyzed with the aid of a model with one African and one European sector producing the same good, both employing labor and land (Lundahl, 1982). The Europeans had two goals. They wanted to increase their numbers through immigration and wanted to increase the land area at their disposal. This increased production in the European sector and increased the return to land there but decreased the wage rate and the income per capita in the African sector. Land alienation from the Africans in turn increased European incomes (the value of European production minus wage payments to the African workers in the European sectors) but decreased the wage rate and the per capita income in the African sector. These results depend critically on the relative land intensity of the two sectors. The natural assumption is that this intensity was higher in the European sector. Then, if land is transferred from Africans to Europeans and the original factor proportions are maintained in both sectors, the African sector will release more labor than the European sector is willing to accept at a constant wage. The wage rate must then fall, increasing both sectors' employment. Incomes are depressed in the African sector, but European incomes are increased. Altogether, from the historical perspective, European immigration and land alienation increased economic inequality between Europeans and Africans.

The second phase of racial discrimination began with the mineral discoveries, which inaugurated a period of exceptionally high growth in the South African economy, a process that accelerated from World War I. Between 1919–1929 and 1959–1969, the growth of real national income was between 5 and 6 percent on average (Houghton, 1976, p. 40). The development was driven by capital formation, but mining also required large amounts of labor. In order to deal analytically with the second phase, which extended approximately until World War II, the European sector had to be split into agriculture and industry (including mining), and capital and skilled labor had to be introduced. As before, African and European agriculture used land and unskilled African labor, whereas the industrial sector used European and African unskilled and skilled labor as well as a given capital stock. The number of both kinds of European workers was also fixed. The discriminatory measures employed were continued land alienation, 'civilized labor policy', that is, the imposition of a given ratio of European to African unskilled workers in industry and the reduction of the number of Africans allowed to hold skilled jobs.

As before, land alienation had a positive impact on European incomes and a negative one on African incomes, provided that European agriculture is the relatively land-intensive sector. (Because of the civilized labor policy, the unskilled African labor released in the process could enter the industry.) A higher ratio of European to African unskilled workers in the industry benefitted the former, and those unskilled Africans were allowed to continue in industry. The agricultural wage was lowered since the African unskilled workers released by the industrial sector had to go into European or African agriculture. So were the per capita income in African agriculture, the return to industrial capital, and the skilled wage rate. The reduction of the number of Africans allowed to hold skilled jobs finally benefitted European skilled workers and farmers. However, it hurt industrial capitalists and unskilled workers in both European sectors and lowered the per capita income in African agriculture. In sum, all three measures tended to hurt the Africans, except those allowed to remain in the industrial sector and to benefit European farmers.

The analysis also points to conflicts between European capitalists and unskilled workers and between skilled and unskilled workers. During the years following World War I, South Africa had a 'poor white problem'. For various reasons, around 200,000–300,000 Europeans were forced to leave the countryside and migrate to the cities, where they had to compete with Africans for unskilled jobs (Wilson, 1975, pp. 126–136). This made the former group push for tightening the civilized labor policy. On the other hand, the mine owners were intent on getting workers at the lowest possible wage. The conflict culminated in the so-called Rand Rebellion in 1922, when the European miners (three-fourths of whom were Afrikaners) went on strike. The strike was crushed violently by the military, and the employment of Africans was increased. In 1924, however, the sitting government lost to a coalition of European workers and farmers (the so-called gold–maize alliance), a strict civilized labor policy was implemented, and the best jobs were reserved for Europeans. The situation of the unskilled European workers improved during the 1930s. At the end of the decade, when the new government had embarked on a policy encouraging manufacturing, the poor white problem was a thing of the past. Since the reservation of unskilled jobs hurt the (mainly English-speaking) skilled workers, whereas the crowding of Africans out of skilled jobs hurt unskilled Europeans (mainly Afrikaners), the simultaneous implementation of both policies also made for an intra-European conflict (Houghton, 1976, pp. 153–155).

The latter conflict would come to the surface in the 1948 elections. The National Party, which had been founded as an ethnic Afrikaner party in 1914, had developed into a party whose main issue was white supremacy and which advocated the total segregation of races in South Africa.[1] It defeated the ruling United Party (a mixture of Boers and Britons) led by Jan Smuts. The elections were the beginning of the third phase of racial discrimination in South Africa. The Africans were disenfranchised. The notorious 'homelands' system was introduced: a system which made it possible to deport millions of Africans to some of the least fertile and most poverty-stricken areas in the country, ten nominally self-governing areas, with separate administrations—areas which in practice worked as reserves of cheap labor for the white economy. The educational system was segregated, with good schools reserved for whites and mediocre schools teaching in African languages instead of in English for Africans. White universities were prohibited from receiving African students. The access to better paid jobs was reserved for whites. The influx of Africans to urban areas was severely limited, and they could be thrown out on the pretext that they constituted a threat to the public order. An internal pass law was introduced, which registered the ethnicity of the passport holder, his or her employment, tax payments, and dealings with the police. The two main African political parties, the African National Congress (ANC) and the Pan Africanist Congress (PAC), were outlawed. South Africa was converted into a police state, and Nelson Mandela was given a lifetime sentence for sabotage.[2]

It was inevitable that the Byzantine apartheid legislation would lead to a highly unequal distribution of incomes and wealth, with huge differences between the races. The wage rate in the South African mines was lower in 1971 than in 1911 and that of African workers in European agriculture stagnated or was reduced until the 1960s (Lipton, 1985, pp. 44, 388). In 1978, South Africa had the most unequal distribution of incomes of all 57 countries for which data were available, with a Gini coefficient of 0.66. At the very end of the apartheid period, in 1993, the situation was very much the same: 0.65—to be compared with 0.38 for the United States, 0.32 for Sweden, and 0.28 for Japan. These figures can be explained largely in racial terms. The latter year, the average Asian per capita income amounted to 40 percent of the white one, that of 'Coloreds' to less than 20 percent, and that of Africans to 8.5 percent (Lundahl and Moritz, 1996, p. 101). The figures for the distribution of wealth convey a similar picture. At the beginning of the 1980s, 5 percent of the population accounted for 88 percent of the privately owned wealth in South Africa, against 54 percent in Great Britain, 44 percent in the United States, and 34 percent in West Germany (Lundahl and Moritz, 1996, p. 103).

In the third—apartheid—phase, the European agricultural sector makes use of sector-specific capital. The poor white problem has been solved so that all whites hold skilled jobs in manufacturing. No more land alienation takes place, but the land areas of both types of agriculture are fixed. The two discriminatory measures employed were control of the influx of Africans to European areas and limitation of the number of Africans in skilled jobs. The latter benefits the European workers and the European farmers but hurts the industrial capitalists, provided that the complementarity of capital and skilled labor is greater than that between capital and unskilled labor at the margin—a plausible condition.

This, in turn, points to the existence of a conflict between European workers and industrial capitalists and between the latter and the European farmers. The latter conflict may be deepened if the possible secondary effects are considered. An increase in the return to capital in agriculture may lead to an increased investment there to the detriment of industry. Capital is not sector-specific in the longer run but 'mobile' through the process of investment and disinvestment (depreciation). Increased agricultural investment will then also draw industrial unskilled labor into agriculture and hurt industrial capitalists and skilled European workers (Lundahl and Wadensjö, 1984, pp. 137–139).

Influx control, in turn, makes no sense since it reduces the remuneration of all European-owned factors. The question then immediately arises as to why it was employed. Was it because of European security considerations or because it allowed European employers to single out the most productive Africans, offering temporary contracts and avoiding the cost of bringing their families in? Or is there any other way of modeling influx control that makes the latter rational from the European point of view? One such attempt is that of Ronald Findlay and Mats Lundahl (1987). They work with a quasi-two-sector model where only the European sector, using capital and unskilled labor, is modeled explicitly, while the wage rate is given in the African sector. It is assumed that the European wage bill is maximized. The latter consists of the marginal product of labor plus a rent equal to the marginal product of labor minus the African wage. This yields an optimal influx. If the model is extended with skilled labor, assumed to be all European while all unskilled workers are Africans, still assuming that the Europeans capture a rent from the Africans, again an optimal influx can be derived.[3]

As could be expected, the resistance against apartheid began immediately after the Nationalist triumph in 1948. It continued for four decades before the system crumbled between 1990 and 1994. In the 1980s, Prime Minister (and later President) P.W. Botha modified it under the pressure of a weak economy and increasing protests. However, it was only when F.W. de Klerk became president in 1999 that measures were taken to scrap the system completely. Nelson Mandela was released from prison after almost 27 years, and negotiations began with the ANC. When the latter party won the 1994 elections with almost two-thirds of the votes, apartheid was a thing of the past (Sparks, 1990, Chapters 13–15; Davenport and Saunders, 2000, Chapters 19–20).[4]

6.2 Discrimination of Blacks in the United States Labor Market

Slavery is the most extreme form of discrimination. In the United States, it existed in the Southern states until 1865. Slavery covered most of the black population in the country until then. There were free blacks in the Northern states but relatively few. The Civil War put an end to slavery but not to the discrimination of blacks, only that the legal form of discrimination changed.

In the South, so-called Jim Crow laws, which segregated the black population from the whites, were introduced in all parts of the public sector, such as schools and transportation. The result was a much lower quality for blacks than for whites with respect to public facilities. Segregation and discrimination continued in several different forms after the end of slavery, for example, in the labor market and the housing market.

Some social scientists, both black and white, analyzed the situation of the black population during the decades after the end of slavery. (See Rutherford, 2023, for a detailed survey.) Some dealt with different forms of discrimination. Others had their point of departure in theories of racial or cultural differences between whites and blacks and, in practice, blamed the blacks for their difficult situation.

The situation changed during World War I, with the beginning of the Great Migration of mainly black workers from the South to the North. They were employed in the manufacturing industry, which expanded during the war and in the 1920s and improved their economic situation, but not to the point where it was comparable with that of white workers. They were subject to segregation in the North as well, both in the labor market and in the housing market, having to live in other parts of the cities than where the white workers stayed,[5] and, of course, segregation continued in the South,[6] where the majority of them continued to live—77 percent in 1940 and 53 percent in 1970—many in rural areas: 49 percent in 1940 (Reich, 1981, p. 63). However, in other areas of the United States, blacks lived in urban areas more than whites (Reich, 1981, p. 65).

In 1937, Gunnar Myrdal was commissioned by the Carnegie Corporation to undertake a study of America's race problem. This study involved many people, both researchers and representatives of civil rights and reform organizations. One was Ralph Bunche, who wrote several manuscripts and a report on Southern politics. The seminal study, *An American Dilemma. The Negro Problem and Modern Democracy* (Myrdal, 1944),[7] dominated the debate on discrimination until the 1960s, when the black civil rights opted for a more radical discourse.

The American dilemma, as Myrdal saw it, was the discrepancy between what he calls the American Creed—democracy, equality, freedom, fair opportunity, and the rule of law—a concept that encompassed equality, and the discriminatory behavior of the individuals in concrete situations which turned the embracement of the creed into nothing but lip service.

Rejecting the notion of stable equilibrium, Myrdal postulated the existence of a circular and cumulative causation process. In this vicious spiral, the dire situation of the blacks led to white prejudice, which in turn led to even more discrimination and, hence, to worsening conditions for the blacks. On the other hand, policies that improved the conditions of the blacks could produce a positive circle of gradual improvement of their conditions.

Myrdal also rejected conventional, purely economic analysis, favoring a holistic approach. Economic, social, cultural, and moral factors all had to be analyzed. It was their interaction—no single part was more important than the other—that produced the outcome. Myrdal (1944, p. 208) identified three groups of factors that contributed to keeping the blacks at the bottom of American society, but which could also interact to produce positive changes: '(1) the economic level; (2) standards of intelligence, ambition, health, education, decency, manners, and morals; and (3) discrimination by whites'. A change in any of these factors would trigger changes in the other two as well, which would in turn feed back, both on the first factor and on each other, etc., in a cumulative fashion to move the entire system in one direction or another.

What Myrdal was after was the solution to the racial problem, and the tool he envisaged was social engineering: a concerted, consciously designed, planned effort striking at the roots of the poverty/discrimination nexus, using the properties of the cumulative process. The attack could be directed at any of the three constitutive elements, but a rational approach should focus on all three simultaneously.

An American Dilemma has been hailed as 'one of the most influential works of social science ever written in America' (Jackson, 1990, p. xi) and as 'one of the few works of scholarship to alter the course of history' (Barber, 2008, p. 64). It directly impacted American legislation and court cases involving discrimination, where Myrdal's work was cited as evidence. The most important—pathbreaking—one was *Brown v. Board of Education of Topeka*, 1954, in the Supreme Court, where Chief Justice Earl Warren argued that segregated schools harmed black children. The court decided that school segregation was unconstitutional (Southern, 1987, p. 127), a decision which was followed by several others that served to reduce the extent of discrimination and segregation in the United States and in addition to elevate Myrdal 'to the status of a prophet in his own time' (Southern, 1987, p. 189).

In 1964, the Civil Rights Act put an end to the Jim Crow laws. Altogether, during the two decades that followed the publication of *An American Dilemma*, important steps were taken against racial discrimination, but they have not eliminated it. (See Leonard, 1991 for an evaluation of the federal anti-bias effort.) Racial discrimination and segregation are phenomena that are still present in the United States.

This can be seen in the labor market. The employment situation for blacks in the United States improved after the end of legal discrimination in the mid-1960s. (See Freeman, 1981 for details.) Still, significant differences between whites and blacks continued in the 1970s and thereafter (von Furstenberg et al., 1974a, 1974b; McGee, 2021). This is partly explained by the fact that social mobility requires time (generations), more so in a country like the United States with low social mobility than, for example, in Scandinavia. However, the continued existence of different forms of discrimination also plays an important role.

One theory may not be able to explain it all. Here, we will deal with three different mechanisms: discrimination based on preferences, monopsonistic discrimination, and statistical discrimination. Gary Becker (1957) has developed a theory of discrimination based on preferences. Employers could have preferences for having employees belonging to the same group as their own compared to having employees belonging to another group and hence be prepared to pay for having employees belonging to the preferred group. This could be due to racism—white people have negative feelings toward black people. (There are many studies on racism—its existence and its origins in the United States. See, for example, Rose, 1964; Sowell, 1975; Reich, 1981; Fredrickson, 2002; Roemer et al., 2007.)

White employers' preferences for having white employees can lead to whites getting higher wages than blacks. If wages are regulated, this can instead lead to differences in unemployment, with blacks being unemployed to a higher extent than whites. Blacks may also be discriminated against in certain occupations but not others (generally not in low-qualification and low-pay branches). Discrimination can also take the form that blacks with high qualifications are hired but not promoted to the extent of whites. They may hit a 'black ceiling' (Woodson, 2023).

The theory, however, has an inherent flaw. This relates to the long-run effects of discrimination. If employers are working in a competitive market, those who do not discriminate will have an economic advantage and will, therefore, expand at the expense of their discriminatory competitors. The wage difference between the favored and the discriminated group will hence tend to disappear in the long run.

In the same way as employers, employees may prefer working with persons belonging to their own group. If white employees discriminate against black employees (demanding higher wages if they are working with black employees), the result will be segregation—white workers work together with other white workers and black workers work together with other black workers in different divisions of the same workplace or different firms.

A third form of preference-based discrimination is consumer discrimination— white people avoid buying if the sales personnel is black. The result could be similar to those of the other forms of preference-based discrimination: lower wages for blacks and blacks working in shops that serve black customers and whites in shops that cater to white customers.

The second theory of discrimination in the labor market builds on the existence of monopsony. It was first developed by Joan Robinson (1933) in the 1930s. She used the theory to explain low female wages. Women had a smaller local market than men since they had to take care of the children in the household and often worked part-time to manage that. Most men worked full time and were able to commute to other local labor markets and hence find better-paid jobs. In the same way, the number of jobs open to blacks may be restricted. Blacks often live in segregated areas and cannot commute to other local labor markets. (Fewer blacks than whites have cars, relatively speaking.) As a result, employers have monopsonistic positions vis-à-vis blacks to a larger extent than toward whites. This can contribute to explaining the low black wages. (See Manning, 2003 for an extensive survey of the theory of monopsony and wages.)

A third theory of labor market discrimination is that of statistical discrimination (Phelps, 1972; Arrow, 1973; Spence, 1974). Employers who want to recruit workers do not know the productivity of the job applicants. Instead, they use measures of their expected productivity and its variation based on the group characteristics of the applicants, for example, whether they are black or white. It is easier to make a better estimate of those who belong to the same group as that of the employer— have the same school tie. Since most employers are white, this leads to discrimination against blacks. It is also important to design policies against discrimination, for example, in the housing market and the judiciary system (Loury, 2008), the educational system and the labor market and to evaluate the effects of such policies as affirmative action (Bergmann, 1996).

The three theories are not mutually exclusive. Discrimination could be explained by a combination of two or more of the three theories. Only empirical studies can answer the question of which theory will best explain the existence and development of discrimination against blacks in a given labor market situation. Having said that, however, the inevitable question must be faced. Has the time come to resurrect the approach of Gunnar Myrdal—and see whether this approach is capable of integrating other approaches to discrimination as building blocks in the construction of a dynamic theory of circular, cumulative causation?

6.3 Present-Day Struggles of Marginalized Groups Worldwide

In this section, we delve into the persistent struggles of marginalized groups worldwide, highlighting the stark reality of institutionalized discrimination, segregation, and systemic oppression that continues today. We focus on the experiences of the Rohingya in Myanmar, the Uyghurs in China, the Dalits in India, Palestinians, and women in Afghanistan, revealing a disturbing pattern of racial, ethnic, and gender-based oppression. These cases echo the systemic discrimination experienced during South African apartheid and the racial segregation faced by blacks in the United States, underscoring their ongoing relevance and urgency in today's society. This comparative analysis not only sheds light on the unique challenges each group faces but also emphasizes the critical need for global awareness and action against these enduring forms of discrimination.

Furthermore, the cases discussed, among many others, illustrate how discrimination, irrespective of the targeted group, is driven by common mechanisms: power imbalances, legal disenfranchisement, cultural and social enforcement, isolation, dispossession, and displacement. These factors significantly impact marginalized groups' quality of life and opportunities. As we delve into contemporary issues of racial, ethnic, and gender discrimination globally, the relevance of economic theories related to apartheid and insights from Gunnar Myrdal's *An American Dilemma*, discussed earlier, becomes evident. These theories offer valuable frameworks for understanding the economic dimensions of discrimination, analyzing its economic foundations and societal impacts.

6.3.1 Rohingya People

The devastating situation of the Rohingya people, an ethnic minority of roughly two million people mainly living in Myanmar (known as Burma before 1989) and Bangladesh, is a heart-wrenching example of extreme discrimination and human rights abuses in contemporary history. Myanmar's population is ethnically diverse, comprising approximately 30 percent ethnic minorities and 70 percent Burmese, with a predominantly Buddhist religious demographic (Mahmood et al., 2017). The Rohingya people are predominantly Sunni Muslims and have lived in the Rakhine State (known as Arakan State before 1989) of Myanmar for centuries. Their history in the region is complex, with some historians suggesting that their presence dates back to the 15th century (Ty, 2019). The roots of their discrimination can be traced back to the post-colonial era, mainly after Myanmar gained independence from Britain in 1948 (Sarmin, 2020). The government's refusal to recognize the Rohingya as a legitimate ethnic group in Myanmar has been a critical factor in their marginalization.

In 1982, the Myanmar government passed a citizenship law that effectively rendered the Rohingya stateless (Sahana et al., 2019). This law identified 135 national races but excluded the Rohingya, denying them fundamental rights and access to citizenship. The Rohingya have faced severe restrictions on their freedom of movement, access to medical care, education, and employment (Mahmood et al., 2017). They have been subjected to arbitrary taxation, land confiscation, forced labor, and other forms of exploitation (Lewa, 2009). Since the late 20th century, there have been numerous military operations in Rakhine state, often resulting in mass killings, rapes, and the burning of Rohingya villages (Sarmin, 2020). The 2017 military campaign was particularly brutal, leading to accusations of ethnic cleansing and genocide (Parmar et al., 2022). Hundreds of thousands of Rohingya fled Myanmar, primarily to Bangladesh, living in overcrowded refugee camps with limited access to necessities (Beyrer and Kamarulzaman, 2017). Today, far more than one million Rohingya refugees are living in Cox's Bazar in Bangladesh, the largest refugee camp in the world (UN News, 2023). Systematic discrimination and violence have led to a massive humanitarian crisis. The conditions in these camps are dire, with rampant health issues, inadequate shelter, and food scarcity (Shohel, 2023).

The Rohingya crisis is a stark reminder of the destructive power of discrimination and statelessness. It underscores the urgent need for a coordinated international response that not only provides immediate humanitarian assistance but also addresses the root causes of the discrimination and seeks a long-term solution for the Rohingya people, including their safe and dignified return to Myanmar with full citizenship rights. In essence, the plight of the Rohingya is a test of the international community's determination to uphold human rights and combat racial and religious discrimination.

The discrimination against the Rohingya in Myanmar mirrors aspects of apartheid in South Africa and the discrimination against blacks in the United States, highlighting a global pattern of racial and ethnic oppression. Like black South Africans under apartheid and blacks during the Jim Crow era, the Rohingya minority face institutionalized discrimination, including statelessness. In Myanmar, as well as in Bangladesh today, the Rohingya are confined to camps, similar to Bantustans in South Africa, and segregated neighborhoods in the United States, limiting their access to resources, movement, and opportunities. Additionally, the Rohingya endure violence and persecution, paralleling the brutal enforcement of apartheid and the struggle for civil rights faced by blacks.

6.3.2 Uyghur People

The Uyghurs, a Turkic ethnic group primarily living in the Xinjiang Uyghur Autonomous Region in northwest China, have faced significant challenges and discrimination over the years (Amnesty International, 2021). Although there are more than ten million Uyghurs, they constitute a minority in China, where more than 90 percent of the population are Han Chinese (Seytoff and Szadziewski, 2018). The

Uyghurs have a rich and extensive history. Traditionally, they have been a group with a distinct cultural and ethnic identity, with their language belonging to the Turkic language family (Ibrahim and Turkel, 2021). Historically, they have been predominantly Sunni Muslim, a significant aspect of their cultural and religious identity (Bellér-Hann, 2020).

The Uyghurs have faced significant efforts from the Chinese government aimed at suppressing their cultural and religious identity (Amnesty International, 2021). Often, the Chinese government justifies these actions as part of its campaign against Islamic terrorism (Roberts, 2020). Human rights violations include not only restrictions on the practice of Islam, the Uyghurs' primary religion, but also efforts to replace the Uyghur language with Mandarin Chinese (Abdulla and Shamseden, 2021; Waller and Albornoz, 2021). Reports also indicate political repression, including the detention of Uyghurs (Amnesty International, 2021; Waller and Albornoz, 2021). In Xinjiang, the government has implemented extensive surveillance systems, using advanced technology to monitor the Uyghur population. This includes GPS tracking, voice and facial recognition, and biometric data collection (Roche and Leibold, 2022; Leibold, 2020).

Many studies have documented the existence of so-called reeducation camps, where more than 1.5 million Uyghurs have so far been incarcerated without trial (Mooney, 2021; Raza, 2019). Indoctrination, forced labor, and abuse within these camps are widespread (Amnesty International, 2021; Waller and Albornoz, 2021). Moreover, economic policies in Xinjiang favored Han Chinese migrants over the native Uyghur population, leading to economic disparities and limited opportunities for the Uyghurs (Tynen, 2020).

Unfortunately, the response of the international community to the situation of the Uyghurs has been mixed (Stern, 2021). While some countries and international organizations have condemned the treatment of the Uyghurs, geopolitical and economic considerations have led others to be more cautious in their approach (Stern, 2021). China's economic power and role in global supply chains have made some countries, not least Muslim countries, hesitant to take decisive action against it over the Uyghur issue (Mooney, 2021).

The discrimination faced by the Uyghur people raises serious concerns about human rights and respect for cultural and religious identities. It is a complex issue that intersects with global politics, economic interests, and the struggle for cultural survival. Addressing this issue requires a concerted effort from the international community, mindful of the geopolitical complexities involved. The global community must balance engaging with China and upholding the principles of human rights and dignity for all, including the Uyghur people.

Like the systemic segregation of apartheid, where black South Africans were denied fundamental rights and freedoms, the Uyghurs in China are subjected to a range of repressive measures, including surveillance, restrictions on religious practices, and forced assimilation policies. The existence of reeducation camps in Xinjiang, where Uyghurs are detained and subjected to indoctrination, parallels the enforced separations and limitations on freedom of movement and expression that characterized apartheid and racial segregation in the United States. Furthermore, the cultural and religious suppression of the Uyghurs, aimed at eroding their ethnic identity, mirrors the efforts in both apartheid South Africa and the United States to undermine the cultural heritage and dignity of black communities.

6.3.3 Dalit People

The Constitution of India ensures that all citizens are treated equally, regardless of their religion, race, caste, sex or birthplace (Sharma, 2022). Nevertheless, the discrimination faced by Dalit (oppressed, broken) people in India is a profound and complex issue that is rooted in the country's historical, social, and cultural contexts (Hanchinamani, 2001). Dalits, who comprise about one-sixth of India's population, epitomize what can be termed 'an Indian dilemma', reflecting the profound challenges within the social fabric of the world's largest democracy.

At the core of this issue lies the caste system, also known as *jati*, a centuries-old social structure deeply ingrained in Indian society (Sing, 2016). Within this system, historically labeled as 'Untouchables', Dalits are positioned at the lowest level. Excluded from the four main *varna*, or broad social classes, they face severe discrimination, social exclusion, and violence (Borooah et al., 2015; Karade, 2015; Thorat and Sabharwal, 2014). The roots of discrimination against Dalits can be traced back to ancient texts and practices that established a rigid social hierarchy (Marriott, 2004). This hierarchy was reinforced during historical periods such as Mughal rule and British colonialism and continues to persist in various forms in modern-day India (Bayly, 2001).

The social exclusion faced by Dalits is pervasive and multifaceted. It is manifested in their negative experiences in housing (Thorat et al., 2015), education (Sukumar, 2023), and access to public facilities like water and basic sanitation (Ghosh et al., 2023; Rao, 2021). Such exclusion not only perpetuates their marginalized status but also limits their opportunity for social mobility. Economic discrimination is another significant challenge, with Dalits often relegated to menial and low-paying jobs (Thorat and Neuman, 2010). This economic marginalization directly results from longstanding prejudices and institutional barriers that restrict their access to resources and opportunities (Mosse, 2018).

Violence and abuses against Dalits are alarmingly common (Narula, 1999). This includes physical assaults, verbal abuse, hate crimes, and massacres, often committed with impunity. The violence is not just physical but also psychological, perpetuating a cycle of trauma and fear that profoundly impacts the mental health of Dalit communities.

In response to these challenges, India's legal framework includes several provisions to protect Dalit rights, such as the Prevention of Atrocities Act. However, the effectiveness of these legal mechanisms is often hampered by inadequate enforcement and societal resistance (Badge, 2020). Alongside legal responses, there have been robust social movements and advocacy efforts led by Dalit leaders and NGOs, striving for equality and justice (Bob, 2007; Mosse, 2018). These movements have played a crucial role in bringing attention to the plight of Dalits and demanding change.

Despite these efforts, the journey toward eradicating Dalit discrimination is long and challenging (Teltumbde, 2020). It requires legal and policy reforms and a fundamental shift in societal attitudes and practices. As we reflect on the future, it becomes clear that addressing this issue is not just a matter of social justice for Dalits but also is essential for the overall health and progress of Indian society. The extreme discrimination faced by Dalits is a stark reminder of the deep-seated inequalities that exist in society. Overcoming this requires a concerted effort from all sectors of society, including government, civil society, and the public, to ensure that the ideals of equality and justice are not just enshrined in law but are also reflected in the everyday lives of all citizens.

The caste-based discrimination in India has historically relegated Dalits to the margins of society, enforcing rigid social and economic barriers. This segregation is an evident ingredient of various aspects of life, from restricted access to public services and education to limitations in housing and employment opportunities, mirroring the enforced separation of races in apartheid and the segregation of blacks in America. Furthermore, the violence and social ostracism faced by Dalits, akin to the brutal enforcement of apartheid and the violence endured by blacks, highlight the pernicious effects of institutionalized discrimination. Both apartheid and the discrimination against American blacks were underpinned by ideologies that sought to justify the suppression of a group based on an inherent characteristic—race in these former cases and caste in the current—creating a deeply entrenched system of inequality and injustice.

6.3.4 Palestinians

As this chapter is being written, a new war has erupted in the 'Holy Land'. This conflict has been and remains complex, sensitive, and dynamic, with ongoing military actions, global diplomatic negotiations, and humanitarian concerns at the forefront. The extreme discrimination faced by the Palestinian people is a multifaceted and deeply rooted issue steeped in a history of conflict, geopolitical interests, and cultural divides. To understand the discrimination against Palestinians, one must delve into the historical context of the Israeli–Palestinian conflict. The roots of this conflict trace back to the early 20th century, with the decline of the Ottoman Empire and the subsequent British mandate in Palestine. The Balfour Declaration of 1917, which expressed Britain's support for a 'national home for the Jewish people' in Palestine, sowed the seeds of future conflicts between Jewish and Arab populations in the region (Gelvin, 2014).

The establishment of Israel in 1948 marked a pivotal moment, leading to the first Arab-Israeli war and the displacement of hundreds of thousands of Palestinians, an event known as *al-Nakbah* or 'the catastrophe' (Allan, 2021). The 1967 Six-Day War (Louis and Shlaim, 2012) and subsequent occupation of the West Bank and Gaza Strip (Efrat, 2006) further exacerbated tensions, laying the groundwork for ongoing discrimination and conflict.

The discrimination against Palestinians manifests itself in various forms, including restricted access to resources, limited freedom of movement, unequal legal rights, and disparate treatment in areas such as housing, employment, and education (Amnesty International, 2022; Human Rights Watch, 2021; Tartir, 2021). The situation is particularly acute in the occupied territories, where Palestinians often face stringent military checks, land expropriation, and settlement expansions that encroach on Palestinian lands (Amnesty International, 2022; Human Rights Watch, 2021; Spangler, 2019). International human rights organizations have widely criticized these practices for perpetuating a cycle of inequality and exacerbating tensions between the two groups. For example, both Amnesty International and Human Rights Watch have accused Israeli authorities of committing crimes of apartheid and persecution (Amnesty International, 2022; Human Rights Watch, 2021).

Palestinians live under a complex web of control that includes physical barriers, such as the separation wall and military checkpoints. Moreover, the economic disparities and restricted access to resources, education, and employment opportunities faced by Palestinians are akin to the economic marginalization of black communities in both South Africa and the United States, stemming from a long history of systemic oppression. These parallels draw attention to the broader themes of racial and ethnic discrimination, where power dynamics and historical contexts create systems of oppression and inequality, profoundly affecting the lives of those subjected to them. The international community's role remains crucial in addressing these injustices, and there is a pressing need for a sustained and collaborative effort to find a just and lasting solution to the Israeli–Palestinian conflict, one that respects the rights and dignity of all people involved.

6.3.5 Afghan Women

Discrimination against women in Afghanistan is a profound and deeply entrenched issue, shaped by a complex web of cultural, religious, and political factors. Historically, Afghan society has been patriarchal, with deeply rooted tribal and ethnic traditions playing a significant role in shaping gender norms (Moghadam, 2002). These traditions often prioritize male authority and control, relegating women to subordinate roles. The advent of the Taliban regime in the 1990s exacerbated this situation dramatically (Skaine, 2002). Under the Taliban, strict interpretations of Islamic law were enforced, severely limiting women's rights and freedoms. The Taliban government collapsed following the aftermath of the 9/11 terrorist attacks in 2001, which gave Afghan women some hope, but the Taliban regained power 20 years later, reinstituting 'gender apartheid' (Akbari and True, 2022).

In today's Afghanistan, women face discrimination in almost every aspect of their lives (Amnesty International, 2023; Shoib et al., 2022). One of the most glaring examples is in education. Afghan girls are denied access to education (Akbari and True, 2022; Najibi and McLachlan, 2023). This denial violates their fundamental right to learn and severely reduces their ability to participate fully in society. In the workforce, Afghan women are significantly underrepresented (Akbari and True, 2022; Amnesty International, 2023). Those who do work often face discrimination and harassment. The societal expectation that women should prioritize domestic responsibilities over professional ambitions further restricts their career opportunities.

The legal system in Afghanistan also reflects and reinforces gender discrimination. Women who seek justice for crimes like domestic violence and sexual assault often face overwhelming challenges (Mukerji et al., 2023). The legal system, influenced by traditional and conservative interpretations of Islamic law, frequently fails to protect women's rights. In many cases, women are blamed for the crimes committed against them, and the concept of 'honor' is often used to justify violence against women.

The political arena in Afghanistan offers little respite from discrimination against women. They are actively excluded from government and political life, and those who attempt to participate often confront significant risks, including threats to their safety (Albrecht et al., 2022). This exclusion from decision-making processes leads to the neglect or disregard of women's needs and perspectives, further perpetuating gender inequality.

Moreover, Afghanistan's health care system is inadequately equipped to meet women's specific health needs (Glass et al., 2023). Cultural norms significantly restrict women's mobility, and combined with the scarcity of female health care professionals, these factors create substantial barriers to health care access (Neyazi et al., 2022).

Furthermore, in Afghanistan, societal norms often impose strict codes of behavior on women, dictating their dress, movement, and social interactions (Amnesty International, 2023). These norms not only violate women's freedoms but also perpetuate a culture of control and oppression. Women facing the consequences of violating these norms are at risk of social ostracism, violence, or even death.

Addressing gender discrimination in Afghanistan necessitates a holistic approach, encompassing education, legal reforms, increased political participation, and a transformation in societal attitudes. The international community plays a crucial role in supporting and advocating for Afghan women's rights. Rigorous efforts at all levels are essential to effectively challenge and ultimately overcome the deep-rooted discrimination against women in the country. Unfortunately, the progress achieved after the initial fall of the Taliban was abruptly reversed with their return to power 20 years later. This reversal underscores the fragility of these gains and the ongoing struggle for women's rights in Afghanistan.

The discrimination against women in Afghanistan is rooted in systemic and institutionalized inequality, similar to apartheid, which legally and socially mandated racial segregation and established the superiority of one racial group over others. The situation in Afghanistan imposes severe, systemic restrictions on women. This segregation comes from not only men but also society at large and even other women, many of whom are primarily confined to their homes. The severity of this situation is underscored by the broad denial of fundamental rights to Afghan women, including equal access to education, health care, political participation, and the right to live free from violence and cruelty.

6.4 Conclusions

The present essay has explored the multifaceted nature of institutionalized and systemic discrimination through a detailed examination of historical and contemporary examples, applying economic theories to discern the underlying mechanisms of systemic injustice. The discussion has illuminated the dangerous and pervasive nature of discrimination, not only as an artifact of the past but also as an ongoing challenge that demands our immediate attention and action.

Economic analysis, as applied to the cases of apartheid in South Africa and racial discrimination in the United States, has proven to be a potent tool for understanding the complexities of discrimination. The neoclassical and holistic approaches provided insights into the economic underpinnings of discriminatory practices and their far-reaching effects on society. These theories highlight how discrimination is a moral or social issue and a significant economic concern, impacting productivity, income distribution, and overall economic growth.

The historical examples of apartheid in South Africa and racial discrimination in the United States, while unique in their contexts, share characteristics common with the ongoing struggles of marginalized groups such as the Rohingya, Uyghurs, Dalits, Palestinians, and Afghan women. This continuity suggests that discrimination, in its various forms, is a persistent global issue. It also indicates that the mechanisms of power, economic exploitation, and social exclusion are universally applicable, transcending geographical and cultural boundaries.

The analysis of these diverse cases underscores the importance of well-crafted policies and international interventions in combating discrimination. While legal frameworks and governmental policies play a crucial role in addressing systemic inequalities, societal attitudes and the complex interplay of historical, cultural, and political factors often limit their effectiveness. The international community's response, or lack thereof, to the plight of these marginalized groups highlights the need for a unified and proactive approach that goes beyond mere condemnation to actionable steps.

The historical insights provided by the analysis of apartheid and racial discrimination in the United States offer valuable lessons for addressing modern forms of discrimination. Understanding the economic, social, and political dynamics that sustain these systems can inform contemporary strategies to dismantle similar structures of oppression. The parallel between historical and current forms of discrimination emphasizes the necessity of learning from history to avoid repeating past mistakes. This analysis concludes that an integrated approach considers economic, social, cultural, and political factors and is crucial in addressing discrimination. The multidimensional nature of discrimination demands an equally nuanced and holistic response. This approach should target the symptoms and the root causes of discrimination, including power imbalances, economic disparities, and cultural prejudices.

In conclusion, the present essay reaffirms that the fight against discrimination is far from being over. It is a battle that requires collective effort, continuous thoughtfulness, and a firm commitment to justice and equality. As the world evolves, so must our strategies and perspectives addressing these deep-seated issues. Only through a collaborative effort that encompasses economic analysis, policy reform, social activism, and international cooperation can we hope to make significant advances toward a more just and equitable world for all.

Notes

1 During the apartheid period, the South African population was officially classified in four official groups: whites, Bantu (Africans), Coloreds (mixed race), and Asians. The latter two groups also suffered discrimination. In the models dealt with presently, they are lumped with the Africans.
2 The construction of the apartheid system is dealt with, for example, in Troup (1975), Chapter 6; Bunting (1986), Thompson (1990), Chapter 6; Sparks (1990), Davenport and Saunders (2000), Chapters 13–15.
3 The model presented here is not the only one that has been used to analyze racial discrimination in South Africa. For an overview of other approaches, see Lundahl (2014).
4 Lundahl and Moritz (1996), Chapter 2, provide a detailed reference list.
5 See, for example, Farley et al. (2000) for a study of residential segregation in Detroit.
6 See Marshall and Christian (1978) for a number of studies of black employment in the South.
7 See Lundahl (2021, Chapter 4) for an analysis of Myrdal's book and its influence on the debate and the development of policy formulation to improve the situation for blacks in the United States. See also Myrdal (1987) and Clayton (1996) for evaluations of the effects of Myrdal's study.

References

Abdulla, M., and Shamseden, Z. (2021). The Rise of Xenophobia and the Uyghur-China Situation. *Social Research: An International Quarterly*, 88(4), 949–972.
Akbari, F., and True, J. (2022). One Year on From the Taliban Takeover of Afghanistan: Re-instituting Gender Apartheid. *Australian Journal of International Affairs*, 76(6), 624–633.
Albrecht, C., Rude, B., and Stitteneder, T. (2022). Women in Afghanistan: Developments Over the Last 20 Years and the Return of the Taliban. *CESifo Forum*, 23(1), 57–62.
Allan, D. (ed) (2021). *Voices of the Nakba: A Living History of Palestine*. London: Pluto Press.
Amnesty International (2021). *Like We Are Enemies in a War—China's Mass Internment, Torture and Persecution of Muslims in Xinjiang*. London: Amnesty International.
Amnesty International (2022). *Israel's Apartheid Against Palestinians: Cruel System of Domination and Crime Against Humanity*. London: Amnesty International.
Amnesty International (2023). *The Taliban's War on Women: The Crime Against Humanity of Gender Persecution in Afghanistan*. London: Amnesty International.
Arrow, K.J. (1973). The Theory of Discrimination. In O. Ashenfelter and A. Rees (eds), *Discrimination in Labor Markets* (pp. 3–33). Princeton, NJ: Princeton University Press.
Badge, U.S. (2020). Human Rights Perspectives of Indian Dalits. *Journal of Law and Conflict Resolution*, 11(2), 26–32.
Barber, W.J. (2008). *Gunnar Myrdal: An Intellectual Biography*. Houndmills, Basingstoke and New York: Palgrave Macmillan.
Bayly, S. (2001). *Caste, Society and Politics in India From the Eighteenth Century to the Modern Age*. Cambridge: Cambridge University Press.
Becker, G. (1957). *The Economics of Discrimination*. Chicago: Chicago University Press.
Bellér-Hann, I. (2020). Uyghur Religion. In S. Feuchtwang (ed), *Handbook on Religion in China* (pp. 338–360). Cheltenham: Edward Elgar.
Bergmann, B.R. (1996). *In Defense of Affirmative Action*. New York: Basic Books.
Beyrer, C., and Kamarulzaman, A. (2017). Ethnic Cleansing in Myanmar: The Rohingya Crisis and Human Rights. *The Lancet*, 390(10102), 1570–1573.
Bob, C. (2007). 'Dalit Rights Are Human Rights': Caste Discrimination, International Activism, and the Construction of a New Human Rights Issue. *Human Rights Quarterly*, 29(1), 167–193.

Borooah, V.K., Sabharwal, N.S., Diwakar, D.G., Mishra, V.K., and Naik, A.K. (2015). *Caste, Discrimination, and Exclusion in Modern India*. New Delhi: SAGE Publications India.

Bunting, B. (1986). *The Rise of the South African Reich*. London: International Defence and Aid Fund for Southern Africa.

Clayton, O. (ed) (1996). *An American Dilemma Revisited: Race Relations in a Changing World*. Washington, DC: Russell Sage Foundation.

Davenport, R., and Saunders, C. (2000). *South Africa: A Modern History*, 4th ed. Houndmills, Basingstoke: Macmillan Press and New York: St. Martin's Press.

Efrat, E. (2006). *The West Bank and Gaza Strip: A Geography of Occupation and Disengagement*. Abingdon: Routledge.

Farley, R., Danziger, S., and Holzer, H.J. (2000). *Detroit Divided*. New York: Russel Sage Foundation.

Findlay, R., and Lundahl, M. (1987). Racial Discrimination, Dualistic Labor Markets and Foreign Investment. *Journal of Development Economics*, 27(1–2), 139–148.

Fredrickson, G.M. (2002). *Racism. A Short History*. Princeton, NJ: Princeton University Press.

Freeman, R.B. (1981). Black Economic Progress after 1964: Who Has Gained and Why? In S. Rosen (ed), *Studies in Labor Markets* (pp. 247–294). Chicago and London: University of Chicago Press.

Gelvin, J.L. (2014). *The Israel-Palestine Conflict: One Hundred Years of War*. Cambridge: Cambridge University Press.

Ghosh, P., Hossain, M., and Sarkar, S. (2023). Inequality Among Social Groups in Accessing Improved Drinking Water and Sanitation in India: A District-Level Spatial Analysis. *Professional Geographer*, 75(3), 361–382.

Glass, N., Jalalzai, R., Spiegel, P., and Rubenstein, L. (2023). The Crisis of Maternal and Child Health in Afghanistan. *Conflict and Health*, 17(1), 28.

Hanchinamani, B.B. (2001). Human Rights Abuses of Dalits in India. *Human Rights Brief*, 8(2), 6.

Houghton, D.H. (1976). *The South African Economy*, 4th ed. Cape Town: Oxford University Press.

Human Rights Watch (2021). *A Threshold Crossed: Israeli Authorities and the Crimes of Apartheid and Persecution*. New York: Human Rights Watch.

Ibrahim, A., and Turkel, N. (2021). The Uyghur People: History, Geography, Religion, Language. In S.E. Brown and S.D. Smith (eds), *The Routledge Handbook of Religion, Mass Atrocity, and Genocide* (pp. 217–224). London and New York: Routledge.

Jackson, W.A. (1990), *Gunnar Myrdal and America's Conscience: Social Engineering and Racial Liberalism, 1938–1987*. Chapel Hill, NC and London: University of North Carolina Press.

Karade, J. (ed) (2015). *Caste Discrimination*. New Delhi: Rawat Publications.

Leibold, J. (2020). Surveillance in China's Xinjiang Region: Ethnic Sorting, Coercion, and Inducement. *Journal of Contemporary China*, 29(121), 46–60.

Leonard, J.S. (1991). The Federal Anti-bias Effort. In E.P. Hoffman (ed), *Essays on the Economics of Discrimination* (pp. 85–114). Kalamazoo, MI: W. E. Upjohn Institute for Employment Research.

Lewa, C. (2009). North Arakan: An Open Prison for the Rohingya in Burma. *Forced Migration Review*, 32, 11–13.

Lipton, M. (1985). *Capitalism and Apartheid*. Aldershot, Hants: Gower/Maurice Temple Smith.

Louis, W.R., and Shlaim, A. (eds) (2012). *The 1967 Arab-Israeli War: Origins and Consequences*. Cambridge: Cambridge University Press.

Loury, G.C. (2008). *Race, Incarceration, and American Values*. Cambridge, MA and London: MIT Press.

Lundahl, M. (1982). The Rationale of Apartheid. *American Economic Review*, 72(5), 1169–1179.

Lundahl, M. (2014). Some Stepping Stones in the Economic Modelling of Apartheid. *Economic History of Developing Regions*, 29(2), 126–145.
Lundahl, M. (2021). *The Dynamics of Poverty: Circular, Cumulative Causation, Value Judgements, Institutions and Social Engineering in the World of Gunnar Myrdal*. Cham: Palgrave Macmillan.
Lundahl, M., and Moritz, L. (1996). *Det nya Sydafrika: Ekonomi och politik efter apartheid*. Stockholm: SNS Förlag.
Lundahl, M., and Wadensjö, E. (1984). *Unequal Treatment: A Study in the Neo-Classical Theory of Discrimination*. London and Sydney: Croom Helm.
Mahmood, S.S., Wroe, E., Fuller, A., and Leaning, J. (2017). The Rohingya People of Myanmar: Health, Human Rights, and Identity. *The Lancet*, 389(10081), 1841–1850.
Manning, A. (2003), *Monopsony in Motion. Imperfect Competition in Labor Markets*, Princeton, NJ and Oxford: Princeton University Press.
Marriott, M. (2004). Varna and Jati. In S. Mittal and G. Thursby (eds), *The Hindu World* (pp. 357–381). New York: Routledge.
Marshall, R., and Christian, V.L., Jr (1978). *Employment of Blacks in the South. A Perspective on the 1960s*. Austin, TX: University of Texas Press.
McGee, H. (2021). *The Sum of Us. What Racism Costs Everyone and How We Can Prosper Together*. New York: Random House.
Moghadam, V.M. (2002). Patriarchy, the Taliban, and Politics of Public Space in Afghanistan. *Women's Studies International Forum*, 25(1), 19–31.
Mooney, M. (2021). Our Collective Failure: Why the International Community Has Not Intervened to Protect China's Uighur Muslims. *International Research and Review*, 11(1), 45–64.
Mosse, D. (2018). Caste and Development: Contemporary Perspectives on a Structure of Discrimination and Advantage. *World Development*, 110, 422–436.
Mukerji, R., Saboor, L., Paphitis, S., Devakumar, D., and Mannell, J. (2023). How Does Domestic Violence Stigma Manifest in Women's Lives in Afghanistan? A Study of Survivors' Lived Experiences of Help-seeking across Three Provinces. *Global Public Health*, 18(1), 2212035.
Myrdal, G. (1944). *An American Dilemma. The Negro Problem and Modern Democracy*. New York: Harper & Row.
Myrdal, G. (1987). *Historien om an American Dilemma*. Stockholm: SNS Förlag.
Najibi, P., and McLachlan, C. (2023). Moving Towards a Sustainable Future for Women in Afghanistan Through Increased Tertiary Education Participation: Challenges and Possibilities. In S. Weuffen, J. Burke, M. Plunkett, A. Goriss-Hunter and S. Emmett (eds), *Inclusion, Equity, Diversity, and Social Justice in Education: A Critical Exploration of the Sustainable Development Goals* (pp. 245–259). Singapore: Springer.
Narula, S. (1999). *Broken People: Caste Violence Against India's 'Untouchables'*. New York: Human Rights Watch.
Neyazi, N., Safi, N., Afzali, A., and Kabir, M. (2022). Gender Barriers are Worsening Women's Access to Health Care in Afghanistan. *The Lancet*, 400(10354), 731–732.
Parmar, P., Mon, S.H.H., and Beyrer, C. (2022). The Rohingya Genocide and Lessons Learned From Myanmar's Spring Revolution. *The Lancet*, 400(10355), 793–795.
Phelps, E.S. (1972). The Statistical Theory of Racism and Sexism. *American Economic Review*, 62(4), 659–661.
Rao, Y.S. (2021). Dalits, Water and Discrimination. *Journal of Language and Linguistic Studies*, 17(1), 738–743.
Raza, Z. (2019). China's 'Political Re-education' Camps of Xinjiang's Uyghur Muslims. *Asian Affairs*, 50(4), 488–501.
Reich, M. (1981). *Racial Inequality. A Political-Economic Analysis*. Princeton, NJ: Princeton University Press.
Roberts, S.R. (2020). *The War on the Uyghurs: China's Campaign Against Xinjiang's Muslims*. Manchester: Manchester University Press.

Robinson, J. (1933). *The Economics of Imperfect Competition*. London: Macmillan.
Roche, G., and Leibold, J. (2022). State Racism and Surveillance in Xinjiang (People's Republic of China). *Political Quarterly*, 93(3), 442–450.
Roemer, J.E., Lee, W., and van der Straeten, K. (2007). *Racism, Xenophobia and Distribution*. Cambridge, MA: Harvard University Press.
Rose, P.I. (1964). *They & We: Racial and Ethnic Relations in the United States*. New York: Random House.
Rutherford, M. (2023). *Racism, Segregation, Acceptance: American Economics and Black Issues, 1890–1945*. http://doi.org/10.2139/ssrn.4528215. Downloaded 24 November 2023.
Sahana, M., Jahangir, S., and Anisujjaman, M.D. (2019). Forced Migration and the Expatriation of the Rohingya: A Demographic Assessment of Their Historical Exclusions and Statelessness. *Journal of Muslim Minority Affairs*, 39(1), 44–60.
Sarmin, A. (2020). Ongoing Persecution of the Rohingya: A History of Periodic Ethnic Cleansings and Genocides. *Intellectual Discourse*, 28(2), 675–696.
Seytoff, A., and Szadziewski, H. (2018). China's Most Oppressed: Uyghur Exclusion and Discrimination. In F. de Varennes and C.M. Gardiner (eds), *Routledge Handbook of Human Rights in Asia* (pp. 75–88). London: Routledge.
Sharma, B.K. (2022). *Introduction to the Constitution of India*. Delhi: PHI Learning.
Shohel, M.M.C. (2023). Lives of the Rohingya Children in Limbo: Childhood, Education, and Children's Rights in Refugee Camps in Bangladesh. *Prospects*, 53(1), 131–149.
Shoib, S., Saeed, F., Dazhamyar, A.R., Armiya'u, A.Y.U., Badawy, M.M., Shah, J., and Chandradasa, M. (2022). Women in Afghanistan: A Call for Action. *The Lancet Psychiatry*, 9(5), 342–343.
Singh, E. (2016). *Caste System in India: A Historical Perspective*. Delhi: Kalpaz Publications.
Skaine, R. (2002). *The Women of Afghanistan Under the Taliban*. Jefferson, NC: McFarland & Company.
Southern, D.W. (1987). *Gunnar Myrdal and Black-White Relations: The Use and Abuse of an American Dilemma, 1944–69*. Baton Rouge, LA and London: Louisiana State University Press.
Sowell, T. (1975). *Race and Economics*. New York: David McKay Company.
Spangler, E. (2019). *Understanding Israel/Palestine: Race, Nation, and Human Rights in the Conflict*. Leiden: Brill.
Sparks, A. (1990). *The Mind of South Africa: The Story of the Rise and Fall of Apartheid*. London: Heinemann.
Spence, A.M. (1974). *Market Signaling. Informational Transfer in Hiring and Related Screening Processes*. Cambridge, MA: Harvard University Press.
Stern, J. (2021). Genocide in China: Uighur Re-education Camps and International Response. *Immigration and Human Rights Law Review*, 3(1), 2.
Sukumar, N. (2023). *Caste Discrimination and Exclusion in Indian Universities: A Critical Reflection*. Abingdon: Routledge.
Tartir, A., Dana, T., and Seidel, T. (eds) (2021). *Political Economy of Palestine: Critical, Interdisciplinary, and Decolonial Perspectives*. Cham: Springer Nature.
Teltumbde, A. (2020). *Dalits: Past, Present and Future*, 2nd ed. London and New York: Routledge.
Thompson, L. (1990). *A History of South Africa*. New Haven, CT and London: Yale University Press.
Thorat, S., Banerjee, A., Mishra, V.K., and Rizvi, F. (2015). Urban Rental Housing Market: Caste and Religion Matters in Access. *Economic and Political Weekly*, 50(26/27), 47–53.
Thorat, S., and Neuman, K.S. (eds) (2010). *Blocked by Caste: Economic Discrimination in Modern India*. New Delhi: Oxford University Press.
Thorat, S., and Sabharwal, N.S. (eds) (2014). *Bridging the Social Gap: Perspectives on Dalit Empowerment*. New Delhi: SAGE Publications India.

Troup, F. (1975). *South Africa: An Historical Introduction*. Harmondsworth: Penguin Books.
Ty, R. (2019). The Rohingya Refugee Crisis. *SUR—International Journal on Human Rights*, 29(16), 49–62.
Tynen, S. (2020). Dispossession and Displacement of Migrant Workers: The Impact of State Terror and Economic Development on Uyghurs in Urban Xinjiang. *Central Asian Survey*, 39(3), 303–323.
UN News (2023). *Rohingya Refugees Share Concerns With UN Rights Commissioner During Visit to Cox's Bazar.* United Nations. 24 November. https://news.un.org/en/story/2022/08/1124822
von Furstenberg, G., Harrison, B., and Horowitz, A.R. (eds) (1974a). *Patterns of Racial Discrimination. Volume I: Housing*. Lexington, MA: Lexington Books.
von Furstenberg, G., Harrison, B., and Horowitz, A.R. (eds) (1974b). *Patterns of Racial Discrimination. Volume II: Employment and Income*. Lexington, MA: Lexington Books.
Waller, J., and Albornoz, M.S. (2021). Crime and No Punishment? China's Abuses Against the Uyghurs. *Georgetown Journal of International Affairs*, 22(1), 100–111.
Wilson, F. (1975). Farming, 1866–1966. In M. Wilson and L. Thompson (eds), *The Oxford History of South Africa. II. South Africa 1870–1966* (pp. 104–171). Oxford: Clarendon Press.
Woodson, K. (2023). *The Black Ceiling*. Chicago and London: Chicago University Press.

7 The Predatory State

A Case of Extreme Inequality

Mats Lundahl

7.1 Putin's Palace

How come that Vladimir Putin is the owner of a kitschy palace that cost 1.4 billion US dollars to construct, with 850-dollar toilet brushes and 1,250-dollar toilet paper holders, located on an area 39 times the size of the principality of Monaco, overlooking the Black Sea, built so that no outsiders can have access to it? Why may the ex-small-time KGB bureaucrat who has ruled Russia since 2000 be the richest man on the planet? His presidential salary amounts to 140,000 US dollars per annum, which points to a savings rate which must be the highest in the world? He is supposedly good for some 200 billion US dollars (Morrow, 2022; cf. Dawisha, 2014 and Åslund, 2019, Chapter 6).

Could it possibly be the case that the money comes from other sources—sources that are not to be revealed? Well, they actually were in Alexei Navalny's documentary *Putin's Palace* (2021), released on 19 January 2021, which instantly became viral. According to Reuters (2021), on 29 January, it had already been watched more than 100 million times.

The answer, my friend, is blowing in the wind. Vladimir Vladimirovich is a simple kleptocrat, the ruler of the predatory state of contemporary Russia—a state which preys on its citizens, and citizens of other countries or, to put it slightly differently, a state which assumes that the citizens exist for the good of the state instead of vice versa. More formally, it is 'the agency of a group or class; its function [is] to extract an income from the rest of the constituents in the interest of that group or class' (North, 1981, p. 22). The predatory states maximizes the income accruing to deserving citizens, that is, to the ruling clique and then distributes it according to some formula such as 'to each one in proportion to his importance for the group'.

Unfortunately, the predatory state, like plagues and diseases, is one of the eternal companions of mankind—ubiquitous both in time and in space. Political scientist Margaret Levi has even suggested that, in principle, all rulers are predatory but that the extent of actual predation depends on the circumstances—the bargaining position of the ruler, his transaction costs and his time preferences (Levi, 1988, Chapter 2).[1] Many rulers during many historical epochs and across a wide geographical territory have created huge fortunes simply by controlling the state apparatus. We will not attempt to be exhaustive here. A few examples suffice to convey the message. They range from ancient Rome, via Chinggis Khan and his Mongols, Tudor and Stuart Britain (notably Henry VIII), Mughal India, the European colonies in Latin America, Asia and Africa (not least the Congo Free State—the personal possession of Leopold II of Belgium)—to Napoleon Bonaparte.

Closer to our own time, we find the *nomenklaturas* of the Eastern European Communist dictatorship, led by such champions as Nicolae Ceaușescu and Slobodan Milošević and their heirs: Vladimir Putin and Alexander Lukashenko. In the Third World, we find such unhampered predators as Juan Perón in Argentina, Marcos Pérez Jiménez in Venezuela, Rafael Trujillo in the Dominican Republic, the two Duvaliers in Haiti, the two Somozas in Nicaragua, Alfredo Stroessner in Paraguay, Fidel Castro in Cuba, Hailie Selassie in Ethiopia, Mobutu Sese Seko in Zaire, Jean-Bédel Bokassa in the Central African Empire, Francisco Macías Nguema in Equatorial Guinea, Idi Amin in Uganda, Félix Houphouët Boigny in Ivory Coast, Robert Mugabe in Zimbabwe, Sani Abacha in Nigeria, Jacob Zuma in South Africa, the last Shah of Iran, Muammar Gaddafi in Libya, Saddam Hussein in Iraq, the House of Saud in Saudi Arabia, Ferdinand Marcos in the Philippines, Suharto in Indonesia, the Kim dynasty in North Korea, Islam Karimov in Uzbekistan and Kurmanbek Bakiyev in Kyrgyzstan. And then we have our contemporaries: Daniel Ortega in Nicaragua, Nicolás Maduro in Venezuela, Teodoro Obiang in Equatorial Guinea, Mohammed VI in Morocco, Bashar al-Assad in Syria, Nursultan Nazarbayev in Kazakhstan and Emomali Rahmon in Tajikistan. The list of corrupt kleptocrats can easily be extended. There is no doubt whatsoever that the predatory state is a very real phenomenon.[2]

7.2 Winner Take Nothing?

When you come out on top of the political game, do you immediately begin to serve the population of your country? Don't be ridiculous. That kind of politicians exist, but how many are they and how far is it between them? Charity begins at home, and all too often it also ends there. We have already made reference to Putin's fabulous alleged net worth, but those playing in the somewhat lower divisions don't fare too bad either.

Thus, Emperor Hailie Selassie of Ethiopia had bank accounts amounting to hundreds of millions of dollars, perhaps more (Kapuśiński, 1983, p. 161). When Juan Perón left Argentina in 1955, he brought along some 700 million dollars, and Marcos Pérez Jiménez had bank assets of around 400 million when he left Venezuela three years later (Andreski, 1966, p. 66). When Rafael Trujillo in the Dominican Republic was murdered in 1961, he in different ways controlled between 65 and 85 percent of the Dominican economy. His private fortune was estimated to be around 800 million dollars (Wiarda, 1968, p. 86). As a comparison, the GDP of the Dominican Republic was estimated at 634 million dollars in 1961 (International Monetary Fund, 1983, pp. 196–197). When he died in 1971, Papa Doc Duvalier in neighboring Haiti had amassed 100–150 million dollars, and when his son Jean Claude, 'Baby Doc', was forced into exile in 1986, he was worth around 1,600 million (Lundahl and Vedovato, 1989, p. 52). When Anastasio Somoza Debayle was forced by the Sandinistas to leave Nicaragua in 1979, the Somoza family fortune amounted to 500–600 million dollars (Rouquié, 1992, p. 262). *Forbes Magazine* in 2006 listed Fidel Castro among the richest leaders in the world, with a wealth of 900 million dollars (Kroll, 2006; Flamer, 2016). In the mid-1980s, the American Ministry of Finance and the IMF estimated the fortune of Mobutu Sese Seko to be four billion dollars (Burns and Huband, 1997). According to the Supreme Court of the Philippines, Ferdinand Marcos had amassed ten billion dollars during his 21 years in office before leaving the country in 1986 (Davies, 2016). Before the 1990–1991 Gulf War, Saddam Hussein was also stated to have had assets amounting to ten billion dollars (*The Economist*, 1991). Again, the list can easily be extended, but that is not necessary. In 2013, Kim Jong-un had five billion dollars' worth of assets scattered in a variety of countries (Celebrity Net Worth, 2023). At the top of the list, we find a number of Arab royal families, headed by the House of Saud. The alleged wealth of the latter is a breathtaking 1.4 trillion dollars! (Awal, 2022).

The pattern keeps repeating itself. In predatory states, the national income is heavily concentrated in the hands of the ruler or the ruling clique.

7.3 The Rationale of Redistribution

Predation implies a redistribution of incomes and wealth from the prey to the predators. This redistribution has its own perverse logic (Olson, 1982, pp. 41–44). One may innocently pose the question whether it would not be in the interest of a predatory regime that the economy grows, but that is far from always the case. Assume that the predator manages to redistribute 100 million dollars to himself, using some of the tricks in his repertoire. This is likely to result in distortions in the economy and loss of efficiency and a concomitant loss of GDP. The question that then arises is how far the predator is prepared to go. How large is the maximum reduction of GDP that he can accept? The answer depends on how much of that GDP accrues to himself. Assume that we are dealing with a predator who is at the beginning of his career and who commands a mere 1 percent of GDP. Assume furthermore that the shrinkage of GDP that results from the redistribution affects him in the same proportion. Then, as long as GDP does not shrink with more than $100 \times 100 = 10$ billion dollars, he makes a gain. A predator who has been in the business for a long time, on the other hand, and who has a substantial share of GDP will be prepared to go less far. Thus, assuming that this share as well as his share of the loss is 50 percent, the maximum GDP loss that he will tolerate is 200 million, since he will have to bear half of that. At the extreme, when the predator owns the entire economy, he will not be prepared to tolerate any loss at all but will attempt to make the economy grow.

Growth is, however, no option for the beginner. Accumulation of 100 million through growth requires that the economy grows by $100 \times 100 = 10$ billion dollars, an option that is much more difficult than redistribution since it requires efficient institutions, something that is not likely to exist in a predatory state. Take the case of Putin's Russia. From 2009 to 2017, the average growth of GDP there was a mere 1 percent (Åslund, 2019, p. 2).

The fact that predators with a low stake in the economy are prepared to inflict more damage than predators with a high stake has a corollary. The situation of the citizens/prey is likely to be better with an established, stable kleptocratic regime than an unstable situation where different cliques are competing with each other for power. In the latter, where nobody has an upper hand, each clique—knowing that it is likely to be ousted quickly—will go for one-shot raids of the treasury, grabbing as much as possible, without regard for the consequences, while an established kleptocrat who does not have to pay much attention to his security situation will do less damage to GDP. A stationary bandit is better from the point of view of those plundered than a series of roving bandits who have no stake in preserving the economy (Olson, 1993).

7.4 Some Steps to Successful Plunder

Predators may come into power in many ways. Sometimes they are elected. At other times, they become rulers after staging a revolution or a coup. Be that as it may. We will not deal with that question presently. Instead, let us simply assume that we have a country ruled by a kleptocrat. How will he behave in order to squeeze as much as possible out of the population—maximize the share of national income that accrues to him and his cronies ('oligarchs')?

It goes without saying that in order to prey successfully on the population, the ruler must remain in power. Predatory states are ruled by cliques, but the ruling clique always risks being thrown out of power by competing would-be ruling coalitions. Thus, we may think of the ruler as having a utility function with two arguments: income and security (the probability of remaining in power).[3] Neither income nor security can be obtained without help. No predator can rule alone. He is dependent on a polity, an army, a police force, etc., to ensure both that he is not deposed and that he can steal from the population at large. The question then is: how many should be cut in on the deal? Which is the optimal size of the ruling clique or 'club'? Beginning with income, the larger and the more powerful the clique, the more can be obtained, but at a decreasing rate. Income redistribution is the subject of decreasing returns, while its marginal cost is increasing. Income as a function of the clique size thus describes an inverted U curve with a maximum where the marginal revenue equates the marginal cost. The same is true for the probability of remaining in power. Increasing the size of your army makes you stronger and makes it harder for revolutions staged by outside groups to succeed, but again decreasing returns prevail. Also, as the size of the ruling clique increases, the clique becomes more difficult for the leader to control. The likelihood that a palace coup, staged by 'insiders', will take place increases at an increasing rate. The probability of remaining in power as a function of clique size thus also describes an inverted U. Only by pure chance will the clique size producing maximum income coincide with that producing maximum security. In the general case there will be a trade-off, where increased security can only be obtained at the expense of reduced income and vice versa. The clique size chosen by the ruler will be decided by which of the curves that peaks first and by the ruler preferences at the margin.

The results are obvious. The criteria of selection vary and with that the size of the clique that pockets the proceeds of plunder. Romania under Ceaușescu was a case of 'socialism in one family'. (For details, see Pacepa, 1988 and Behr, 1991.) Rafael Trujillo, François Duvalier and Anastasio Somoza also chose to keep the spoils of office within their families. (See, e.g., Wiarda, 1968; Lundahl, 1979, Chapter 7; Rouquié, 1992.) Ferdinand Marcos' economic system, 'crony capitalism', extended to a wider range of people (Boyce, 1993). Putin's circle is also wider. It consists of three elements: his old friends from the St. Petersburg KGB who control the security agencies, the loyalists who run the state enterprises and transfer money from them to private beneficiaries, and private businessmen who have become billionaires through shady deals with the government (Åslund, 2019, pp. 6, 47).

There are devices which the ruler may use to shift the income-security trade-off outwards so as to make possible a higher income and/or security at any given clique size. The simplest one is obfuscation: hiding what you are doing (Danielson and Lundahl, 1994). The methods used by predators to obtain incomes may be arranged according to their degree of transparency or obfuscation. For example, much of the wealth of Vladimir Putin is not held by him personally but by his cronies (Åslund, 2019, Chapter 6). The more obscure the method, the easier it becomes to raise a given sum of money but at a decreasing rate. Likewise, more obscure methods can be devised only at an increasing marginal cost. By the same token, more obscure methods reduce the likelihood that it will be revealed to the citizens in general what the ruler is up to and hence the resistance to him. On the other hand, the ruler needs inside helpers to carry out his monkey business, and these may see that his incomes are increasing so that their willingness to depose him may increase. Again, we get two inverted U curves whose peaks are not likely to coincide, and the ruler must make a choice to arrive at his optimal degree of obfuscation in his effort to shift the income-security trade-off.

Other possible shift parameters are the creation of an 'ideology' which serves to rally the citizens around the flag and the use of repression to intimidate them. (For examples of both, see Lundahl, 2019, pp. 71–72.) Kleptocracies have secret police forces and paramilitary militias. There are no uprisings in concentration camps. The use of brute force is generally more expensive than the development of an 'ideology' because the latter entails economies of scale. Repression is always local, directed toward determined groups or individuals with views which run counter to those of the ruler, even when employed on a national scale.[4] Ideology, on the other hand, can be propagated on a massive scale through the institutions of the country: the educational system, the media, art, music, literature, and it serves to make people act contrary to their beliefs in the 'interest of the nation'. Once established, ideology is a flexible and powerful instrument for the ruler to use in order to ensure that the citizens are loyal and back him against possible contenders.

To sum up, the typical predatory state is ruled by a clique which attempts to maximize its income. In order to do so, the clique must remain in power. The ruling clique is an analogy to a club with limited membership. There is an optimal clique size which maximizes incomes and another one which maximizes the probability that this clique will remain in power. At the margin, the ruler is faced with a choice between the two. Both incomes and security can be increased with the use of obfuscation of the methods of plunder and by the use of repression and ideology.

7.5 The Methods of Plunder: Taxation and Borrowing

Assuming that the objective of the predatory state is to maximize the income accruing to the members of the ruling clique, which methods does the ruler have at his disposal? The most important asset that he has is his control of the state. History abounds with examples of how different cliques have combated each other in the struggle for political control. This is of course no coincidence, since it is the use of the state machinery for private purposes that produces the income which is distributed among the members of the ruling clique (Lundahl, 2019, pp. 107–108).

Most important of all is that control of the state also implies control—monopolization—of the tax machinery. In predatory states, taxes are not collected for productive purposes, for stabilization purposes or for redistribution to economically weak groups. The tax machinery will instead be devised in a way which minimizes the cost of raising a given revenue (the transaction cost). The tax administration in predatory states is usually weak and corrupt, that is, highly inefficient. This in turn tends to rule out sophisticated, skill-intensive, methods of taxation, such as income taxation, which furthermore has high administration costs. The latter requires on the one hand an honest collection and control apparatus and, on the other hand, widespread literacy and familiarity with paperwork among the citizens, since the large number of people subject to taxation means that the system must rest on self-declaration. Thus, income taxes tend to be low and flat and collection inefficient in predatory states. Value-added taxes are cheaper to administer, but trade taxes are even cheaper.[5] All you have to do is to put customs houses at border crossings, in ports and in airports. Not surprisingly, on low-income levels, trade taxes tend to be the most important source of government revenues (Tanzi, 1987, p. 217), and this is even more pronounced in predatory regimes, as witnessed, for example, by the Dominican Republic and Haiti during the late 19th century, where their shares frequently exceeded 90 percent (Lundahl, 2019, p. 108).

The avoidance of trade taxes can also contribute to kleptocrat incomes: more or less organized smuggling of goods subject to import charges. This was the case of Baby Doc Duvalier in Haiti, Jomo Kenyatta and Daniel arap Moi in Kenya, Manuel Noriega in Panama and the military junta in Burma in the 1980s and 1990s (Lundahl, 2019, pp. 108–109).

Another method of taxing the citizens without their consent is that of debasing the currency. Inflation is a tax on cash holdings. In order to obtain money, the citizens must part with real resources, and holding money instead of spending it directly entails a loss of purchasing power as the price level increases. This method has been used as long as money has existed. A flagrant, illustrative, case is that of Idi Amin in Uganda who kept increasing the government budget deficit through unhampered spending and kept printing money in a desperate, misdirected, effort to close it. Another case is that of Buenaventura Báez and Ulises Heureaux in the Dominican Republic during the second half of the 19th century, who both made systematic use of large monetary emissions with the result that the currency depreciated systematically (Lundahl, 2019, pp. 108–109).

Perhaps the most efficient way of reducing tax collection costs is tax farming. The government sells the right of taxation directly to the collectors. In this way, you avoid the costly creation of a tax bureaucracy. This is a time-honored way of doing things, used all the way from Antiquity (the Greeks and the Romans). It was resorted to in Europe during the late Middle Ages and the early Modern Age by the Ottoman Empire and by European colonial powers in Africa. The alternative to tax farming is the sale of public offices: creating a bureaucracy where the positions are thereafter sold directly to those who will hold them and who are allowed to use them at their own discretion. All public jobs in the Philippines had price tags in the 1970s. In post-independence India, a price had to be paid for transfer to more lucrative positions. In the Soviet republics of Georgia and Azerbaijan, even positions in the very power hierarchy were for sale in the 1970 (Lundahl, 2019, pp. 109–110).

Finally, the most direct form of 'taxation' is outright confiscation of desirable assets, either without compensation or with a compensation which amounts to a mere fraction of the real value. The method was extensively practiced, for example, by Rafael Trujillo in the Dominican Republic, Anastasio Somoza in Nicaragua and Idi Amin in Uganda (the expulsion of the Asians in 1972). In 2003, Vladimir Putin had the richest man in Russia, Mikhail Khodorkovsky, the owner of the Yukos oil company, arrested and confiscated Yukos, transferring its assets to state-owned Rosneft (Åslund, 2019, p. 28). Between 2004 and 2007, state-owned Gazprom was stripped of 60 billion dollars' worth of assets which were put into private hands ((Åslund, 2019, p. 32).

Alternatively, citizens are blackmailed, asked for 'voluntary contributions' or 'donations'. During the Papa Doc era, the richest man in Haiti, Osvald Brandt, had to purchase an entire issue of state bonds, all salary earners had to purchase 'economic liberation bonds' and all public employees had to purchase the second volume of Duvalier's 'Essential Works'. In Putin's Russia, a slightly different method has been used to bring companies under thief control. Between 2009 and 2013, 670,000 cases of 'fraud' were opened against Russian businessmen, 146,000 of which went to court (Åslund, 2019, p. 32). Alternatively, companies that resisted state takeover were hit by enormous tax bills until they sold out (Åslund, 2019, p. 99).

The main alternative to taxation is borrowing, at home or abroad, in non-predatory states as well. The difference between the latter and predatory states, however, is that in predatory states, the loans are not used for productive purposes. The proceeds end up in the pockets of the rulers and their cronies, and the repayment bill is footed by the taxpayers. Good examples are provided by the Dominican Republic and Haiti during the late 19th and early 20th century. Thus, foreign loans were taken (on disastrous conditions) by the Dominicans in 1869, 1888, 1890, 1893, 1894 and 1897 and by the Haitians in 1874, 1875, 1896 and 1910. In the Haitian case, they were complemented with domestic loans in 1874, 1912, 1913 and 1914 (four loans) (Lundahl, 2019, pp. 112–113).

7.6 Rent Creation

Scarcity rents of various kinds exist in all economies. They, however, acquire a very special significance in predatory states. A scarcity rent arises when the supply of a good or a service is limited in relation to the demand for it. Take the situation when imports are subjected to quantitative restrictions. Those who lay their hands on the available import licenses are the ones who pocket the rents: the difference between the domestic sales price and the regulated import price. The existence of rents leads to rent-seeking or directly unproductive profit-seeking (DUP) activities (Krueger, 1974; Bhagwati, 1982). Competition is shifted from the economic arena—cost minimization and product improvement—to the political one, wooing the political establishment in order to obtain whatever special favors that are needed to pocket the scarcity rents. Company activities concentrate on lobbying instead of on production, lobbying directed both at obtaining existing rents and on persuading the government to create new ones by interfering with the market mechanism. This reduces competition in the economic arena, and the economy moves away from the efficient competitive equilibrium.

In the predatory state, the government makes systematic use of rents. If you possess the political power, you also have the power to create rents, rents which can be distributed at will to the ruling clique or to outsiders ('oligarchs') who are willing to pay kickbacks to their benefactors. The methods are manifold. In Putin's Russia, 'there are four sources of crony enrichment: privileged public procurement, stock manipulation, asset stripping, and privileged trade', summarizes Anders Åslund in his study of the Russian kleptocracy (Åslund, 2019, p. 154). The rents are 'auctioned'—sold to the highest bidder, and the state maximizes its income. In the end, a corrupt bureaucracy is created which routinely distributes privileges in a standardized fashion (Schleifer and Vishny, 1993, pp. 605–607).

7.7 The Use of Foreign Aid

On the international scene, for developing countries, the alternative to borrowing is obtaining foreign aid, preferably with no strings attached. The latter, however, is not easy for predatory regimes. It usually requires special circumstances. One such circumstance was the Cold War, with the United States and the Soviet Union competing for support in international organizations. When the United States needed the Haitian vote in the Organization of American States (OAS) in 1962, to impose sanctions on Cuba, Papa Doc obtained American aid by threatening to join the Soviet camp. In 1972, when Idi Amin found that Great Britain and Israel wanted to find out what their aid money went to, he instead turned to Gaddafi in Libya, threw the Israelis out of Uganda and assumed a strongly anti-Jewish position. Jean-Bédel Bokassa in the Central African Republic (Empire from 1976) systematically blackmailed potential donors. He converted to Marxism and 'scientific socialism' in

1969, but the move produced no financial results, so he had to embrace capitalism again. Thereafter, he converted to Islam, spurred by Gaddafi, but failing to obtain enough money from Libya, he again became a devout Catholic.

The best solution for a predator is to obtain untied loans which can be used at his own discretion. When that is not possible, funds are often diverted to unintended uses with the aid of obscure criteria. Thus, during the early 1990s, the Swedish aid agency, SIDA, discovered a well-developed system which rested on nepotism and tribalism in Kenya, involving public officials on many levels and a suspect collaboration among politicians, public servants and private companies in a web where allocation of funds was based on kickbacks instead of competitive bidding (Lundahl, 2019, pp. 113–115).

7.8 The Flexible Budget

Aid funds are not the only funds diverted by kleptocrats to unbudgeted uses. They form part of a wider pattern which includes domestic funds as well, a pattern which on the one hand reallocates funds more or less secretly, from budgeted to unbudgeted uses, and on the other hand employs funds without budgeting their use. In the early 1970s, Bokassa routinely transferred funds from one use to another even when this meant that projects were left unfinished. Idi Amin, in turn, spent as much as 50 percent of the budget on the army, a much higher figure than the budgeted one. An even better example of budget manipulation is Papa Doc Duvalier in Haiti. He ruled by decree during most of his presidency and could hence easily switch items, particularly in favor of his militia. He also used the government tobacco monopoly to collect taxes on a wide variety of goods ranging from milk to cement, funds that were never accounted for in any budget but were pocketed and used at will by the president (Lundahl, 2019, pp. 115–116).

7.9 State-Owned and Private Enterprises

State enterprises tend to be an excellent instrument for fund diversion, especially when they are given monopoly privileges. Ferdinand Marcos in the Philippines used sugar and coconut monopolies to channel funds directly to his own family. Other state enterprises were exempt from auditing (the national oil corporation) or from taxes and fees (the amusement and gambling corporation). Rafael Trujillo in the Dominican Republic was the most important sugar exporter in the country, Forbes Burnham in Guyana between 1971 and 1976 nationalized a number of bauxite and sugar companies whose exports he employed to pay the ruling clique, and Baby Doc Duvalier in Haiti during the last years before his fall in 1986 used a large number of state-owned companies to siphon off money to his family and his close supporters (Lundahl, 2019, pp. 116–117).

Private enterprises can be used as well. We have already dealt with the use of them to divert aid funds, and it is even easier to use them to steal domestic money. General Yakubu Gawon in Nigeria in 1975 placed a cement order abroad that amounted to two-thirds of the needs of all of Africa and which exceeded the total production capacity of Western Europe and the Soviet Union together, at a price way above the one prevailing in the world market. The total cost was two billion dollars or one-fourth of Nigeria's oil revenue. Between 1979 and 1983, Nigerian oil was sold to unauthorized dealers at a price which exceeded the official one. A shortage of oil was created inside Nigeria. Ferdinand Marcos paid far more to Westinghouse for a contract for a nuclear power station than what the lowest bidder, General Electric, was asking, and Mobutu in Zaire allowed the German rocket company OTRAG to use an area larger than West Germany in his country for an outrageous price. François 'Papa Doc' Duvalier in Haiti systematically wooed foreign investors to become involved in dubious projects, the main purpose of which was to generate kickbacks to himself (Lundahl, 2019, pp. 116–119).

Vladimir Putin, in turn, has spun an intricate web of obscure operations of a combination of state enterprises, private enterprises and offshore companies registered in tax havens combined with fake ownership by front men to siphon off wealth and transfer it abroad, mainly to the United States and Great Britain, where property rights are much stronger than in Russia (Åslund, 2019, Chapters 4 and 6).

7.10 The Economic Effects of Predation

In the foregoing, we have already pointed to two of the main economic consequences of the predatory state: the concentration of incomes in the hands of the members of the ruling clique and the negative effects on growth and production. The first one is obvious: a fact that does not require any details. It speaks for itself. The second consequence is more complicated. Many mechanisms are at work. Plunder by the state affects the efficiency of the allocation of resources, investment, migration and technological change negatively.

Predation builds on intervention in the market mechanism. Distortions are created which in various ways create an inefficient allocation of resources. The latter are not directed to the most efficient producers but to producers who are favored by the political establishment because they share their profits with the latter. Alternatively, state-owned enterprises are created which channel money directly to the rulers. Under free economic competition, resources will be devoted to cost reduction and development of new products. In the predatory state, efficiency is systematically sacrificed on the altar of redistribution of the existing resources. In a celebrated article, William Baumol (1990) makes the distinction between productive, unproductive and destructive entrepreneurship. The predatory state is a prime example of the third category. The state signals that it is more lucrative for entrepreneurs to compete for government-created rents than to concentrate on production, and the proceeds are split between them and the ruling clique. In the worst case, the process degenerates to something resembling pure criminal activities, like when the Burmese military junta and Noriega in Panama got involved in drug traffic (Lundahl, 2019, p. 120). When destructive rent-seeking stands out as more lucrative than production, more and more people will be drawn into the former type of activity and fewer and fewer into the latter. Resources are used up without creating any new value. Production and growth suffer.[6]

In the market economy, prices play a fundamental role as bearers of information. They tell producers what and how much to produce, consumers what and how much to consume and factor owners how much they should ask for their services and how many of them to supply. In the predatory state, prices become misleading. Kleptocrats distort the price mechanism (Lundahl, 2019, pp. 121–122):

> High tariffs are imposed to boost profits, notably in manufacturing. Agricultural producers receive low prices for their efforts while at the same time the high costs of parastatal marketing boards hide substantial corruption. Agricultural exports are taxed severely unless they happen to come from firms owned by the rulers themselves or their cronies. Real interest rates are negative and credits are systematically channeled to the least needy. Domestic currencies are overvalued, often to the point where the supply of foreign currency is rationed, and whatever is available is allocated to luxury imports by the predators. Arbitrary (often completely illicit) taxes, that end up in the pockets of the members of the ruling clique and their supporters, as well as subsidies to inefficient companies via government contracts distort domestic relative prices.

The distorted price mechanism provides misleading information about relative scarcity. The criterion that governs the allocation of resources is not profits in a market economy where the latter reflect efficiency but the relative contribution of activities to the incomes of the ruling clique. The wrong kind of goods is produced, and the welfare of the citizens decreases. In addition, the efficiency of investment is lowered, which hampers growth.

Not only will predation affect allocative efficiency negatively. It will also affect X-efficiency, that is, the output produced by a given amount of resources in a given sector. Thus, tariff production of a sector will reduce the incentives to cut costs. The same is true for monopoly privileges. Frequently, the two are combined. Even worse is the case when assets are simply confiscated and transferred into inexperienced and uninterested hands.

The X-efficiency of the public sector will also be affected. The functioning of the predatory machinery requires corruption. The bureaucrats become the agents of the ruler who is corrupt himself. Corruption in the predatory state is not only simple petty corruption but it also trickles down from the top. The ruler sets the standard, and the underlings behave accordingly. Organized theft is institutionalized, and the proceeds trickle up to the top. In addition, however, the corrupt civil servants will do private business on the side. No services will be performed without payments from the citizens. The cost of producing services will increase.

Both private and public investments suffer in the predatory state. A study by Paulo Mauro (1995) of 67 countries for the years 1980–1983 combines indices of corruption, red tape and the state of honesty in the judiciary into a single measure of inefficiency. This measure (as well as the simple corruption index) was strongly negatively correlated with investment and the growth of GDP per capita. Investment shrinks, since nobody will invest in a situation where it is not certain that you will reap what you sow, in the best case a fraction of what normally would accrue to you, in the worst nothing at all. Public investment is likely to suffer as well unless it is made in projects that directly benefit the ruling class. It will not be directed toward the socially highest-yielding activities. Quite probably, investment in infrastructure will be held back unless it can be used for some kind of racket, and this will in turn decrease such private investment that is dependent on water, electricity, etc.

Investment in human capital will also suffer. Education may make people think on their own and analyze the state of affairs in the predatory state. Ignorant people are more easily tamed than educated people. But not only that. The demand for education is also likely to be reduced. It makes no sense to invest in education if it does not take you anywhere. In the predatory state, it is much better to spend your money and energy on making the right kind of connections. The skills taught in school matter little. Also, part of the human capital already accumulated will disappear. In order to get the highest return on their education, people will leave the country: a brain drain process will begin, like in Papa Doc's Haiti, Idi Amin's Uganda and Francisco Macías Nguema's Equatorial Guinea. (In the latter, not a single university graduate is reported to have remained in the country.)

One of the most important determinants of economic growth in the longer run is technological change. Predatory behavior by the state acts as a brake on the development of new products and methods. Innovating firms need all kinds of permits and licenses to be able to operate, and these can be obtained only upon more or less transparent payments to the government. Innovating firms are often new and without any channel to the political establishment (whereas established firms have easy access to politically created rents). They often have problems obtaining credits which in turn makes it difficult to pay to a government which is likely to charge as much as the traffic can bear. Also, innovation is a long-term venture, which means that fees can be extracted over an extended period of time, and successful innovators always run the risk of being expropriated or 'bought out' by the government. None of this is conducive to a climate which will promote innovations and long-run growth.

7.11 Increased Informality

The existence of a predatory state will make the citizens invent countermeasures. They will think of ways which make it possible, to the largest possible extent, to escape plunder. One such measure consists in operating outside the formal economy in order to avoid taxation. The degree of informality will tend to increase. However, working in the informal economy is an imperfect weapon. The reason is that the formal and informal sectors are interdependent. It is difficult to work only in the informal part of the economy. Douglas Marcouiller and Leslie Young (1995,

p. 631) have argued that this is the case when the two sectors produce imperfect substitutes:

> Suppose that the elasticity of substitution between the two goods is low, as might be the case if the production of some essential goods is difficult to conceal from official surveillance. Then exploitation of the formal sector by official taxation and unofficial bribes which reduce formal output could drive down rapidly the relative price of informal goods, thereby impoverishing informal workers even faster than it impoverishes formal workers. With secession from the formal sector thus impeded by price effects, the predatory state can always rake off more by increasing the rate of taxation.

Marcouiller and Young postulate that the state only maintains law and order in the formal sector—in order to increase productivity there—but it does not necessarily pay to do so. The ruler maximizes his revenue by equalizing the marginal revenue and the marginal cost of providing order, but in the case where the marginal revenue curve does not rise above the marginal cost curve, the optimum amount of order is zero, and the formal sector ceases to exist. The entire economy becomes informal. The state, however, remains predatory. The only difference is that the means of predation are likely to become cruder: simple confiscation instead of taxation. It is also possible that the state will encourage exit from the formal into the informal sector. By refraining from harassing the informal sector too much, the government may increase production there, which will in turn lower the relative price of informal goods and make workers go into the formal sector where they will increase the tax base at the disposal of the rulers. Encouragement of informal activities may thus under certain circumstances form part of the revenue-maximizing strategy of a predatory government.

7.12 Epilogue: The End of Predation

Will predation go on forever? Is Putin safe in the saddle? For the time being, probably yes. In the longer run, possibly but not certainly. He has made a complete fool of himself by starting the war in Ukraine. He has already experienced the aborted coup of the Wagner group, and if too many Russian soldiers return home in caskets instead of as 'heroes', the public opinion may slowly begin to swing. He may be faced with yet another 'geopolitical catastrophe': his own demise. But we don't know.

One fact that bodes well is that the recent historical evidence is against him. Kleptocrats tend to be thrown out of office, more or less violently. Marcos Pérez Jiménez, Juan Perón, Idi Amin, Baby Doc Duvalier, Alfredo Stroessner, the Shah of Iran, Ferdinand Marcos, Jean-Bédel Bokassa. Mobutu Sese Seko and Kurmanbek Bakiyev were forced into exile. Hailie Selassie was deposed and imprisoned. Manuel Noriega was arrested after a United States intervention and given a 40-year prison sentence in the United States, mainly for drug trafficking. Slobodan Milošević was arrested after suffering an electoral defeat and extradited to the UN International Criminal Tribunal for the Former Yugoslavia at The Hague for crimes against humanity, genocide and war crimes. Suharto, Robert Mugabe and Hosni Mubarak were forced to resign. Rafael Trujillo was shot to death in an ambush. Anastasio Somoza García ('Tacho') was murdered and so was his son Anastasio Somoza Debayle ('Tachito'), after having been toppled by the Sandinistas and forced into exile. Francisco Macías Nguema was deposed and shot. Nicolae Ceaușescu was overthrown in a revolution and executed. Saddam Hussein was captured and hung after the American conquest of Baghdad during the Iraq War. Muammar Gaddafi was savagely killed upon capture during the Libyan civil war.

There is no rule without exception, however. The House of Saud has ruled Saudi Arabia since 1932, and the Kim dynasty has ruled North Korea since 1948.[7] There is, however, a fundamental difference between the two. Due to its oil, Saudi Arabia is a rich country, while North Korea is poor, with starvation always lurking around the corner, a threat exacerbated by the disastrous behavior of the Kim family. Thus, at the beginning of 2023, Amnesty International estimated that 40 percent of the North Korean population suffers from 'malnutrition amid widespread food insecurity' (Amnesty International, 2023). The downfall of predatory rulers, as exemplified by Idi Amin, Macías Nguema, Mobutu and Bokassa (Lundahl, 2019, pp. 131–132), frequently goes hand in hand with economic chaos and loss of political control. Two present-day cases are Somalia, a country in constant civil war since the early 1990s, and Haiti, where the government has gradually lost control over the territory since 2010—prime examples of failed states, arguably worse than those ruled by well-established predators. Will the Russian economy collapse? What may come after Putin? Conceivably, another corrupt predatory regime. As history has proved, kleptocracy is difficult to uproot.

To conclude, there is nothing new under the sun. The predatory state is a perennial companion of mankind. Ruling cliques maximize government revenue and pocket it, with the aid of an infinite array of ingenious devices. Incomes are grotesquely concentrated in the hands of small minorities at the expense of the common citizens who have to shoulder the burden in a way that leads to serious impoverishment and destitution.

Notes

1 The last of the three limitations states that a ruler who extracts large sums in the present runs a higher risk to be thrown out than one who extracts less during each period.
2 Lundahl (2019, pp. 151–153) provides a selective bibliography of great men. For the nomenklatura, see Voslensky (1984).
3 For details of the following, see Lundahl (1985).
4 Putin's Russia provides a good case study of how visible journalists, representatives of the opposition, oligarchs and other perceived enemies have been murdered or given long prison sentences. Sergei Skripal, double agent for Russia and Britain in 2004, was sentenced to 14 years in prison and subsequently, in 2018, poisoned with Novichok. Mikhail Khodorkovsky, reputedly the richest man in Russia and a political activist, was sentenced to 9 years in 2005, extended by another 10 years in 2010 (pardoned in 2013, stripped of his Yukos company). The journalist Alexander Litvinenko, former FSB agent and defector, was poisoned with polonium in London in 2006. His colleague Anna

Politkovskaya was murdered (shot at point-blank range) in 2006. Sergei Magnitsky, an auditor who exposed the corruption of leading Russian government officials, was arrested in 2008 and died in prison less than a year after, having been denied medical attention. The opposition politician and outspoken Putin critic Boris Nemtsov was shot to death in the back in 2015. The historian Yury Dmitriev, who worked on Stalin's execution sites in Karelia, was sentenced to 15 years in 2021. The same year, the ex-municipal deputy Ksenya Fadeyeva from Tomsk was arrested and charged with organization of an 'extremist organization'. The trial against her began in August 2023. The artist Sasha Skochilenko was arrested and brought to a psychiatric hospital (and denied medical attention) on pretrial detention (until October 2023) in 2022 for having protested against the Russian war against Ukraine. The opposition politician Ilya Yaashin was given 8.5-year sentence in 2022 for 'spreading knowingly false information' about the war. The journalist and opposition politician Vladimir Kara-Murza was sentenced to 25 years in 2023. His colleague Dmitri Glukhovsky, after being forced into exile, was given an 8-year sentence the same year. The most important opposition leader, the very symbol of resistance to the scared little man in the Kremlin, Alexei Navalny, was poisoned with Novichok in 2020 and subsequently given jail sentences which in practice amounted to lifetime had he survived the infrahuman conditions of Russia's political prisons (3.5 + 9 + 19 years), before his death in prison on 16 February 2024 under circumstances that the Russian authorities have failed to explain. His former campaign chief Lilia Chanysheva received a 7.5-year sentence in 2023, for 'creating an extremist organization'. On top of all this, the leader of the Wagner Group, Yevgeny Prigozhin, together with a number of his closest collaborators, was killed in an airplane crash in August 2023, either by a bomb inside the plane or by a Russian antiaircraft gun—a direct result of the group's march on Moscow in June.
5 Thus, a World Bank study from 1988 (World Bank, 1988, p. 85) calculated the administrative costs of income taxation to be 10 percent of the revenue, that of value-added taxation 5 percent and that of taxes on international trade 1–3 percent.
6 The following draws on Lundahl (2019, pp. 119–128).
7 See, for example, Lacey (1981), Aburish (1994) for the former, and Martin (2004), Fifield (2019) for the latter.

References

Aburish, S.K. (1994). *The Rise, Corruption and Coming Fall of the House of Saud*. London: Bloomsbury Publishing.
Amnesty International (2023). *North Korea: Deteriorating Human Rights Situation Calls for International Attention*. 7 February. www.amnesty.org/en/latest/news/2023/02/north-korea-deteriorating-human-rights-situation-calls-for-international-attention/. Downloaded 13 July 2023.
Andreski, S. (1966). *Parasitism and Subversion: The Case of Latin America*. New York: Pantheon Books.
Åslund, A. (2019). *Russia's Crony Capitalism: The Path from the Market Economy to Kleptocracy*. New Haven, CT and London: Yale University Press.
Awal, A. (2022). The 10 Richest Royal Families in the World Ranked by Their Net Worth 2022. *The Family Nation*. 15 July. https://thefamilynation.com/richest-royal-families-in-the-world-ranked-by-their-net-worth. Downloaded 27 July 2023.
Baumol, W.J. (1990). Entrepreneurship: Productive, Unproductive and Destructive. *Journal of Political Economy*, 98(5), 893–921.
Behr, E. (1991). *'Kiss the Hand You Cannot Bite': The Rise and Fall of the Ceausescus*. London: Hamish Hamilton.
Bhagwati, J.N. (1982). Directly Unproductive, Profit-seeking (DUP) Activities. *Journal of Political Economy*, 90(5), 988–1002.

Boyce, J.K. (1993). *The Philippines. The Political Economy of Growth and Impoverishment in the Marcos Era*. Houndmills, Basingstoke and London: Macmillan.
Burns, J., and Huband, M. (1997). La véridique historire du maréchal Mobutu qui a construit une fortune de 4 milliards de dollars en pillant son pays. *Le Monde*, 18–19 May.
Celebrity Net Worth (2013). *Kim Jong-un Net Worth $5 Billion*. www.celebritynetworth.com/richest-politicians/presidents/kim-jong-un-net-worth/. Downloaded 27 June 2023.
Danielson, A., and Lundahl, M. (1994). Endogenous Policy Formation and the Principle of Optimal Obfuscation: Theory and Some Evidence from Haiti and Jamaica. *Comparative Economic Studies*, 36(3), 51–78.
Davies, N. (2016). The $10bn Question: What Happened to the Marcos Millions? *The Guardian*. 7 May. www.theguardian.com/world/2016/may/07/10bn-dollar-question-marcos-millions-nick-davies. Downloaded 26 June 2023.
Dawisha, K. (2014). *Putin's Kleptocracy: Who Owns Russia?* New York: Simon and Schuster.
The Economist (1991). Give a Little, Take a Lot. 30 March.
Fifield, A. (2019). *The Great Successor: The Divinely Perfect Destiny of Brilliant Comrade Kim Jong Un*. New York: PublicAffairs.
Flamer, K. (2016). 10 Surprises About Fidel Castro's Extravagant Life. *Forbes Magazine*. 26 November. www.forbes.com/sites/keithflamer/2016/11/26/10-surprises-about-castros-extravagant-life/. Downloaded 27 June 2023.
International Monetary Fund (1883). *International Financial Statistics Yearbook*. Washington, DC: International Monetary Fund.
Kapuśiński, R. (1983). *The Emperor: Downfall of an Autocrat*. New York: Harcourt Brace Jovanovich.
Kroll, L. (2006). Fortunes of Kings, Queens and Dictators. *Forbes Magazine*. 5 May. www.forbes.com/2006/05/04/rich-kings-dictators_cz_lk_0504royals.html. Downloaded 28 June 2023.
Krueger, A.O. (1974). The Political Economy of the Rent-Seeking Society. *American Economic Review*, 64(3), 291–303.
Lacey, R. (1981). *The Kingdom*. New York and London: Harcourt Brace Jovanovich.
Levi, M. (1988). *Of Rule and Revenue*. Berkeley, CA: University of California Press.
Lundahl, M. (1979). *Peasants and Poverty: A Study of Haiti*. London: Croom Helm.
Lundahl, M. (1985). Government and Inefficiency in the Haitian Economy: The Nineteenth-Century Legacy. In M.B. Connolly and J. McDermott (eds), *The Economics of the Caribbean Basin* (pp. 175–218). New York: Praeger Publishers.
Lundahl, M. (2019). *Predators and Terrorists: Essays in Economic Pathology*. Montreal: CIDIHCA.
Lundahl, M., and Vedovato, C. (1989). The State and Economic Development in Haiti and the Dominican Republic. *Scandinavian Economic History Review*, 37(3), 39–59.
Marcouiller, D., and Young, L. (1995). The Black Hole of Graft: The Predatory State and the Informal Economy. *American Economic Review*, 85(3), 630–646.
Martin, B.K. (2004). *Under the Loving Care of the Fatherly Leader North Korea and the Kim Dynasty*. New York: Thomas Dunne Books, St Martin's Press.
Mauro, P. (1995). Corruption and Growth. *Quarterly Journal of Economics*, 110(3), 681–712.
Morrow, A. (2022). How Much Is Vladimir Putin Worth? Almost No One Knows for Sure. *CNN Business*. 28 February. https://edition.cnn.com/2022/02/28/business/vladimir-putin-wealth-sanctions/index.html. Downloaded 22 June 2023.
North, D.C. (1981). *Structure and Change in Economic History*. New York and London: W.W. Norton.
Olson, M. (1982). *The Rise and Decline of Nations. Economic Growth, Stagflation and Social Rigidities*. New Haven, CT and London: Yale University Press.
Olson, M. (1993). Dictatorship, Democracy, and Development. *American Political Science Review*, 87(3), 567–576.
Pacepa, I.M. (1988). *Red Horizons*. London: Heinemann.

Putin's Palace (2021). www.youtube.com/watch?v=mMxqTae75Fs. Downloaded 21 June 2023.

Reuters (2021). Online Film about Alleged Putin's 'Palace' Watched Over 100 Mln Times—Data. www.reuters.com/world/online-film-about-alleged-putins-palace-watched-over-100-mln-times-data-2021-01-29/. Downloaded 21 June 2023.

Rouquié, A. (1992). Dynasty: Nicaraguan Style. In H.M. Hamill (ed), *Caudillos: Dictators in Spanish America* (pp. 257–269). Norman, OK and London: Oklahoma University Press.

Schleifer, A., and Vishny, R.W. (1993). Corruption. *Quarterly Journal of Economics*, 198(3), 599–617.

Scott, J.C. (1972). *Comparative Political Corruption*. Englewood Cliffs, NJ: Prentice-Hall.

Tanzi, V. (1987). Quantitative Characteristics of the Tax Systems of Developing Countries. In D. Newbury and N. Stern (eds), *The Theory of Taxation for Developing Countries* (pp. 205–241). New York: Oxford University Press.

Voslensky, M. (1984). *Nomenklatura: Anatomy of the Soviet Ruling Class*. London: Bodley Head.

Wiarda, H. (1968). *Dictatorship and Development: The Methods of Control in Trujillo's Dominican Republic*. Gainsville, FL: University of Florida Press.

World Bank (1988). *World Development Report, 1988*. New York: Oxford University Press.

Part IV
Geographical Inequalities

8 Regional Inequalities

Daniel Rauhut and Alois Humer

8.1 Introduction

The disadvantages rural, peripheral and remote places have when it comes to their distance to the market reduce their competitiveness and hence their economic growth (Krugman, 1991). The economic policies in the EU favour bigger cities and regions with bigger cities (Rauhut and Humer, 2020; Vedrine and Le Gallo, 2021) and in peripheral regions, few cities have been able to benefit from these policies (Nagy and Benedek, 2021). After the financial crisis 2008–2009, it was clear that the economic crisis hit different types of regions in Europe unevenly (Hadjimichalis, 2011, Christophers, 2015; Gruber et al., 2019). Many regions experienced rapid growth of unemployment and lost welfare benefits (Essletzbichler et al., 2018); some regions suffered massive job destruction (Fratesi and Rodríguez-Pose, 2016). Simultaneously, a retrenchment of the public sector and a shrinking state occurred (Lobao et al., 2018). Many regions were labelled as having 'no future'; they were 'places that don't matter' (Rodríguez-Pose, 2018; Mattila et al., 2023). Economic diversification, the quality of production factors hosted, the density of external cooperation networks and the quality of urban infrastructure give greater economic resilience to cities and to the regions hosting them (Capello et al., 2015). The regional disparities regarding welfare provision (e.g. healthcare and education) and network services (e.g. IT and communications) have increased (Marques da Costa et al., 2015), and especially rural and peripheral areas have experienced a deterioration of services (Clifton et al., 2015).

The marketisation of services of general interest (SGI), or social overhead capital, and public sector retrenchment hit weak regions the hardest (Rauhut, 2019). The problematisation of regional disparities has usually gone hand in hand with the legitimisation and/or de-legitimisation of some political powers, especially when 'justice' is related to issues such as, for example, regional development, regional disparities, infrastructure, production and accessibility of services and welfare, as well as participation (Gyuris, 2014). The market cannot make profit in, for example, peripheral, remote and lagging regions; the 'third sector' cannot accumulate sufficient money for investments and hence is unable to meet the needs of the population (Borges et al., 2015).

Moreover, much of what we know about spatial differentiation of welfare implicitly takes a centralist perspective, that is it takes the 'urban' or 'metropolitan' as a starting point when discussing regional inequalities (Powell and Boyne, 2001). How disrupting these problems and challenges are depends on what scale we analyse, and where we draw the boundaries between different types of territory. This leads to the delicate question on how to define such boundaries (Bell and Davoudi, 2016). A person's life chances and quality of life depend more upon the region one grew up in than class distinctions (Andersson and Malmberg, 2018).

This chapter discusses the key challenges regarding regional inequalities today from a European perspective. We will start discussing what a region is, what types of regions there are and the impact of scale. Then we will turn the discussion to what kind of inequalities we can expect from a regional perspective and what have caused them. After this, we will discuss some thematic cases that regions struggle with today regarding regional inequalities followed by a discussion and conclusion.

8.2 Regions and Types of Regions

There is a plurality of answers to what a 'region' is in geography and spatial sciences. A region is a clearly or softly delineated space by scale in between a local to global level. For a conceptual typology, we will distinguish among Euclidian, networked and perceived regions. Euclidian spaces are like containers, which feature clear borders and a definite distinction between out and in. We know these kinds of spaces from formal, multi-hierarchical governance entities. There are local entities like municipalities, maybe federal meso-scaled entities like Swiss Cantons, and a national entity of the nation state. None of these Euclidian entities are necessarily called regions; rather, what is called regions is right in between those common vertical state scales: regions maybe larger than single municipalities but smaller than federal or nation state. As well, regions may be larger than nation states, in case of EU's macro regions, for example, or in global scale on a continental level. For administrative-organisational and statistical reasons, states delineate such container spaced regions. Most prominently, the vertical spatial subdivisions defined by Eurostat 'NUTS' are complementing the state entities with regions in-between. In some Member States, a NUTS 1 region is a true political state space, and in some it is a mere statistically delineated space. Despite the seemingly arbitrary delineation of administrative, statistical regions, the political power going through these kinds of regions is strong when it comes to connected funding schemes and legal regulations.

In contrast to Euclidian spaces, networked spaces have a certain genesis beyond a plane political decision of delineation. They may form through functional relations of a historical, economic and/or geographical genesis. Historically networked regions can go back to cultural aspects of languages or pre-modern societies, partly connected to political history—for example the Maramureș region in today's cross-border situation between Romania and Ukraine. Economically networked regions constitute through their shared industrial heritage—like for example the German Ruhr area. In geographical terms, regions can form through environmental connectivity like mountainous, coastal, island, water catchment or similar features, for example the Scottish Highlands. As well, in terms of urban geography, functional regions form through morphological connectivity, that is when the built environment of a city exceeds the urban boundaries like in the case of Paris metropolitan area. The same can count for rural peripheral regions despite their lack of urban centres—like for example some Italian inner peripheries.

A third type of regions is the perceptual regions, that is, an area which is imagined, subjective, and informal. Examples of perceptual regions is 'the bible belt', the 'rust belt' or a tourist hotspot area. This kind of region emerges from one's informal sense of place rather than a scientific model. A perceptual region is an area defined by subjective perceptions that reflect the feelings and images about key place characteristics. Both locals and residents make up such feelings and images, as well as visitors or people who live far away and have never been to the area (Knox and Marston, 1992).

By now, we have analytically distinguished the constitution of a region by separately speaking about the Euclidian, networked and perceived characteristic. De facto, regions show more than one such feature but constitute through a plurality of features. A region can be a geographically functional entity and at the same time a homogenous area in terms of industrial development. We could combine each single feature with one another and find examples of European regions. Yet, there is no cases of a region that functions through all of these features at once. This is the crucial finding to be aware of when investigating regions and when arguing about regional development and inequalities. Even more so, various features of region-building may oppose each other, as seen for example when political municipal borders cut off the core city from its functional hinterland or when national borders cut through historical–cultural regions.

Despite the complexity of what to call a region, there exist many regional typologies in order to systematise regions in a given territory, like the European continent. Very commonly, regions are sorted into different types according to their degree of urbanisation, from large urban metropolises to rural peripheries. Eventually, some typologies pick up economic, geographical or political features by identifying old-industrial regions, mountainous regions or border regions. The different typologies share the idea of using a city or urban area as a point of reference for the other types, which can be consecutively suburban areas, semi-peripheral areas, rural areas in vicinity to a city, etc. As long as these typologies are used for scientific analytical purposes only, the variety of typologies and underlying logics is an advantage. However, when regional types are used in regional policy terms to redistribute funding or target certain strategies, the delineation of regions does matter a lot in practical terms and for the people living in these regions. There is no optimal solution per se. The largest regional policy mechanism, the EU Cohesion and Regional Policy, is relying on the NUTS nomenclature, which is a (necessarily) simple form of regional typology that covers the whole of Europe in four hierarchies from NUTS 0 (nation states), NUTS 1, NUTS 2, NUTS 3, until NUTS 4 (i.e. LAU, local municipalities). Especially the semi-large regions of NUTS 2 level are a prime container for delivering EU funding to people. Yet, in some EU member states, the NUTS 2 regions are at the same time also political entities, like the Austrian Länder, and in some they are a mere statistical artificial delineation of areas, like in many New-EU member states of Central East Europe. To conclude, speaking about regional development or inequalities is always a matter of what is considered a region.

8.3 The Causes of Regional Inequalities

Policies and practices that are supposed to stimulate economic activity appear not as effectful as they once did. The increasing regional economic inequalities in the EU and the unsettled questions of disintegration, discontent and discretion pose a long-term threat to economic progress, social cohesion and political stability in Europe (Humer et al., 2021). Existing theories, both mainstream and heterodox, appear unable to explain the existence of different regional trajectories and how to stimulate regional convergence processes (Iammarino et al., 2019). However, regional inequalities and how they change over time are not a new phenomenon. Myrdal (1957) argued that economically expanding regions will attract capital and labour from lagging regions; investments are made in prosperous regions simply because investments have been made there before, and the migrants are in their prime working age with demanded human capital and skills. Lagging regions will further drop behind as the flow of human resources and capital tend to favour the more prosperous regions. In other words, polarization between regions will increase. Moreover, mature economies display fewer regional inequalities and a higher degree of regional economic convergence than developing economies. Worth noting is that 'developing' also refers to regions within a fully industrialised country but undergoing different forms of structural change. 'Increasing regional inequality is generated during the early development stages, while mature growth has produced regional convergence or a reduction in differentials', concludes Williamson (1965, p. 44).

The regional inequality in the industrialised world started to increase in the 1970s and only started to accelerate since the turn of the millennium (Cörvers and Mayhew, 2021). Usually, this is explained by globalisation and technological change, and this development has hit small- and medium-sized manufacturing cities and their surroundings hard (Iammarino et al., 2019). Parallel to this, many large metropolitan areas have experienced a significant economic growth and dynamic development in terms of job creation and income (Dijkstra et al., 2015). In the conventional economic theories, greater agglomeration and population density generate the externalities which are behind the dynamism of large cities and regions (Glaeser, 2011; Duranton and Puga, 2001; Fujita et al., 1999). The positive economic effects are then, theoretically, assumed to trickle out to the surrounding regions (Rauhut and Humer, 2020). In many cases, however, lagging regions must display agency and actively try to reach out to more prosperous regions. This can be challenging for regions with limited resources (Ek and Rauhut, 2023).

Regional characteristics and macroeconomic trends interact and hence create a geography of countries, cities and regions, holding different structural positions and operating at different levels in the hierarchy of economic roles and functions in a modern market economy (Scott and Storper, 2003). Many studies have identified the economic, demographic and policy-oriented forces in motion when discussing the increasing regional inequality between regions.

The economic forces in motion that impact regional inequalities relate to the long-term cyclical development in the economic structure (Storper, 2018). The current economic long cycle started in the mid-1970s and is built around biochemistry and the microchips (Schön, 2012).[1] The economic structure during this cycle has stimulated the concentration of high-technology and knowledge-intensive sectors in large metropolitan areas (Storper, 2018), leading to a centripetal movement of highly skilled labour and non-routine and creative jobs towards economic cores (Krugman, 1991). Previously dominant manufacturing industries have experienced automation, which revolutionised trade costs and led to the substitution of routinised medium- and low-skilled jobs in most of the former industrial hubs of Europe. Manufacturing activity has experienced an increase in third-world countries, leading to the demise of the more routine industry jobs across most of Europe (Iammarino et al., 2019) and the United States (Storper, 2018). Parallel to these macroeconomic trends, regional economic development is also affected by these long-cycle economic movements. The aforementioned deindustrialisation has hit different regions differently, leading to higher unemployment rates (Essletzbichler et al., 2018) and job destruction (Fratesi and Rodríguez-Pose, 2016). Place-specific endowments of people and skills and firms and industries are affected, and so are changes in formal and informal institutions as well as the capability for innovation and the reaction to change when experiencing completely new conditions (Storper, 2018; Iammarino et al., 2019). These place-specific endowments vary between the different economic long cycles (Schön, 2012) and can hence be assumed to impact convergence/divergence at a regional level.

Demographic aspects also matter when discussing regional inequalities. Not only population size but also its age structure and human capital matter. Many left-behind regions suffer from population aging and population decline, both in terms of a negative natural population balance and in terms of an outmigration of young adults. The remaining workforce in these regions will experience a gradually increasing comparative disadvantage in terms of (outdated) human capital (Böhm et al., 2021), which will cause the regions to fall further behind economically. National one-size-fits-all policies may cause more harm than good in this context (Mitze et al., 2018).

Traditional top-down regional policies have been replaced by place-based policies. In the lagging regions, regional policy was inextricably bound up with traditional industrial policy. Many of these interventions attempted to boost sectors and activities that did not match local economic strengths and which became in perpetual need of assistance to survive. There was a widespread belief that decentralisation and local initiatives would serve these lagging regions better (Vanthillo et al., 2021). In relation to this, the EU Cohesion Policy also shifted focus from cohesion to competitiveness (Faludi et al., 2015). While many of these lagging regions suffer from missing markets and market failure (Borges et al., 2015), a parallel process of public sector retrenchment hit the lagging regions especially bad (Lobao et al., 2018). The place-based cohesion policy has favoured bigger city regions in central Europe, while rural, peripheral and remote regions have lost out (Rauhut and Costa, 2021) or have been left alone (Gruber et al., 2019).

8.4 Regions, Inequalities and Quality of Life

The quality of life or well-being reflects, in broad terms, what welfare an individual enjoys. The welfare an individual enjoys may be actual or perceived, that is, objective and subjective in character (Hanell et al., 2022). The distribution of welfare in a population is not by random; class, social-economic background, etc., play an important role here (Barr, 1998; Sen, 1993). However, so does the geographical place in which the individual lives (Hanell et al., 2022; Powell and Boyne, 2001; Sen, 1998). The life chances and quality of life of a person depend more upon the region you grew up in than class distinctions (Andersson and Malmberg, 2018). A person's reference frame, to a large degree, dictates the norm against which one's own situation is assessed. Hence, assessments of welfare at the regional or local level are most likely to provide a more accurate reference framework than corresponding assessments where the nation average constitutes the comparable analytic entity, since 'sub-national measures are also more likely to correspond to what people experience in their day-to-day lives [in a situation where] few can identify with the national average' (CEC, 2013, p. 22).

Welfare services includes a rather wide set of services. Moreover, these services can be provided by different actors—public, private and NGOs (Borges et al., 2015). Generally, social policy seldom acknowledges geographical differences in service provision; usually, service provision is set by a nation average (Powell and Boyne, 2001). The spatial organisation of welfare services never fully addressed problems relating to the historic pattern of spatial (un)evenness on the 'supply side', that is, in the geographical distribution of adequate services, state-of-the art technologies and qualified welfare professionals. 'Equity versus efficiency' questions thus continue to form the locus for all public service provision decisions (de Vries and Nemec, 2013) as equal provision across a territory is rarely possible, given the vagaries of geography, historic patterns of physical and institutional endowment and differences in administrative capacity or fiscal capability. This means that difficult choices must be faced over what is funded and how and where is it delivered. What then constitutes a workable balance between equity or 'fairness' in accessibility terms and efficiency in provision, given that requirements necessarily differ between the potentially multifarious groups of people located within any given territory? This problem is often tackled in the context of distinguishing between inequity and inequality where the former represents an unfair or ethically problematic difference in health while the latter a mere difference in welfare (Rauhut and Smith, 2018; Rauhut and Komornicki, 2015). The issue here is determining what is 'unfair' in welfare provision seen from a geographical perspective.

Most welfare services are under a strong influence of centripetal forces, which makes them cluster on bigger cities, urban agglomerations and in areas with relatively high population density (Branco and Marques da Costa, 2023). Economies of scale matter when it comes to the production of welfare services. The welfare producer can achieve economies of scale by increasing production and lowering costs. This happens because costs are spread over a larger number of goods. In remote, peripheral and disadvantageous regions with a relatively low population density, the planning, production and financing become costlier than in bigger cities, urban agglomerations and in areas with relatively high population density because of the absence of economies of scale (Humer, 2014). To obtain economies of scale, that is to ensure an economically efficient provision, the welfare services are allocated to the regional population centre (Brovarone and Grunfelder, 2021; Kompil et al., 2019). By necessity, the accessibility will be reduced compared to bigger cities, urban agglomerations and in areas with relatively high population density (Rauhut and Komornicki, 2015).

8.5 Three Examples of Inequality in Regions Left Behind

In awareness of the various regional conceptualisations as presented in Section 8.2, this section will showcase three examples of regions left behind and what inequalities the processes being left behind will generate. We will discuss three regions of various size and types, from Austria, Portugal and Sweden.

8.5.1 Dalarna, Sweden: A Laggard in Economic Development

Dalarna is an administrative region on central Sweden, and it is a rural and semi-peripheral region. During the industrial economy, the region was relatively opulent and flourishing. The relative immobility of capital required the labour force to move to the production sites during the industrial society. Housing was then built close to the production sites to accommodate the workers, and the increasing public sector provided services related to child and elderly care, education and medical care. Deindustrialisation started to hit the Swedish region Dalarna in the mid-1970s, and the process is still ongoing. Primarily, deindustrialisation hit labour-intensive and low-productive companies operating in areas with a strong international competition (Johansson, 1996). However, still today, business life is dominated by small one-mill-towns (20–50,000 inhabitants). Employment has declined sharply in most of these towns; often, one company that has dominated the job market in the town and that has taken on a large social responsibility in the locality. When this company has reduced both the number of employees and social responsibility, this has hit these places hard (Region Dalarna, 2022).

The economic structure in Dalarna is characterised by a negative structure and the fact that there are slower branch changes in the region than at the national level. Both the structural and branch effects reinforce each other in slower growth than in the national economy. The branch structure is obsolete, has a slow branch growth and is losing out relative to other regions in the same country (Rauhut and Kahila, 2008). Although the sector is still declining, manufacturing will remain an engine in Dalarna's regional economy, and most of the production targets the export market. Dalarna has a cluster of specialisations in the extraction and processing of raw materials (e.g. not only the extraction of sand and gravel but also stone and porcelain manufacturing). This cluster shares competences with the textile industry, metalwork and a smaller competence cluster linked to forest industries (forestry service, sawing and planning, and forestry) (Region Dalarna, 2022). However, these products are also produced in other countries and usually at a lower cost. Moreover, the low share of population with tertiary education obstructs a transition towards a more knowledge-intensive economy. Both the knowledge-intensive economy and simple service sector jobs have predominantly generated jobs in the three metropolitan areas in Sweden (Greater Stockholm, Greater Gothenburg and Greater Malmö), leaving Dalarna behind (Broström and Rauhut, 2018).

The traditional state-centred top-down regional policy was dismantled after Sweden became an EU member in 1995. Instead, regional policy became based on a growth-oriented policy with a strong bias on competition (Foss et al., 2004). The shift in the EU Cohesion Policy 2009 in the wake of the financial crisis and austerity policies further emphasised competition, cities and place-based policies (Gruber et al., 2019), which requires the capacity to mobilise endogenous resources (economically, politically, institutionally and socially). It also requires functioning markets and market actors. In the absence of cities, functioning markets and competitive business life in relation with few and weak resources to mobilise, the region and its inhabitants have become poorer relative the capital region and the other Swedish regions (Broström and Rauhut, 2018). The increasing regional inequalities Dalarna experiences are related not only to the poor economic structure of the region but also to a policy failure.

8.5.2 Süd Burgenland, Austria: A Border Region Without Urban Centres

Burgenland is the most eastern Federal State of Austria, bordering to mainly Hungary with self-governmental rights. By EU statistical type, it is a NUTS 2 region. Thus, the political and statistical delineation are identical. These are good preconditions for doing regional development. However, in geographical and historical–cultural terms, Burgenland is disfavoured. It lacks larger urban areas, advanced industries and infrastructure networks. Instead, it is still dominated by agricultural and touristic activities and a very scattered settlement structure of low density (Swiatek et al., 2013; Gruber et al., 2019).

Burgenland is not an old region but was founded in 1921 by merging several former Hungarian regions into one new Austrian region according to the Peace Treaty of Versailles. However, the few urban centres of the former Hungarian regions remained with Hungary; only the rural hinterland formed the new Burgenland. The largest municipality of this designed Federal State, Eisenstadt with just a few thousand inhabitants, became the capital. Since its constitution, Burgenland has faced all difficulties of a peripheral, lagging behind region in national and European terms. During Interwar and World War II times, this meant quite some hardship for their people. Also later, Burgenland could not participate in the economic uplift as other Austrian Federal States could, neither rebuilding their industrial nor exploring touristic potential. The major urban and labour market centres for Burgenland are still Vienna and Graz (Gruber et al., 2013).

The EU accession of Austria in 1995 made Burgenland a major receiver of EU Cohesion funding and indeed helped stimulating the economy to some extent. The re-integration with Hungary and Slovakia through EU enlargement in 2004 slowly recreated the connectivity of the former urban centres of Györ, Sopron, and not least Bratislava for the hinterland of Burgenland. Yet, there is a long way to go, and the Burgenland has been cut off for (too) long from its centres (Stepniak and Rosik, 2013). Still in the funding period 2021–2027, the NUTS 2 region of Burgenland is considered a phasing-out Cohesion region in EU terms with a GDP per capital of less than 90 percent of EU average.

Together with the increasing focus on urban-centred regional policy (Rauhut and Humer, 2020), the inner-Austrian policy mode of subsidiarity and federalisation is a challenging environment for Burgenland to catch up. Rather, regional disparities are likely to increase. Despite the meanwhile strong local level and bottom-up initiatives in Burgenland, which partly is a seed of EU funding, this peripheral region is in a constant dependency on redistribution mechanisms from national and European levels (Gruber et al., 2019). Without inter-regional solidarity, cross-border cooperation, and top-down care taking, Burgenland can hardly escape its fate of a lagging region.

8.5.3 *Alentejo, Portugal: Stuck in the Primary Sector*

The NUTS2 region Alentejo extends to about one-third of continental Portugal's area. However, the population density is relatively low for Portuguese standards. The two biggest cities are Èvora and Santarém, both with approximately 60,000 inhabitants each. The countryside varies from the open rolling plains of the south of Alentejo to the granite hills that border Spain in the northeast. In the north, the economic activity is dominated to be more livestock-based production, for example cattle, sheep and pig farming; in the south, agriculture may be more predominant. Cork, wines and tourism are important economic sectors in Alentejo (OECD, 2022). The regional GDP/capital is low relative to other regions in Portugal as well as from an EU perspective (CEC, 2022). Both when it comes to basic infrastructure networks and social services, Alentejo performs poorly compared to the other regions in Portugal (Humer and Palma, 2013); the two biggest cities Èvora and Santarém perform well, but not the rest of Alentejo.

Alentejo has benefited from EU investments by the Regional Smart Specialisation Strategy (RIS3). These investments should help the region to 'attract foreign investments to its territory which will provide the development and modernization of traditional sectors of the regions' (Sarkar et al., 2021, p. 462). According to data from the Portuguese Regional Innovation Scoreboard, the North, Centre and Lisbon areas are the areas that have strong innovation, while the rest regions of the country display a moderate innovation. Nonetheless, an improvement in innovation was registered between 2016 and 2019 in all regions except Alentejo and Algarve (Gomes et al., 2022). Moreover, it seems as if the survival of the entrepreneurs in Alentejo supported by the LEADER+ programme is dependent not only on how much money is invested in them but also on the frequency of the investments made (Santos et al., 2016).

Alentejo is a high-potential area for tourism development, but only now it has begun to be implemented. However, to profit from the full potential of tourism, several preconditions must be fulfilled. One is a national tourism strategy, another is a policy to avoid speculation in the real estate market and a third is foreign investments (Serdoura et al., 2009). In some very niched sectors, the innovations are at the front of the development, such as biomass gasification of biomass waste, but it has no competitive advantages towards regions in other countries (Rijo et al., 2023). Another example is the wine industry in Alentejo which produces good products, but this sector is insufficient to lead the regional development. The regional development strategies are supposed to utilise regional specificities and local institutions; this is the basis for the place-based regional development. However, these endogenous development strategies usually underestimate the importance of transregional relations and institutions. This is where Alentejo's wine sector encounters problems (Marques and Barberá-Tomás, 2022).

The main sectors dominating the economic activities in Alentejo are all labour-intensive and low-productive and require low-skilled labour. None of these sectors will generate a Rostovian 'take-off' economically. There are no bigger cities in the region with a dynamic service sector; the supply of services is in a very basic state in most towns. It is easy to fall in love with Alentejo's lovely food and wines as well as the adorable scenery, but economically, Alentejo is stuck in the primary sector.

8.6 Discussion and Conclusion

The three selected case regions display several similarities. They are all located in the backwaters of the capital region, the economic structure is dominated by relatively labour-intensive and low production and services and they have problems of attracting investments. The population has a lower education level than the national average, and the GDP/capita is lower than the national average. None of the regions have any airport nor high-speed train; Alentejo and Dalarna have small regional university colleges and neither Burgenland nor Dalarna has any motorway. These aspects play a crucial role when it comes to attract investments and human capital.

Alentejo, Burgenland and Dalarna all have a relatively low social overhead capital, that is capital goods of types which are available to anybody, hence social, and are not tightly linked to any particular part of production, hence overhead. Because of their broad availability, they often must be provided by the state. Examples of social overhead capital is, among others, basic infrastructure and network services (roads, airports, harbours, dams, air-water deterrents, water sewage works, transportation, communication facilities and other high-cost slow-self-liquidating equipment) as well as long- run service installations related to health, education and welfare together with libraries, museums and parks.

> [T]he State is uniquely capable of appraising the intrinsic value of social overhead capital from a broad and long view as of financing costly social overheads out of taxes and/or deficits/. . ./the private sector is supplementary capable of forming some social overhead capital of a rather quick-yielding nature.
>
> (Kurihara, 1970, p. 398)

However, this social overhead capital is not evenly spread across the territory. While some parts of the social overhead capital (or services of general interest in the EU terminology) are dispersed across all types of territory, other parts of the social overhead capital are concentrated to bigger cities. Hence, the life conditions as well as the quality of life for the inhabitants differ depending on where they live geographically (see Figure 8.1). The aggregate demand in remote and sparsely populated regions is simply not sufficient to run, for example, airports, theatres or specialised hospitals (Milbert et al., 2013), and hence the accessibility for the population living in these areas will be significantly lower than for the urban population (Breuer and Milbert, 2013; Stepniak and Rosik, 2013). Although research has pointed at the low profitability for the market in remote and peripheral regions, reducing the willingness for the market and private actors to invest in these regions (Borges et al., 2015), the EU strategies, based on the place-based approach (Barca, 2009), focus on a strong, willing and helping hand from the private sector to invest in these lagging regions (German Presidency, 2020; CEC, 2021, 2022). To invest in the social overhead capital, which would help these regions, is primarily the task of the state (Kurihara, 1970; Rauhut, 2019; see also Sen, 1998). It is very unlikely indeed that regions like Alentejo, Burgenland and Dalarna will be able to mobilise the needed resources endogenously to finance the needed social overhead capital to attract foreign and national investors as well as human capital to their regions.

A person's life chances and quality of life depend on social class distinctions but more so on the region one grew up in. Perspectives of the 'urban' or 'metropolitan' are

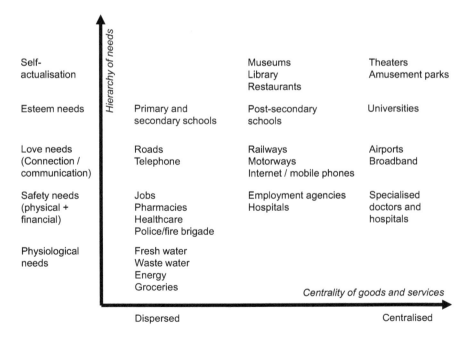

Figure 8.1 Two-dimensional ranking of services of general interest and Maslow's hierarchy of needs

Source: Modified after Milbert et al. (2013).

a starting point when discussing geographical inequalities vis-à-vis rural, peripheral regions; the accessibility and availability of, for example, welfare services, high-speed trains and airports as well as universities cannot be the same due to differing aggregate demand in 'urban' or 'metropolitan' areas relative to 'rural' or 'peripheral' areas. How disrupting these problems and challenges are on the one (urban) and the other (rural) end of the geographical scope depends on what scale we analyse and where we draw the boundaries between different types of territory (Euclidian/administrative, networked/functional or perceived regions). The problematisation of regional inequalities has usually gone hand in hand with the legitimisation and/or de-legitimisation of some political powers, especially when 'justice' is related to issues such as regional development, production and accessibility of welfare services and infrastructure, as well as public participation. The marketisation of welfare services and infrastructure as well as public sector retrenchment in advanced economies hit weak regions the hardest. The market cannot make profit in peripheral, remote and lagging regions; the 'third sector' cannot accumulate sufficient money for investments and hence is unable to meet the needs of the population. If the state cannot level out regional disparities, who will? It means that we will have to accept regional inequalities, but how much and what kind of inequalities are acceptable is a delicate question for future research to address.

Note

1 The first economic long cycle was built around steel and steam (from late 18th century to mid-19th century), the second was electricity and chemistry (mid-19th century to ca. 1930), a third was built around motorism and mass-consumption (ca. 1930 to ca. 1975) and the fourth—the contemporary one—is built on the microchips and biochemistry (since 1975) (Schön, 2006). A qualified guess is that the present economic long cycle will be replaced by one building its economic activity on AI and nanotechnology.

References

Andersson, E.K., and Malmberg, B. (2018). Segregation and the Effects of Adolescent Residential Context on Poverty Risks and Early Income Career: A Study of the Swedish 1980 Cohort. *Urban Studies*, 55(2), 365–383. http://doi.org/10.1177/0042098016643915

Barca, F. (2009). *An Agenda for a Reformed Cohesion Policy: A Place-Based Approach to Meeting European Union Challenges and Expectations*. Independent Report Prepared at the Request of Danuta Hübner, Commissioner for Regional Policy. Brussels: DG Regio.

Barr, N. (1998). *The Economics of the Welfare State*. Oxford: Oxford University Press.

Bell, D., and Davoudi, S. (2016). Understanding Justice and Fairness in and of the City. In S. Davoudi and D. Bell (Eds.), *Justice and Fairness in the City*. Bristol: Policy Press.

Böhm, M., Gregory, T., Qendrai, P., and Siegel, C. (2021). Demographic Change and Regional Labour Markets. *Oxford Review of Economic Policy*, 37(1), 113–131. http://doi.org/10.1093/oxrep/graa063

Borges, L., Humer, A., and Smith, C.J. (2015). Europe's Possible SGI Futures: Territorial Settings and Potential Policy Paths. In H. Fassmann, D. Rauhut, E.M. da Costa and A. Humer (eds), *Services of General Interest and Territorial Cohesion: European Perspectives and National Insights* (pp. 123–146). Göttingen: V&R Unipress.

Branco, P., and Marques da Costa, E. (2023). Social Services of General Interest in European Regions: A Look at 'Territorial Cohesion' in the Economic Crisis Context. *European Journal of Spatial Development*, 20(1). http://doi.org/10.5281/zenodo.7684275

Breuer, I.M., and Milbert, A. (2013). Services of General Interest Indicators: Methodological Aspects and Findings. *Europe XXI*, 23, 29–46.

Broström, L., and Rauhut, D. (2018). Policy Changes and Implications on Poverty in Sweden 1991–2014. In D. Rauhut and N. Hatti (eds), *Poverty, Politics and the Poverty of Politics* (pp. 99–124). New Delhi: B.R. Publishing.

Brovarone, E.V., and Grunfelder, J. (2021). Accessibility Challenges in European Rural Regions. In E.V. Brovarone, G. Cotella and L. Staricco (eds), *Rural Accessibility in European Regions* (pp. 21–38). London: Routledge.

Capello, R., Caragliu, A., and Fratesi, U. (2015). Spatial Heterogeneity in the Costs of the Economic Crisis in Europe: Are Cities Sources of Regional Resilience? *Journal of Economic Geography*, 15(5), 951–972. http://doi.org/10.1093/jeg/lbu053

CEC (2013). *Commission Staff Working Document*. Progress on 'GDP and Beyond' Actions. Brussels, 2.8.2013, SWD(2013) 303 final, Volume 1 of 2.

CEC (2021). *Long-Term Vision for Rural Areas: For Stronger, Connected, Resilient, Prosperous EU Rural Areas*. https://rural-vision.europa.eu/index_en. Downloaded 18 July 2023.

CEC (2022). *Cohesion in Europe Towards 2050*. Eighth Report on Economic, Social and Territorial Cohesion. Luxembourg: Publications Office of the European Union.

Christophers, B. (2015). Geographies of Finance II: Crisis, Space and Political-Economic Transformation. *Progress in Human Geography*, 39(2), 205–213. http://doi.org/10.1177/0309132513514343

Clifton, J., Díaz-Fuentes, D., and Fernández-Gutiérrez, M. (2015). Public Infrastructure Services in the European Union: Challenges for Territorial Cohesion. *Regional Studies*, 50(2), 358–373. http://doi.org/10.1080/00343404.2015.1044958

Cörvers, F., and Mayhew, K. (2021). Regional Inequalities: Causes and Cures. *Oxford Review of Economic Policy*, 37(1), 1–16. http://doi.org/10.1093/oxrep/graa067

de Vries, M., and Nemec, J. (2013). Public Sector Reform: An Overview of Recent Literature and Research on NPM and Alternative Paths. *International Journal of Public Sector Management*, 26(1), 4–16. http://doi.org/10.1108/09513551311293408

Dijkstra, L., Garcilazo, E., and McCann, P. (2015). The Effects of the Global Financial Crisis on European Regions and Cities. *Journal of Economic Geography*, 15(5), 935–949. http://doi.org/10.1093/jeg/lbv032

Duranton, G., and Puga, D. (2001). Nursery Cities: Urban Diversity, Process Innovation, and the Life Cycle of Products. *American Economic Review*, 91(5), 1454–1477. www.jstor.org/stable/2677933

Ek, R., and Rauhut, D. (2023). Regional Development, Power and Topological Reach: To Reach Out or Fold In? *Regional Studies*. EPub ahead of print. http://doi.org/10.1080/00343404.2023.2231504

Essletzbichler, J., Disslbacher, F., and Moser, M. (2018). The Victims of Neoliberal Globalisation and the Rise of the Populist Vote: A Comparative Analysis of Three Recent Electoral Decisions. *Cambridge Journal of Regions, Economy and Society*, 11(1), 73–94. http://doi.org/10.1093/cjres/rsx025

Faludi, A., Stead, D., and Humer, A. (2015). Conclusions: Services of General Interest, Territorial Cohesion and Competitiveness in Europe. In H. Fassmann, D. Rauhut, E.M. da Costa and A. Humer (eds), *Services of General Interest and Territorial Cohesion: European Perspectives and National Insights* (pp. 259–267). Göttingen: V&R Unipress.

Foss, O., Johansen, S., Johansson, M., and Svensson, B. (2004). Regionalpolitikk ved et vegskille: Går Sverige og Norge i forskjellige retninger? In R. Amdam and O. Bukve (eds), *Det regionalpolitiska regimeskiftet—tilfellet Noreg* (pp. 107–128). Trondheim: Tapir Akademisk Forlag.

Fratesi, U., and Rodríguez-Pose, A. (2016). The Crisis and Regional Employment in Europe: What Role for Sheltered Economies? *Cambridge Journal of Regions, Economy and Society*, 9(1), 33–57. http://doi.org/10.1093/cjres/rsv032

Fujita, M., Krugman, P., and Venables, A.J. (1999). *The Spatial Economy; Cities, Regions, and International Trade*. Cambridge, MA: MIT Press.

German Presidency (2020). *Territorial Agenda 2030*. Agreed on at the Informal Meeting of Ministers Responsible for Spatial Planning, Territorial Development and/or Territorial Cohesion 1 December 2020, Germany.

Glaeser, E.L. (2011). *The Triumph of the City: How Our Greatest Invention Makes Us Richer, Smarter, Greener, Healthier, and Happier*. London: Penguin.

Gomes, S., Lopes, J.M., Ferreira, L., and Oliveria, J. (2022). Science and Technology Parks: Opening the Pandora's Box of Regional Development. *Journal of Knowledge Economy*. https://doi.org/10.1007/s13132-022-00995-y

Gruber, E., Humer, A., and Fassmann, H. (2013). *Case Study Report: Austria, Annex 6a to SeGI Scientific Report*. Luxembourg: ESPON.

Gruber, E., Rauhut, D., and Humer, A. (2019). Territorial Cohesion under Pressure? Welfare Policy and Planning Responses in Austrian and Swedish Peripheries. *Papers in Regional Science*, 98(1), 115–132. http://doi.org/10.1111/pirs.12344

Gyuris, F. (2014). *The Political Discourse of Spatial Disparities. Geographical Inequalities Between Science and Propaganda*. Heidelberg: Springer Verlag.

Hadjimichalis, C. (2011). Uneven Geographical Development and Socio-Spatial Justice and Solidarity: European Regions after the 2009 Financial Crisis. *European Urban and Regional Studies*, 18(3), 254–274. http://doi.org/10.1177/0969776411404873

Hanell, T., Makkonen, T., and Rauhut, D. (2022). Geographies of Well-Being and Quality of Life. *Social Indicators Research*, 164(3), 1–10. http://doi.org/10.1007/s11205-022-02966-x

Humer, A. (2014). Researching Social Services of General Interest: An Analytical Framework Derived from Underlying Policy Systems. *European Spatial Research and Policy*, 21(1), 65–82. http://doi.org/10.2478/esrp-2014-0006

Humer, A., and Palma, P. (2013). The Provision of Services of General Interest in Europe: Regional Indices and Types Explained by Socio-Economic and Territorial Conditions. *Europa XXI*, 23, 85–104.

Humer, A., Rauhut, D., and Sielker, F. (2021). Unsettled Questions of Disintegration, Discontent and Discretion. In D. Rauhut, F. Sielker and A. Humer (eds), *The EU's Cohesion Policy and Spatial Governance: Territorial, Economic and Social Challenges* (pp. 272–275). Cheltenham: Edward Elgar.

Iammarino, S., Rodríguez-Pose, A., and Storper, M. (2019). Regional Inequality in Europe: Evidence, Theory and Policy Implications. *Journal of Economic Geography*, 19(2), 273–298. http://doi.org/10.1093/jeg/lby021

Johansson, M. (1996). Residence, Employment and Migration in Four Types of Localities 1972–1992. In M. Johansson and L.O. Persson (eds), *Extending the Reach. Essays on Differing Mobility Patterns in Sweden* (pp. 69–95). Stockholm: Fritzes.

Knox, P.L., and Marston, S.A. (1992). *Human Geography*. Upper Saddle River, NJ: Pearson.

Kompil, M., Jacobs-Crisioni, C., Dijkstra, L., and Lavalle, C. (2019). Mapping Accessibility to Generic Services in Europe: A Market-Potential Based Approach. *Sustainable Cities and Societies*, 47, 101372. http://doi.org/10.1016/j.scs.2018.11.047

Krugman, P. (1991). *Geography and Trade*. Cambridge, MA: MIT Press.

Kurihara, K.K. (1970). Social Overhead Capital and Balanced Economic Growth. *Social and Economic Studies*, 19(3), 398–405. www.jstor.org/stable/27856439

Lobao, L., Gray, M., Cox, K., and Kitson, M. (2018). The Shrinking State? Understanding the Assault on the Public Sector. *Cambridge Journal of Regions, Economy and Society*, 11(3), 389–408. http://doi.org/10.1093/cjres/rsy026

Marques, P., and Barberá-Tomás, D. (2022). Innovating But Still Poor: The Challenges of Regional Development in Regions with Mature Industries. *Transactions of the Institute of British Geographers*, 47, 440–454. https://doi.org/10.1111/tran.12507

Marques da Costa, E., Palma, P., and Marques da Costa, N. (2015). Regional Disparities of SGI Provision. In H. Fassmann, D. Rauhut, E.M. da Costa and A. Humer (eds), *Services of*

General Interest and Territorial Cohesion: European Perspectives and National Insights (pp. 91–121). Göttingen: V&R Unipress.

Mattila, H., Purkarthofer, E., and Humer, A. (2023). Governing 'Places that Don't Matter'—Agonistic Spatial Planning Practices in Finnish Peripheral Regions. *Territory, Politics, Governance*, 11(4), 813–832. http://doi.org/10.1080/21622671.2020.1857824

Milbert, A., Breuer, I.M., Rosik, P., Stepniak, M., and Velasco, X. (2013). Accessibility to Services of General Interest in Europe. *Romanian Journal of Regional Science*, 7(special issue), 37–65.

Mitze, T., Dall Schmidt, T., Rauhut, D., and Kangasharju, A. (2018). Ageing Shocks and Short-Run Regional Labour Market Dynamics in a Spatial Panel VAR Approach. *Applied Economics*, 50(8), 870–890. http://doi.org/10.1080/00036846.2017.1346360

Myrdal, G. (1957). *Economic Theory and Underdeveloped Regions*. London: Duckworth.

Nagy, J.A., and Benedek, J. (2021). Can EU Cohesion Policy Fight Peripheralization? In D. Rauhut, F. Sielker and A. Humer (eds), *The EU's Cohesion Policy and Spatial Governance: Territorial, Economic and Social Challenges* (pp. 142–155). Cheltenham: Edward Elgar.

OECD (2022). *Regions and Cities at a Glance: A Country Note on Portugal*. Paris: OECD.

Powell, M., and Boyne, G. (2001). The Spatial Strategy of Equality and the Spatial Division of Welfare. *Social Policy and Administration*, 33(2), 181–194.

Rauhut, D. (2019). A Rawls-Sen Approach to Spatial Injustice. *Social Science Spectrum*, 4(3), 109–122.

Rauhut, D., and Costa, N. (2021). What Regions Benefit from the Post-Crisis Cohesion Policy? Evidence from a Territorial Cohesion Development Index. In D. Rauhut, F. Sielker and A. Humer (eds), *The EU's Cohesion Policy and Spatial Governance: Territorial, Economic and Social Challenges* (pp. 185–198). Cheltenham: Edward Elgar.

Rauhut, D., and Humer, A. (2020). EU and Spatial Economic Growth: Trajectories in Economic Thought. *European Planning Studies*, 28(11), 2116–2133. http://doi.org/10.1080/09654313.2019.1709416

Rauhut, D., and Kahila, P. (2008). *The Regional Welfare Burden in the Nordic Countries* (Nordregio Working Paper 2008:6).

Rauhut, D., and Komornicki, T. (2015). *The Challenge of SGI Provision in Rural Areas*. A Paper Prepared for the 55th European Congress of Regional Science International, 25–29 August 2015 in Lisbon, Portugal.

Rauhut, D., and Smith, C.J. (2018). *Spatial Challenges to Universal Health Care in Finland and Sweden*. A Paper Prepared for the Regional Studies Association's Annual Conference 2018, 3–6 June 2018 in Lugano, Switzerland.

Region Dalarna (2022). *Smart specialisering i Dalarna—en analys av nuläget i Dalarnas näringsliv*. www.regiondalarna.se/contentassets/6b34eb5b3d1b4fe9b6ed7f3bd284cc85/smart-specialisering-kunskapsunderlag-jan-2022.pdf. Downloaded 13 February 2023.

Rijo, B., Alves, O., Garcia, B., Lourinho, G., Brito, P., and Nobre, C. (2023). Technical and Market Analysis of Biomass Gasification: Case Study in Alentejo, Portugal. *Journal of Cleaner Production*, 417, 138007. https://doi.org/10.1016/j.jclepro.2023.138007

Rodríguez-Pose, A. (2018). The Revenge of the Places that Don't Matter (and What to Do about It). *Cambridge Journal of Regions, Economy and Society*, 11(1), 189–209. http://doi.org/10.1093/cjres/rsx024

Santos, A., Neto, P., and Serrano, M.M. (2016). A Long-Term Mortality Analysis of Subsidized Firms in Rural Areas: An Empirical Study in the Portuguese Alentejo Region. *Euroasian Economic Review*, 6, 125–151. https://doi.org/10.1007/s40822-015-0035-4

Sarkar, S., Bilau, J.J., and Basílio, M. (2021). Do Anchor Infrastructures Matter for Regional Smart Specialisation Strategy? The Case of Alentejo. *Regional Studies*, 55(3), 453–464. https://doi.org/10.1080/00343404.2020.1722804

Schön, L. (2006). *Tankar om cykler*. Stockholm: SNS.

Schön, L. (2012). *An Economic History of Modern Sweden*. London: Routledge.

Scott, A., and Storper, M. (2003). Regions, Globalization, Development. *Regional Studies*, 37(6–7), 579–593. http://doi.org/10.1080/0034340032000108697a

Sen, A. (1993). Capability and Well-Being. In M. Nussbaum and A. Sen (eds), *The Quality of Life* (pp. 30–53). Oxford: Clarendon Press.

Sen, A. (1998). *Development as Freedom*. Oxford: Oxford University Press.

Serdoura, F., Moreira, G., and Almeida, H. (2009). Tourism Development in Alentejo Region: A Vehicle for Cultural and Territorial Cohesion. In S. Lehman, H. Al Waer and J. Al-Qawasmi (eds), *Sustainable Architecture and Urban Development*, vol. 2 (pp. 619–633). Amman: CSAAR Press.

Stepniak, M., and Rosik, P. (2013). Accessibility of Services of General Interest at Regional Scale. *Europe XXI*, 23, 131–148.

Storper, M. (2018). Separate Worlds? Explaining the Current Wave of Regional Economic Polarisation. *Journal of Economic Geography*, 18(2), 247–270. http://doi.org/10.1093/jeg/lby011

Swiatek, R., Komornicki, T., and Silka, P. (2013). Services of General Interest: Empirical Evidence from Case Studies of the SeGI Project. *Europa XXI*, 23, 105–130.

Vanthillo, T., Beckers, J., and Verhetsel, A. (2021). The Changing Nature of Regional Policy in Europe. *Oxford Review of Economic Policy*, 37(1), 201–220. http://doi.org/10.1093/oxrep/graa058

Vedrine, L., and Le Gallo, J. (2021). Does EU Cohesion Policy Affect Territorial Inequalities and Regional Development? In D. Rauhut, F. Sielker and A. Humer (eds), *The EU's Cohesion Policy and Spatial Governance: Territorial, Economic and Social Challenges* (pp. 156–170). Cheltenham: Edward Elgar.

Williamson, J.W. (1965). Regional Inequality and the Process of National Development: A Description of the Patterns. *Economic Development and Cultural Change*, 13(4, pt 2), 1–84. www.jstor.org/stable/1152097

9 Housing and Inequality

The Case of Portugal

Sónia Alves and Pedro Guimarães

9.1 Introduction

Numerous definitions of inequality exist, but at its core inequality refers to 'the phenomenon of unequal and/or unjust distribution of resources and opportunities among members of a given society' (Koh, 2020, p. 269), limiting the possibility for disadvantaged individuals or groups to benefit from certain opportunities in life (health, education, housing, etc.).

In the fields of urban studies, sociology and geography, the study of inequality has been a constant, giving rise to a vast research programme that has developed various new approaches. Inspired by Milanovic (2012), we can identify three types of approach.

In one type of approach, *inequality is examined as a dependent variable*. This is, for example, the case for studies that use neo-Marxist theory to explain inequality as the consequence of class exploitation and class struggle due to the imperatives of capitalist accumulation (Linklater, 1990; Piketty, 2014), or structural–functionalist theory to explain inequality as the outcome of public administration that leads to processes of social stratification and social reproduction (Merton, 1968; Fournier, 2013).

In other approaches, *inequality appears as a variable that explains other social, economic and urban phenomena*. In these approaches, inequality is seen as a variable that either stimulates or prevents some desirable economic outcome, such as economic growth, collective efficiency and so on. Hamnett (2019), for example, claims that educational attainment and economic development within a society are not random but patterned and constrained by the impact that poverty and inequality have on the access of both youth and adults to the education system. 'People who live in nice houses in wealthy areas are likely to be healthier and have better education levels' he argues (p. 246).

Finally, there is a third way in which inequality enters the realm of social scientists. That is when they *raise and address ethical issues related to inequality and social or territorial injustice*. In this type of approach, researchers problematise the role that public policies have played (through the distribution of resources such as income or housing) in producing inequality, pointing out that this has limited the prospects of past, current and future generations. Alves (2017b) makes the point that discriminatory attitudes towards the Gypsy/Roma have delayed this population's ability to settle and confined them to the least desirable social/public rented housing, far from the privileged white neighborhoods with better connections to the labour market. Meanwhile, Van Baar (2011) claims that the nomad theory, which argues that Gypsy/Roma are 'nomads' who can only survive in segregated 'camps' (Van Baar, 2011, p. 207), isolating them from mainstream society, has helped marginalise or even dehumanise this population, limiting their opportunities for social integration and social mobility.

Human geographers' writing on inequality has been rich and varied. Many have been concerned with the effects of capitalist state and market intervention on different stages of urbanisation, with a focus on urban decline or growth, as well as how the characteristics of different types of settlements at each moment in time (in terms of demographics, housing quality, and access to services) is echoed in new dimensions of inequality and social injustice (Hopkins, 2021).

In the early decades of the 20th century, scholars from the Chicago School tried to explain the urban distribution of social structures (Park, 1915; Park and Burgess, 1925), noting, as emphasised by Pacione (2005), that this distribution was explained not just by spatial factors—such as where a particular group is located in the present—but also by temporal ones—such as how long this particular group has been located in this area.

With the rise of radical political-economic inquiry in human geography during the 1970s and 1980s, growing attention was directed to the rights to the city and the just city (Harvey, 2012; Fainstein, 2014). Already in 1973, Harvey, in 'Social Justice and the City', pointed out that while the Chicago school (see Park and Burgess, 1925) drew heavily on urban geography's developments of location theory and central place theory and 'elaborated an interpretation of city form in ecological terms'—claiming that the competition for land and urban resources between social groups led to the division of urban spaces into distinctive ecological niches (identifying, e.g., the concentration of low-income groups and various ethnic groups within particular sectors of the city)—they were mainly concerned 'to find out who ended up where and what conditions were like when they got there' (Harvey, 1973, p. 131), and this did not offer an explanation for the real constitutive forces that shaped urban inequality. Harvey (1973) also makes the point that several decades before the Chicago school, Engels had shown greater interpretative capacity when he sought to explain the patterns and living conditions of low-income groups in Manchester, emphasising the causal mechanisms that gave rise to them. They resulted from the exploitation of the stronger and more powerful few who '[tread] the weaker under foot . . . while to the weak many, the poor, scarcely a bare existence remains' (Harvey, 1973, p. 134).

It is from this more critical and reflexive perspective that Harvey challenges us to interpret the spatial structure of cities from a more economic and cultural point of view—one that takes into consideration, for example, how urban land use is determined through a process of competitive bidding, and how this process pushes low-income groups towards smaller, poorer-quality housing in less attractive areas: 'when the poor group is forced to live on high rent land, the only way they can adjust to this is to save on the quantity of space they consume and crowd into a very small area' (Harvey, 1973).

The relationship among capital, the proletarian class and the right to housing and the city is even more complex because, as Dear and Scott (1981) discuss, the proletarian class is composed of different social groups, among which the capital–labour relation may be different, and the state often takes on the role of a regulator, a moderator, whose intervention in society aims at 'the protection and reproduction of the social structure', supporting the maintenance and reproduction of existing inequalities in order—allegedly—to maintain its socio-economic efficiency.

9.2 Theoretical and Methodological Considerations

We know that the dimensions of inequality are intertwined, intersect (e.g. racial discrimination in the employment and housing markets) and are related to geography, as places differ in terms of the qualities and opportunities that they offer to individuals (Andersen et al., 2020).

We also know that inequality—that is the unequal and/or unjust distribution of resources and opportunities among members of a given society and across neighborhoods (communities)—is shaped by public policy. Even though, as Malpass and Murie (1999) emphasise,

> [T]he word 'policy' is notoriously difficult to define with any precision . . . . A starting point is to say that it generally implies action in relation to a particular problem which it is intended to solve or ameliorate in pursuit of some objective.
>
> (p. 5)

Policy, therefore, involves the formulation of a problem, policy goals and policy tools, which Bali et al. (2021) describe as the set of techniques and means by which governing authorities exercise their power to ensure that policy objectives are achieved. Bali et al. (2021) distinguish substantive tools that are used to directly affect policy outcomes (such as regulations and subsidies) from procedural tools that are used to alter aspects of a government's own workings and policymaking processes (Bali et al., 2021).

Taking these two facts into consideration, we are able to formulate a working hypothesis for this chapter: that social and spatial inequalities are the result both of a succession of political, social and economic conjunctures and of policy measures designed and implemented to modify the quality, quantity, price, and ownership of housing—measures that shape the way housing is produced and consumed.

Three specific goals guide our empirical research on the specific case of Portugal:

1) To detect contradictions between the scope and content of housing policy, on the one hand, and housing needs, on the other.
2) To analyse the effect of different generations of housing policy on inequality, distinguishing between policies that construct the idea of housing: (i) as an economic good subject to market mechanisms—which gives rise to policies that mostly respond to the demand of a population that can afford

it; (ii) as a social right—which gives rise to policies that mostly aim to support groups that have limited economic, social or cultural resources (such as low- and middle-income families, young people, immigrants, the elderly and so on).
3) To show how housing policy both reflects and generates social inequality, trying to identify the key causal mechanisms that have given rise to inequality in the construction of housing policies.

Even though geographers have addressed questions of inequality at a finer spatial scale—for example in studies of residential segregation and neighbourhood development—this is not the case with this chapter. Instead, our aim is to problematise choices made at the level of policy design in a country where insufficient attention has been paid to ex-ante, ongoing and ex-post evaluation (Alves, 2017a). The lack of systematic data collection by local and central authorities over time—particularly about volume of investment, the form this investment takes and its impacts—complicates the analysis.

Methodologically, our research uses a constructionist/interpretivist approach, complemented by a historical perspective, to provide an account of inequality as the outcome of current and earlier public policies.

We will develop a historical overview of the main housing policies in Portugal based on two main sources of information: documentary sources such as legislation and written policy texts, which will allow us to uncover the reasons behind the development of housing policies—an essential part of the process tracing method; and statistical and administrative data, which will allow us to reveal the political rationality of policies.

To do so, we will adopt the process tracing method as presented by Palier and Trampusch (2018), according to whom a given context or outcome is the result of a sequence of events or actions. Our research will trace the main events/milestones that have led to the current housing context in Portugal. According to Trampusch and Palier (2016), the process tracing method can be either deductive or inductive. We will use an inductive approach to identify the social mechanisms that give rise to social inequalities in access to housing, looking in particular for two kinds of event, as discussed by Bengtsson and Ruonavaara (2017, p. 52): (1) *critical junctures*: crucial moments, such as crises, at which decisions are taken that decisively influence the path followed and make it difficult to annul or minimise the resulting effects; (2) *political focal points*: 'decision points, where the restricting role of dominant institutions is made explicit'. In addition to identifying these two types of event, we will also adopt Somerville and Bengtsson's (2002) concept of 'contextualised rational action'. That is actors' actions stem in part from the goals they intend to achieve but are 'largely shaped by the situation in which they find themselves' (Bengtsson and Ruonavaara, 2017, p. 51). Moreover, for these authors, we need to recognise the temporal dimension of action. For instance, actions taken at a certain point in time are, to some extent, a consequence of a prior decision and, simultaneously, will set some basis for a decision yet to be taken.

9.3 Housing as a Key Structural Domain of Inequality and Exclusion

Hamnett (2019) claims that 'it is impossible to look at urban inequality without analysing the role of government policy' (p. 250). James et al. (2022), in a systematic review of the literature on housing inequality, note that over a quarter of papers frame housing inequality as an unintentional product of public policy, that is 'the way housing issues are problematized, represented and operationalized in public policy processes such as, agenda-setting and issue framing, and policy implementation' (p. 9).

As with other types of social policy (e.g. education, healthcare, social protection), housing policy reflects the ideological choices of those who govern under specific socio-economic and political circumstances. As theorised by Kemeny (1992), ideologies are not merely abstract systems of thought but also provide motivation for action and can channel that action into the creation or legitimation of various combinations of state intervention. Kemeny distinguishes two philosophies in housing policy, in terms of their policy aims and objectives, stressing how they help shape the structure of inequality. In one philosophy, it is argued that the state should take direct responsibility for providing rental housing to the neediest and, to this end, should organise non-profit rental housing in the form of a state or local monopoly. In the other philosophy, it is argued that the state should not itself be a major provider or, if it is, then access to such housing—often provided on a non-profit basis—should not be limited to needy families but should be accessible in a more universal way to families from different socio-economic backgrounds.

Before moving on to our empirical analysis, four preliminary points should be noted. First, policy goals and tools are multi-level in nature. As Howlett emphasises (2009), policy goals and means are formulated and implemented at different levels of government and are co-dependent. For example, at a higher level, the overarching policy regime and governance models set the outside boundaries for the lower level of policy objectives and policy targets. From this perspective, a policy regime preference for a market governance model at the national level, with certain corresponding policy targets and policy tools (which are often set in legislation), restricts the range of choices available for policy design and implementation at the local level.

Second, housing inequality itself is a multi-layered phenomenon. It is often related to wealth inequality (think about the appreciation of property values for homeowners versus skyrocketing housing prices and the problem of housing unaffordability for tenants), to issues of economic globalisation and—as James et al. (2022) emphasise—to: (1) the failure of governments, regulators and markets to adopt fair policies; (2) the tension between home understood as a social right and a place to live, and housing seen as an investment and financial asset.

Third, the literature on inequality shows that it is a structural phenomenon characteristic of Portuguese society. Inequalities of access are present in the social protection system and in all other public sector services (e.g. healthcare), since protection covers the various groups in society differently, leaving some of them less protected or not protected at all (Alves, 2010). Allen et al. (2004, pp. 8–10) describe Southern European policies as suffering from a deficit of stateness in the sense that state regulation of land use and social protection are weak. Several studies (Srinivas, 2008) on social protection argue that the welfare state has been shaped by the dualism between protected and unprotected workers (including the precarious, long-term unemployed, etc.), noting that the labour market and social protection are together responsible for failing to protect a wide range of people (especially young people, women with difficulties in accessing employment, and people with disabilities).

Fourth, in a country where the economy has been based on construction, real estate and tourism, there are major inequalities in access to, and the condition of, housing (in terms of its cost and quality). In this chapter, we argue that the inequality of access to housing and housing conditions is the result of a historical trajectory of social inequalities—a trajectory that originates in social, economic and political spheres that are beyond the control of the population most affected by the phenomenon.

9.4 Housing Inequality in Portugal

The housing policies we discuss in this chapter date back to as far as roughly a century ago. A set of critical junctures appear to have been fundamental in the formulation of new policies and implicit political rationales, as Figure 9.1 show us. Our analysis begins in 1910, with the beginning of the 1st Republic. The second critical juncture occurred in 1933, when an authoritarian regime began to administer the country. The end of WWII marks the third critical juncture in a period that extends to 1974, when the carnation revolution—which corresponds to the fourth critical juncture—occurred. The entry into the EEC is the fifth crucial moment we identified. The world financial crisis of 2008 and the regulation of the New Generation of Housing policies in 2018 that has placed the issue of housing again on the national political agenda are identified as the sixth and seventh critical junctures. We should add that, despite the fact that critical junctures are specific moments temporally defined as lasting a number of days or years, their effects are wider. As such, the solutions adopted in response to them extend until the next critical juncture occurs.

The solutions adopted during each of these critical junctures are further analysed and discussed later. Although apparently obvious, this is particularly relevant when analysing the housing sector, as housing shortages or specific housing conditions in a given period of time will strongly impact the actions taken foremost.

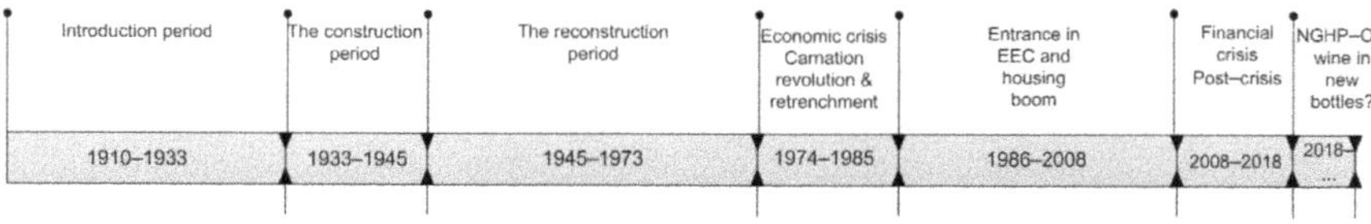

Introduction period	The construction period	The reconstruction period	Economic crisis Carnation revolution & retrenchment	Entrance in EEC and housing boom	Financial crisis Post–crisis	NGHP–Old wine in new bottles?
1910–1933	1933–1945	1945–1973	1974–1985	1986–2008	2008–2018	2018–

Figure 9.1 Temporal segmentation of housing policies in Portugal

9.5 The Introduction Period 1910–1933

During this period, housing has become a political issue. Political interventions are made in the housing market during the 1st Republic (1910–1926), but there is no significant state support for intervention. The priority given to housing as a political issue begins in the last years of this period, with the focus on planning new cities and expanding existing cities.

The institutionalisation of housing policies occurred in Portugal during the 'Estado Novo' (New State), a right-wing authoritarian regime that ruled Portugal for 41 years (1933–1974). The regime implemented a statist development strategy based on a significant programme of public works, including housebuilding.

The 1930s was a period of intense legislative activity in the fields of planning and land policy. The Expropriation Act (1933) allowed for the compulsory purchase of land at existing use value, and the 1934 Town Planning Act established the legal obligation for local authorities with over 2,500 inhabitants to make plans for their consolidated urban areas and contiguous areas of expansion. In cities where the Urbanization Plan was executed (even though seldom officially approved), it guided new housing schemes, general constructions and protected areas of architectural and urban value.

9.6 The Construction Period 1933–1945

During this period, a housing system was developed that supported the very creation of the territorial planning system aimed at expanding cities. In the 1933–1945 period, there was a marked ideological association between the house/yard model (detached houses with gardens) and the affordable-rent model (build-to-rent), which resulted in the exclusion of low-income populations from accessing the housing that was built with public subsidies.

In this period, the main concern of housing policy was both to counteract housing shortages by boosting housing production as much as possible and to support the construction of housing for the upper-middle class (those with better jobs and income), who were regime's main supporters. The *Estado Novo* proclaimed that ownership was the ideal tenure for achieving social stability and, inspired by the ideas of the garden city movements, that the neighbourhood was the basic unit of planning. The main housing programme from this period, the *Programa de Casas Económicas* [Low-cost Houses Programme] (1935–1965), promoted the construction of detached houses with gardens for civil servants and the most skilled segments of the working class. The houses were paid for through monthly rents over a period of 25 years, eventually becoming the property of the family. The production of housing during this period resulted from a strong alliance among banks, employee pension funds, local authorities and real estate companies, under strong central government leadership. The main housing programme not only played an important role in economic dynamics but also became a step on the way to homeownership for working- and middle-class households.

9.7 The Reconstruction Period 1945–1973

After World War II, the emphasis in many countries was put on reconstruction. Although Portugal had not been destroyed, it still had a major housing shortage because of a sharp increase in the population in the main cities due to the rural exodus. Internationally, there was a consensus across the political spectrum in favour of housing construction initiatives and tenants' support—a consensus that, according to Piketty (2014), would not have been possible under different circumstances and one that produced equalising results (a reduction in inequalities). In Portugal, the aim was to promote access to rental housing for income groups that until then had been unable to find homes either through the free market or in state-subsidised housing. Two programmes are worth mentioning. The first is the 1959–1969 *Programa de Renda Económica* [Low-cost Rental Housing Programme], which promoted the construction of three-storey buildings and was created to attract the accumulated investment of the Federation of Pension Funds. The second is the 1945 *Programa Casas dos Pobres* [Poor People's Houses Programme]. Its houses were built and managed by municipalities for the lowest paid workers. However, the scale of this intervention was very small in view of the magnitude of the problem.

Because the large majority of low-income households in Portugal were not able to afford or access these houses, they turned to the illegal self-built home markets (Barata-Salgueiro, 1977). A lack of enforcement and a general unwillingness to find solutions to the problem led to widespread abuse (illegal construction). Cities grew through the illegal genesis of urban areas. These illegal constructions expanded into the suburbs and throughout the inner city (Teixeira, 1992). In 1966, there was an estimated housing shortage of 500,000 dwellings. This led to the creation, in 1969, of the *Fundo de Fomento da Habitação* [Housing Development Fund], an agency which directly promoted not only housing but also the development of mono-functional housing projects that did not include public services, transportation or other amenities and fostered segregation (Branco and Alves, 2020).

9.8 Economic Crisis. Carnation Revolution and Retrenchment 1974–1985

In April 1974, the Carnation Revolution put an end to the dictatorial regime that had ruled the country for 41 years with disappointing results in terms of wages, education, life expectancy, rates of poverty and housing conditions (Branco and Alves, 2020) and marked the introduction of democracy in Portugal.

As many families had to rely on self-building, a large percentage of permanent housing in Portugal of 1970s still had no basic facilities, such as running water (47 percent), a bath or shower (32 percent) or sewers (60 percent of the total housing stock). The development of the welfare state in Portugal in the 1970s occurred during a very adverse international macroeconomic and ideological period, characterised by the shift from the previous post-war consensus (of Keynesian politics) to a neoliberal context of strong confidence in the market. The acute shortage of decent, affordable housing was amplified by internal and international migration flows related to a large rural exodus and the movement of hundreds of thousands of refugees and '*retornados*' (returnees) fleeing from liberation struggles in the former Portuguese colonies (Alves, 2017a).

9.9 Portugal's Entrance Into the EEC and the Housing Boom 1986–2005

This period is marked by Portugal's accession to the European Economic Community in 1986, which was followed by a cycle of continuous growth and low unemployment rates (Portugal had one of the lowest unemployment rates in the EU in 1991, around 4 percent), which saw real wages and the purchasing power of households increase. In a context of deregulation of the credit market and low interest rates, a decade of centre-right governments promoted homeownership through a disproportionate investment in subsidised loans/mortgages and tax deductions. Between 1987 and 2011, almost three-quarters of the Portuguese housing budget was spent on subsidising mortgages, only 8.7 percent on subsidising rent and 17.9 percent on direct housing provision.

Between 1992 and 2002, the number of homes built annually for family housing rose from 52,000 to a record 126,000, while the number of urban buildings sold rose from 166,000 to over 254,000. New building was mostly directed at owner-occupants (Alves, 2022). The volume of mortgage loans grew from €5 billion in 1990 to €104 billion in 2008—an increase of more than 2,000 percent in national spending, while the increase in population was only 10 percent. Approximately half of all mortgage contracts signed in that period were supported by the state through subsidised mortgage loans and tax deductions (Allegra et al., 2020). In 2011, owner-occupancy became the dominant tenure in Portugal by far, accounting for 76 percent of the total housing stock, and covering all strata of the population, but mostly those with middle-to-high incomes (Garha and Azevedo, 2021).

It is important to note that in the 1990s, many small construction companies were working in the informal market. This was a period of rapid suburbanisation, facilitated by a first generation of municipal comprehensive plans, in which the supply of public housing remained low. Many families that could not access loans had to rely on an informal housing sector and self-construction, with support from their family/community, in most cases without the prior construction of infrastructure or state authorisation. Many cities saw the rapid expansion of shanty towns and squatter settlements in the suburbs.

In terms of housing policy, there was a trend in this period towards decentralisation of the state's housing stock to the municipalities and the sale of housing at discount prices to tenants (along the lines of the right-to-buy policies implemented in other countries), which further reduced a public housing stock that was already residual in relation to housing needs.

This was a period generally characterised by (1) an abundance of land for new housebuilding and widely granted construction permissions (even in areas of low demand); (2) a lack of strategic vision with regard to conservation and the enhancement of areas of natural and historic significance and to flood risks; (3) dispersed growth in peripheral areas that later led to cumulative public expenditure on infrastructure and services such as garbage collection, recycling, waste management, water supply, postal services and transportation and (4) narratives that emphasise, in Portugal's semi-peripheral economy, the importance of the construction sector and tourism gains, which, in a context of development planning, favours an increase in the number of seasonal dwellings and vacant dwellings at the expense of securing land for social and affordable housing within market developments, as seen elsewhere (Alves, 2022).

In the 1990s, the national government launched an emergency program of urban clearance (of shanties)—the so-called *Programa Especial de Relojamento* [Special Rehousing Programme] (Allegra et al., 2022). This programme typically built new council housing estates on areas where cheap land was available, displacing slum dwellers to areas in the periphery characterised by a lack of infrastructure and reinforcing the segregation of people along lines of class, income and ethnicity (Branco and Alves, 2020).

9.10 The Management and Retrenchment Period After the 2008 Global Economic and Financial Crisis

The slowdown in the pace of housing licensing and construction started in 2002 when the Portuguese government stopped the interest subsidisation on mortgages for new contracts. It was then reinforced by the economic and financial crisis triggered by the subprime crisis in 2008, which had dramatic effects, leading to the destruction of jobs, higher unemployment rates, wage cuts and so on in Portugal. With the reduction in wages and the rise in unemployment rates, a significant share of households experienced difficulties in repaying their mortgages. The risk of default was particularly high for families at risk of poverty but also for upper-middle-class families facing unexpected situations such as unemployment, divorce, illness, etc. The percentage of households overburdened by housing (i.e. with housing expenses exceeding 40 percent of disposable income) was particularly high among low-income households, who became particularly vulnerable to losing their home.

The global financial crisis also had dramatic impacts on the country's financial situation, as Portugal was in a state of near bankruptcy and had to accede to a programme of economic and financial adjustment imposed by the 'Troika' (the European Commission, the European Central Bank and the International Monetary Fund) and to a package of austerity measures (Allegra et al., 2020).

The economic adjustment programme required a political–ideological reorientation towards: (1) the retraction of the state, namely a reduction of the strong tenant protection that had existed until then, with the introduction of a new landlord–tenant regime that permitted the ending of old contracts for structural works; and (2) the adoption of a pro-growth and pro-market agenda, which involved the introduction of legislative reforms and stimuli in the rehabilitation sector (for more details, see Cocola (2023), Branco and Alves (2020).

Austerity policy also led to a rupture or interruption in the construction trajectory of the social housing system, with government grant funding for social housing no longer available. In this context of austerity, housing policies were mainly made up of tax exemptions or discounts (e.g. tax benefits in special rehabilitation areas that are broadly defined to attract private investment for rehabilitation) and of deregulation and privatisation policies, which even involved the sale of public property as this was seen as the most efficient way to counteract inner-city decline associated with building degradation. Overall, this was an agenda that stimulated the financialisation of housing markets (Canelas et al., 2023) and brought with it the emergence of new social risks.

The impacts of this agenda began to be particularly visible from 2015, when the country offered strong incentives for foreign investment through investor visas (e.g. the golden visa, non-habitual residents' visa). These achieved their objectives by attracting an increasing volume of investment and foreign players to the Portuguese property market, turning certain cities and areas into hotspots for international investment in the process.

However, the increase in demand from foreign investors and immigrants with greater purchasing power, which was associated with an increase in the volume of transactions and housing prices, hampered or prevented access to housing markets especially in areas with high market demand. Those excluded were families in a more precarious situation in the labour and housing markets; the main winners were property-owning families and companies, who saw an unprecedented increase in the value of their real estate assets.

Purchase and rehabilitation were mainly driven by activities and interests linked to the tourism industry. The transformation of the housing stock—in physical terms and in terms of tenures and occupancy—was driven by short-term rental activities that generated higher profitability. Deregulatory policy facilitated gentrification in previously marginalised or declined areas. The tourism industry takes on the role of a key driver of economic growth and the renaissance of historic cities (Montezuma and McGarrigle, 2019) but brings with it the displacement of the working-class people who used to live in these areas.

9.11 A New Generation of Housing Policies (NGHP): 'Old Wine in New Bottles?'

In 2018, after several years of market-oriented strategies and an intensifying housing crisis—which was more manifest in Lisbon, Porto and Algarve where house prices have risen faster (Allegra et al., 2020; Mendes, 2020)—the socialist government launched the so-called New Generation of Housing Policies (NGHP) to address the challenges related to the structural shortages of permanent housing both for the more vulnerable groups and for the middle-class groups. In a context of an increasing share of population overburdened by housing costs and poor housing conditions, the Portuguese government, recognising that 2 percent of public housing within the total housing stock is clearly insufficient to address even the needs of the most deprived and at risk of social exclusion, set the political ambition of increasing the proportion of publicly subsidised housing from 2 percent to 5 percent of the total national stock.

A national survey of housing needs showed a first figure of 26,000 families living in sub-standard conditions in Portugal. But more detailed surveys carried out later, at the level of local housing strategies, showed that the number of families living in unsuitable conditions (e.g. unhealthy and insecure houses, overcrowding, inadequacy of housing for the special needs of residents with disabilities or reduced mobility, homeless) is much higher than this figure. With the Recovery and Resilience Plan (PRR) funding, for which component 2 is devoted to housing issues, the government channelled investment in threefold programmes:

1 The Support Programme for Access to Housing (an expected investment of 1.211 million euros): the *1° Direito* (First Right) is the central programme and allows the construction of new buildings or the renovation of existing dwellings, as well as, whenever necessary, the acquisition of new buildings or the lease of buildings to sublease. The programme's main objective is to provide mainly social housing accommodation but also financial support for renovation or construction to the identified target groups that do not have the financial capacity to guarantee their own housing. The government maintains the aim of providing for at least 26,000 households by 2026.
2 The National Emergency and Temporary Accommodation Grant (176 million euros): the objective of this investment is to provide not only temporary or emergency accommodation to the vulnerable population groups in mainland Portugal, including victims of domestic violence, victims of human trafficking, homeless persons; fulfilling needs for urgent and temporary accommodation for persons at imminent and actual risk of being left without accommodation or in the process of de-institutionalisation but also housing indispensable to the public interest targeted at state officials and agents;
3 Loans for public affordable housing (775 million euros): the *Programa de Arrendamento Acessível* (Affordable Housing Program) offers tenancies at rents of up to 80 percent of market rent levels within the local area, lease contracts of five years and a tenant's affordability ratio (i.e. the ratio between housing costs and household income) between 15 percent and 30 percent.

Another objective of the PRR is to increase the supply of student accommodation at affordable prices throughout the construction of new dwellings and rehabilitation of existing ones. The implementation of Portugal's PRR is underway, however with some delays, and with the risk of not achieving some targets, namely related to the investments in social housing (26,000 dwellings for social housing) and the 12,500 student accommodation places, due to the lack of human resources and capabilities in many municipalities to carry out plans of investment, as well as high inflation of construction costs (raw material and labour).

Some criticisms related to the rationale or logic of intervention of the programmes should be identified. This includes the way problems and needs are defined by the government, including their underlying causes, what they are expected to achieve and their potential impacts related to the segmentation of the provision of social housing, affordable housing and market housing. Other criticisms include the fact that the available budget for the acquisition of land, constructing, rehabilitation or acquisition of dwellings targeted at low-income families will be insufficient considering the level of housing needs identified by municipalities. It is also criticised the fact local housing strategies (*Estratégias Locais de Habitação*) drawn by local authorities in some municipalities have not included in their targets (in terms of the number of dwellings and families), Roma families living in informal or illegal settlements or dwellings (characterised by lack of running water, electricity, and other basic infrastructure). In addition, the possibility is also to be considered that the investments in housing could eventually lead to an increased concentration or further physical isolation of marginalised groups.

So far, the results of the Affordable Housing Program's implementation have shown that: (1) in overheated housing markets, rental values at 20 percent below market level are still inaccessible to most families, including the middle-income families that allegedly are targeted by the programme; (2) low-income families, even those in urgent need, are excluded from this programme and have to apply for social housing, thus, this new affordable housing provision is not tackling the lack of housing options for low-income people; (3) unlike in other countries that seek to integrate social and affordable housing provision to promote social mix (not to mention different tenures of not-for-profit housing within market housing), in Portugal there are no central government requirements to do so—for example in Lisbon we have seen the choice of a segregated model that does not seek to promote socio-spatial inclusion (for more details, see Alves, 2021). On the ground, we have seen in several cities that affordable-rent homes that cannot be let at more than 80 percent of market rents have been provided at a faster pace than social housing. However, 80 percent of market rents are not genuinely affordable in many parts of Portugal, such as the metropolitan areas of Porto and Lisbon and Algarve (Travasso et al., 2020), which means that this is not an inclusive model.

9.12 Conclusion

The analysis and selection of policy objectives and policy instruments have been portrayed as a rational, linear, technical exercise. This is a characterisation that Peters (2002) describes as oversimplified, noting that instrument selection and evaluation are inherently a political exercise influenced by five 'Is'—ideas, institutions, interests, individuals and the international environment. Also, Cairney (2021) makes the point that policymakers exhibit bounded rationality: they only have the ability to pay attention to a tiny proportion of available facts, are unable to separate those facts from their values, struggle to make clear and consistent choices and cannot anticipate fully the effects of their decisions.

In contemporary democratic political systems, policy agendas are focused on the 'problems', policy goals and instruments that leaders and stakeholders believe are worthy of attention and debate (Head, 2019). A central theme within the policy studies literature, including that on housing policy, has been to contest and problematise how problems are understood, defined and shaped in processes of agenda-setting, asking what impacts policy design choices have (in terms of beneficiaries and tools)—and specifically whether they reinforce or mitigate inequality within both residential space and society as a whole. This chapter has sought to answer this question for the case of Portugal over the past century.

The empirical research presented in this chapter confirms that housing policy, 'a field located at the junction between welfare and spatial planning' (Allegra et al., 2022, p. 331), has the potential not only to modify the quality, quantity, price and ownership of housing but also to shape the understanding of housing as a policy matter that is governmentally constructed, in terms of their objectives, instruments, and expected outcomes.

Our case shows that the state can enforce laws that privilege the right to property, reinforcing housing as an economic good subject to market mechanisms, which has given rise to policies that mostly respond to the demand of a population that can afford it, and itself has made housing increasingly unaffordable for a large proportion of the population, over the idea of housing as a social right, jeopardising the right to decent housing at affordable prices, which is key to the sustainability of communities and neighborhoods. Thus, our case study shows that the way housing policy has been designed and implemented reflects and generates social inequality and preconceptions about social and economic issues.

The analysis developed in this chapter has shown that housing policies have been in existence for over a century and that they have arisen as a result of different concerns, policy goals and instruments that were similar between different political regimes (both authoritarian and democratic) and political parties (both left- and right-wing). It has also shown that even though regulation and direct provision have helped to respond to chronic housing crises, associated to housing quality, availability and costs, their coverage and main beneficiaries have varied significantly. Some groups have been excluded from support that has been made conditional on income or other criteria (such as behaviour), and there have been contradictions between the scope and the content of policy, on the one hand, and housing needs, on the other.

We cannot say that all political regimes and political parties have a similar inclination towards an unequal distribution of housing subsidies and opportunities. But what the empirical analysis does show is that the promotion of housing stock under most political regimes has failed adequately to counteract the inequality of access to a safe, stable and healthy place to live. This failure has limited generally desirable economic, social and urban outcomes related to economic growth, collective efficiency and social cohesion.

The Portuguese case study, analysed in this chapter throughout a historical perspective, demonstrates that the basic assumptions made by researchers and planners regarding a greater or lesser public intervention in housing are simplistic and not very helpful, when they don't address the content and the expected effects of policies in terms of either improving or building basic services (water supply, sewage, etc.) and thus living conditions or reducing socio-economic and spatial inequalities.

The chapter further adds to the existing body of literature about inequality by providing new evidence and insights about the potential impact of housing policy's formulation and implementation. The chapter fills a gap in current knowledge from a policy perspective in ways that haven't been explored before and that have the potential to generate more critical debates about the causes and the effects of housing inequality. In terms of contributions for real-world scenarios, the chapter offers practical recommendations to inspire practical change regarding the adoption of non-discrimination and non-segregation principles. In what concerns research paths to study housing inequality, future research should bridge interdisciplinary gaps and integrate knowledge from various sources to engage in a more constructive and useful debate.

Acknowledgements

Our analysis is enriched by the knowledge obtained from a four-year research project conducted in Portugal, delving into the effects of housing and urban policies and practices on citizens with high levels of vulnerability—SUSTAINLIS, sustainable urban requalification and vulnerable populations in the historical centre of Lisbon (PTDC/GESURB/28853/2017).

Sónia Alves also acknowledges financial support from the Fundação para a Ciência e Tecnologia, under the Norma Transitória [DL 57/2016/CP1441/CT0017, and Marie Skłodowska-Curie Actions (MSCA) research and innovation programme of the European Union's Horizon Europe, under the grant agreement ID 101086488: Delivering sAfe and Social Housing (DASH).

References

Allegra, M., Tulumello, S., and Allegretti, G. (2022). Housing Policy in the Political Agenda: The Trajectory of Portugal. In F. Gelli and M. Basso (eds), *Identifying Models of National Urban Agendas. A View to the Global Transition* (pp. 311–332). Cham: Palgrave Macmillan.

Allegra, M., Tulumello, S., Colombo, A., and Ferrão, J. (2020). The (Hidden) Role of the EU in Housing Policy: The Portuguese Case in Multi-Scalar Perspective. *European Planning Studies*, 28(12), 2307–2329.

Allen, J., Barlow, J., Leal, J., Maloutas, T., and Padovani, L. (2004). *Housing and Welfare in Southern Europe*. Oxford: Blackwell.

Alves, S. (2010). *O social, o espacial e o político na pobreza e na exclusão: avaliação de iniciativas de regeneração de áreas urbanas "em risco" na cidade do Porto*. ISCTE-IUL: Lisboa. Tese de doutoramento. www:<http://hdl.handle.net/10071/4412>. ISBN 978-989-732-193-1

Alves, S. (2017a). Spaces of Inequality: It's Not Differentiation, It Is Inequality! A Socio-Spatial Analysis of the City of Porto. *Portuguese Journal of Social Science*, 15(3), 409–431.

Alves, S. (2017b). Ethnic Housing Segregation and the Roma/Gypsy Population: A Portuguese Perspective. In *Spaces of Dialog for Places of Dignity: Fostering the European Dimension of Planning*. 30th Annual AESOP 2017 Congress. Book of Proceedings, pp. 1472–1480. Lisboa: Universidade de Lisboa.

Alves, S. (2021). *Solo municipal e o Programa de Renda Acessível de Lisboa*. Blogue ATS. https://ambienteterritoriosociedade-ics.org/2021/09/22/solo-municipal-e-o-programa-de-renda-acessivel-de-lisboa/. Downloaded 24 November 2023.

Andersen, H., Fallov, M., Jørgensen, A., Neergaard, M., and Nielsen, R. (2020). Cohesion in the Local Context: Reconciling the Territorial, Economic and Social Dimensions. *Social Inclusion*, 8(4), 178–182.

Bali, A., Howlett, M., Lewis, J., and Ramesh, M. (2021). Procedural Policy Tools in Theory and Practice. *Policy and Society*, 40(3), 295–311.

Barata-Salgueiro, T. (1977). Bairros clandestinos na periferia de Lisboa. *Finisterra*, 12(23), 28–55.

Bengtsson, B., and Ruonavaara, H. (2017). Comparative Process Tracing: Making Historical Comparison Structured and Focused. *Philosophy of the Social Sciences*, 47(1), 44–66.

Branco, R., and Alves, S. (2020). Urban Rehabilitation, Governance, and Housing Affordability: Lessons from Portugal. *Urban Research & Practice*, 13(2), 157–179.

Cairney, P. (2021). *The Politics of Policy Analysis*. Cham: Springer Nature.

Canelas, P., Alves, S., and Azevedo, A. (2023). Lisbon. In C. Whitehead, K. Scanlon, M. Voigtländer, J. Karlsson, F. Blanc and M. Rotolo (eds), *Financialization in 13 Cities—An International Comparative Report* (pp. 128–131). Realdania and London School of Economics and Political Science. https://repositorio.ul.pt/handle/10451/58433

Cocola-Gant, A. (2023). Place-Based Displacement: Touristification and Neighborhood Change. *Geoforum*, 138, 103665.

Dear, M., and Scott, A. (1981). Towards a Framework for Analysis. In M. Dear and A. Scott (eds), *Urbanization and Urban Planning in Capitalist Society* (pp. 3–16). New York: Methuen.

Fainstein, S. (2014). The Just City. *International Journal of Urban Sciences*, 18(1), 1–18.

Fournier, M. (2013). *Émile Durkheim. A Biography*. Oxford: Polity Press.

Garha, N., and Azevedo, A. (2021). Population and Housing (Mis)match in Lisbon, 1981–2018. A Challenge for an Aging Society. *Social Sciences*, 10(3), 102.

Hamnett, C. (2019). Urban Inequality. In *Handbook of Urban Geography* (pp. 242–254). Cheltenham: Edward Elgar Publishing.

Harvey, D. (1973). *Social Justice and the City*. London: Edward Arnold.

Harvey, D. (2012). *From the Right to the City to the Urban Revolution*. London: Verso.

Head, B. (2019). Forty Years of Wicked Problems Literature: Forging Closer Links to Policy Studies. *Policy and Society*, 38(2), 180–197.

Hopkins, P. (2021). Social Geography III: Committing to Social Justice. *Progress in Human Geography*, 45(2), 382–393.

Howlett, M. (2009). Governance Modes, Policy Regimes and Operational Plans: A Multi-Level Nested Model of Policy Instrument Choice and Policy Design. *Policy Sciences*, 42, 73–89.

James, L., Daniel, L., Bentley, R., and Baker, E. (2022). Housing Inequality: A Systematic Scoping Review. *Housing Studies*, 19(24), 16627.

Kemeny, J. (1992). *Housing and Social Theory*. London: Routledge.

Koh, S. (2020). Inequality. In A. Kobayashi (ed), *International Encyclopedia of Human Geography*, 2nd ed. (pp. 269–277). Amsterdam: Elsevier.

Linklater, A. (1990). Marxist and Neo-Marxist Theories of Inequality and Development. In *Beyond Realism and Marxism* (pp. 97–118). London: Palgrave Macmillan.

Malpass, P., and Murie, A. (1999). *Housing Policy and Practice*. Basingstoke: Bloomsbury Publishing.

Mendes, L. (2020). Bye Bye Lisbon: Tourism Gentrification Impacts on Lisbon's Inner-City Housing Market. In *Handbook of Research on the Impacts, Challenges, and Policy Responses to Overtourism* (pp. 136–155). Hershey: IGI Global.

Merton, R. (1968). *Social Theory and Social Structure*, Enlarged ed. New York: Free Press.

Milanovic, B. (2012). *Ter Ou Não Ter, Uma breve história da desigualdade*. Lisbon: Bertrand.

Montezuma, J., and McGarrigle, J. (2019). What Motivates International Homebuyers? Investor to Lifestyle 'Migrants' in a Tourist City. *Tourism Geographies*, 21(2), 214–234.

Pacione, M. (2005). *Urban Geography*, 2nd ed. Oxon: Routledge.

Palier, B., and Trampusch, C. (2018). Tracking Causal Mechanisms. The Different Uses of Process Tracing. *Revue française de science politique*, 68, 967–990.

Park, R. (1915). The City: Suggestions for the Investigation of Human Behavior in the City Environment. *American Journal of Sociology*, 20(5), 577–612.

Park, R., and Burgess, E. (eds) (1925). *The City*, 1st ed. Chicago: University of Chicago.

Peters, B. (2002). The Politics of Tool Choice. In L. Salamon (ed), *The Tools of Government: A Guide to the New Governance* (pp. 552–564). New York: Oxford University Press.

Piketty, T. (2014). *Capital in the Twenty-First Century*. Cambridge, MA: Harvard University Press.

Somerville, P., and Bengtsson, B. (2002). Constructionism, Realism and Housing Theory. *Housing, Theory and Society*, 19(3–4), 121–136.

Srinivas, S. (2008). Urban Labour Markets in the 21st Century: Dualism, Regulation and the Role(s) of the State. *Habitat International*, 32(2), 141–159.

Teixeira, M.C. (1992). As estratégias de habitação em Portugal, 1880–1940. *Análise Social*, XXVII(115), 65–89.

Trampusch, C., and Palier, B. (2016). Between X and Y: How Process Tracing Contributes to Opening the Black Box of Causality. *New Political Economy*, 21(5), 437–454.

Travasso, N., Oro, A.V., de Almeida, M.R., and Ribeiro, L.S. (2020). Acesso ao mercado de arrendamento em Portugal: um retrato a partir do Programa de Arrendamento Acessível. *Finisterra*, 55(114), 105–126.

Van Baar, H. (2011). Europe's Romaphobia: Problematization, Securitization, Nomadization. *Environment and Planning D: Society and Space*, 29(2), 203–212.

10 Liberty, Equality, Fraternity, and Globalization

Arne Bigsten

The period since the 1980s has seen dramatic changes in the global economy. These have concerned both the national scenes and the ways in which countries interact. We saw a combination of the opening of up to international markets of countries and regions that were previously not highly integrated with the world economy such as China and Eastern Europe, combined with a communication revolution which made it possible to combine economically over long distances. This period was the most intense globalization period ever. Initially the globalization process proceeded rather smoothly, but there has been a certain backlash against globalization in recent years.

This chapter discusses how key aspects of global development have changed during this period of globalization. I take account of the recent increase in populist and anti-globalist sentiments in the North and their impacts on the global liberal and multilateral system that has served the world economy well since World War II.

First, I set up an analytical framework for discussion based on the dictum of the French Revolution of 'Liberty, Equality, and Fraternity'. Based on this setup, I look at four outcome dimensions, namely inequality, freedom, national fraternity, and international fraternity. I discuss changes of global inequality over time and the impacts of these changes on politics and the policy discussions in Western countries. Here, I consider how economic, social, and political developments have fed populist and anti-globalization feelings. Then I discuss whether our freedom is challenged at present by the changes that the world economy is undergoing and what is required to enhance or maintain freedom. Next, I discuss how the global changes have affected the feeling of fraternity, nationally and internationally, and whether the sense of fraternity or brotherhood is in decline.

After having looked at the populism impacts regarding our welfare dimensions, I move on to discuss the policy challenges that I think are implied. I also touch briefly on the question whether they have already initiated a retreat from the globalization era. Here, I also consider what policymakers can do to counter the populist and anti-globalization sentiments. I conclude by summarizing the conclusions of the analysis and the challenges ahead.

10.1 Analytical Framework

The slogan of the French revolution was 'liberty, equality, and fraternity'. The reason for its longevity is that these goals capture the most essential dimensions of development that governments seek to achieve by their policymaking. The slogan represents three positive aspects of society, and the political debate is largely about how one should trade off these broad goals against each other to deliver the best possible social welfare.

To simplify, I focus on broad features of what could be included under the three headings. Freedom is a good in itself, but it is also essential for economic efficiency by producing an environment, where economic agents are allowed to maximize their income under a system of secure property rights. We simply measure liberty with the outcome variable per capita income and assume that the welfare of an individual increases with income. Comparing two countries with the same income distribution, most people would agree that the one with the highest per capita income has the highest welfare.

What can we say about two countries with different income distributions? If they have the same per capita income, the country with the most equal income distribution has the highest welfare, assuming citizens consider an equal distribution to be preferable to an unequal one, *ceteris paribus*. Such an evaluation is, of course, not self-evident. People's attitudes to redistribution are, for example, affected by the way the high incomes are earned. People feel that incomes from hard work or innovations are more deserved than, for example, income from increased property values in towns unrelated to the owners' efforts. Still, there is at least concern about unjustified inequality.

We also have the third dimension in our dictum, fraternity, or brotherhood. If a broad spectrum of people in a society agrees on the meaning of fraternity, the inclusion of this dimension leads to a three-way trade off between goals. However, I would argue that this simple interpretation of fraternity has broken down or split in recent decades due to technical changes and globalization, as well as socioeconomic changes.

This dimension in our discussion relates to lifestyle and identity issues. In accordance with our dictum, I call this the fraternity dimension. The question is what citizens see as their fraternity. There is a political science model indicating that the left–right (equity-efficiency) dimension should now be complemented by a GAL–TAN dimension (green, alternative, liberal vs. traditional, authoritarian, nationalist) crossing the left–right dimension. If we accept that this dimension largely is about fraternity (although other aspects are normally also included), the breakdown of this dimension into two dimensions gives us four policy goal directions rather than just three. According to the TAN-view, the fraternity only includes nationals, while fraternity according to the GAL-view is more inclusive and could even mean fraternity on a global scale. There is, of course, a continuum of positions as to how much you weigh global solidarity versus national (or local) solidarity. We refer to these two dimensions as national fraternity and global fraternity.

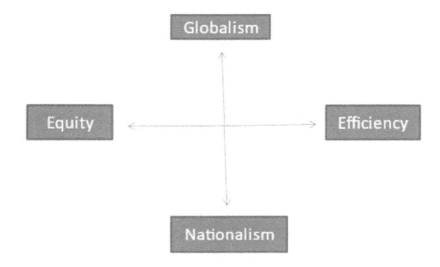

Figure 10.1 Four policy dimensions

Therefore, overall, we may talk about four dimensions for policymakers to consider, namely liberty (efficiency), equality, national fraternity, and global fraternity (see Figure 10.1). The question is how to weigh the goals or outcomes in these dimensions together. Politicians who put larger weight on the distribution dimension could be referred to as the left and those who put relatively more weight on the aggregate income (efficiency) dimension for right. The ones who focus primarily on the national brotherhood we may call nationalists, while the global fraternity group could be called globalists. Still, all political parties or directions we have mentioned have to consider all aspects to some extent. Still, the parties are defined or characterized on the basis of where they are located relative to the four goals in our four-way diagram.

How citizens and politicians value these four different dimensions of development depends partly on their self-interest. The poor might, for example be more concerned than the rich about equity relative to efficiency. However, citizens may also prefer an egalitarian society for altruistic or justice reasons. Whatever the motivation for their preferences, I would argue that the preferences of citizens and politicians could be mapped into the four broad dimensions identified here. I will discuss different policy areas in relation to these four dimensions.

10.2 Changes in Global Inequality

Global inequality among the citizens of the world can be decomposed into inequality within and inequality between countries. Milanovic (2016) begins his book on global inequality with a discussion about the evolution of inequality within countries. He starts from the Kuznets hypothesis, which states that changes in inequality over time have an inverted U pattern. He thinks some of the aspects of Kuznets story make sense, but he feels that the hypothesis cannot explain why inequality has started to increase again after about 1980. He also critically discusses Tinbergen's approach, which says that increases in inequality can be explained by a model where there is a race between education and skill-biased technological progress. However, the skill-premium has not been forced down over time despite increasing supply of skilled labour. Piketty (2014, 2020) argues that the decline in inequality up to 1980 was driven by political forces of wars, taxation to finance the wars, socialist ideology, and economic convergence. When these forces weaken, the normal capitalist pattern emerges again says Piketty, and inequality goes up. Milanovic objects that there are periods when inequality under capitalism has gone down driven by economic forces. So, it is not correct to say that inequality must increase under capitalism.

Milanovic argues that there are essentially three factors that determine the evolution of inequality, namely technology, openness, and policy. Milanovic's theory is that the development can be described as a Kuznets wave, that is alternating increases and decreases in inequality. The Kuznets waves are driven by an interplay between economic and political factors.

Before the industrial revolution, wages were stagnant, and inequality fluctuated around a basically fixed real wage level. In pre-industrial societies, inequality fell during plagues, which reduced the labour force and increased real wages. War reduced capital returns by destroying capital and by reducing the returns on what was left.

The pattern of development changed with the industrial revolution. There was more room for higher inequality as productivity increases pushed average incomes up. The movement of labour to a more diversified sector also increased inequality. Eventually, there emerged demands for redistribution, and the return to capital went down. There were thus a set of 'benign' mechanisms reducing inequality. But there were also 'malign' mechanisms like wars and revolutions doing the same. There have been policy interventions (such as the New Deal), increased bargaining power of organized labour, higher tax rates, and globalization, which have pushed inequality down. Milanovic's summary of the global experience is that the reduction of inequality that we saw up until the 1980s was due to the two wars, higher taxation, reduced incomes from capital, stronger trade unions, and the expansion of the welfare state.

Around 1980, says Milanovic, a second Kuznets wave started, driven by the second technological revolution (information technology), globalization, and the increasing importance of heterogenous jobs in the service sector. The new technology rewarded skilled labour and drove up returns to capital, and the economies were opened to competition from low-income countries. Globalization made it hard for individual countries to put high taxes on mobile actors. Instead, pro-rich policies supporting the trend were instituted.

The second wave started like the first one with technological innovation, substitution of labour by capital, and the transfer of labour between sectors. There were also pro-rich changes in policies. Milanovic suggests that we should consider the changes described by Piketty as endogenous responses to what is happening in the economy, while Piketty sees them as exogenous. Piketty thinks that the 'ideology' of society shapes policies and thus economic outcomes.

The new increase in inequality is due to higher wage dispersion, greater concentration of capital income, and an association of incomes from both labour and capital in the same individuals. There has probably also been more of behavioural changes such as more assortative mating as well as changes in norms and ethics. However, Milanovic (as well as Piketty) thinks that high inequality will eventually become unsustainable and tends to bring about reactions to reverse the trend towards ever higher inequality.

To achieve such a reversal, certain policies need to be implemented. Milanovic (2016) provides the following list of national forces which can bring inequality down: (1) higher taxation, (2) more rapid increases in the supply of skills—because of the race between skills and education, (3) the dissipation of rents accrued in the early stages of the industrial revolution, (4) reduced income gaps between the rich and the developing countries, and (5) low skill-biased technological progress. The key question when it comes to the evolution of inequality concerns the urge and willingness of voters and thus politicians to push egalitarian policies such as social programmes, public education, and health services.

Milanovic also discusses inequality among countries. The main story here is that around 1820, when the industrial revolution started, 80 percent of global inequality was due to inequality within nations while only 20 percent was due to inequality among nations. By the middle of the 20th century, these figures had been reversed, and then 80 percent of global inequality was due to the gaps between nations. The industrial revolution really led to Divergence Big Time (Pritchett, 1997)! The main divergent force during this period was thus the divergence of the mean incomes of countries.

Global inequality (the combined effect of inequality within and between countries) increased from the beginning of the industrial revolution and peaked around the 1980s. From the late 1980s until the turn of the century global inequality was rather constant, but then it started to decrease. First China and then India were the main equalizers with per capita incomes growing substantially faster than those in the West.

One can say that there is a citizenship premium, that is, where we live 'explains' more than two-thirds of the variation in incomes across country percentiles. It is also noteworthy that the poor in Sweden (being a welfare state) have a larger advantage relative to the poor in say Congo, than what the average Swede has relative to the average Congolese. This means that it becomes particularly attractive to those who expect to end up at the bottom of the distribution or are poorly educated to move to a welfare state such as Sweden rather than to more unequal countries.

Do voters and politicians in the North care about the global inequality of opportunities? Yes, to some extent they do, but not so much that they are willing to go for completely open borders. On the contrary, in the last few years, the rich countries have instead started to build walls and make it harder for poor people to migrate to developed countries.

This is, of course, a moral problem, but politically it seems at the present time impossible to change attitudes against open borders. Milanovic argues that it may be possible to let more people migrate if one opens for some differences in treatment or access to welfare services in the recipient countries. Doing this, inequality would increase, and this may be a problem for the welfare states, since they typically see equality within their borders as an important good in itself. The migration issues will certainly feature prominently in the future.

The inequality trends and policies in the developed countries are influenced by what is happening in the major industrial economy, the United States. Milanovic lists five factors explaining why we have seen increasing inequality in the United States in recent years. They are the high elasticity of substitution between labour and capital, which means that increased capital intensity increased the capital share of income. Capital incomes will remain concentrated. More individuals receive both high labour incomes and high capital income. Highly skilled people tend to marry each other. Concentration of incomes reinforces the political power of the rich, and this means that they may get even richer.

The reduction of the importance of the middle class may mean that the stability of democracy decreases.

Milanovic is concerned about the problems of Europe in absorbing migration flows. Different cultural norms may undercut the sustainability of the welfare state. Homogeneity increases affinity (or fraternity) in the population and makes most people observe the same norms. The welfare state has been important in strengthening democratic capitalism in Europe.

Finally, in his book, Milanovic discusses the future of global inequality. He says that its future development will be determined by two forces, namely convergence and Kuznets waves. He feels that the rich countries' middle classes will continue to see their position weaken. Although there is a strong reduction in the inequality of education of the rich and the middle classes, there may still be large gaps because of luck/chance and family background. So, Milanovic believes that in the new capitalism, inequality will remain high or increase. However, he also says that 'It is hard to imagine that a system with such high inequality will be politically stable' (Milanovic, 2016, p. 217). The system could possibly be changed, if there is technological progress creating demand for the labour of the middle classes, and it may also depend on the ability of the losers to get organized. The increasingly important winner-takes-all rule makes it harder to equalize wages, and this depends on the scalability of jobs.

Inequality can be decreased with the help of taxes and transfers, but capital and even skilled labour are getting harder to tax since these factors are so internationally mobile. It may make more sense to try to attack the inequality of ownership of assets and education, by, for example higher inheritance taxes, corporate tax policies, taxes, and administrative policies that make it easier for the middle classes to hold financial assets. So, to move towards a more egalitarian society, we need some combination of more equal ownership of assets and education to reduce inequality and to create a sustainable society.

However, it has become harder to implement such policies in recent decades due to the changes in the attitudes of the population, even if it seems that the anti-establishment attitudes have been driven to some extent by the globalization impacts on inequality. There is a stronger populist pressure for anti-immigration policies than for socio-economic equalization policies. It has been hard to establish broad coalitions for a more egalitarian policy. Even the classical social-democratic parties in northern Europe have come to put less emphasis on equalization. But if we believe observers like Milanovic, Piketty, and Atkinson, there will eventually be a revival of policies focusing on equity. The challenge is to formulate policies that do not have too high efficiency costs.

10.3 Is Freedom Under Threat?

Freedom is one of the key dimensions in our framework. Freedom not only is a value in itself, but it also is a factor that contributes to the economic development of societies. Acemoglu and Robinson (2019) discuss how freedom in society can emerge and be preserved, but it can also be blocked. We are here concerned with what their analysis says about the situation in the West today.

To make it possible for citizens to be free, they must be able to control that state to make sure it delivers freedom to the citizens. The maintenance of freedom requires a society where citizens engage in politics, demonstrate against measures they disapprove of, and vote governments out of office if needed.

Acemoglu and Robinson (2019) argue that you need both a strong state and a strong society. The state controls the tools of violence, upholds the laws, and provides public services, which are needed to make it possible for the citizens to make and undertake their choices. The society (citizens) needs to be strong to be able to control that state.

The main point of Acemoglu's and Robinson's analysis is thus that there must be a balance between the power of the state and the power of society. If the latter is too small relative to that of the state, that country may end up under despotism, and if the society is too strong relative to the state, you may end up in a situation without societal steering ('the law of the jungle'). With an appropriate balance between state and society, you end up in the narrow corridor where freedom can be achieved and maintained. The borders of the corridor show which combinations of power for the state and the society lead to a development where freedom is maintained or increased.

The controlled state solves conflicts in society in a fair way, provides public services and economic opportunities, and hinders the domination of citizens. The controlled state gives increased security and freedom, at the same time as it gives economic opportunities. A lot of the discussion of development in recent years has also focused on the importance of secure property rights for efficiency and growth. The balance between state and society is thus crucial for development.

Acemoglu and Robinson (2019) discuss how the dynamic between state and society looks. They argue that both state and society need to develop at approximately the same rate for the balance between them to be maintained. If one of them lags, you risk ending up outside the narrow corridor where freedom is preserved, and you may end with either despotism or disorganization.

The power of society is a combination of the mobilization of society, institutional power, and ability to control the hierarchies of the state. The power of the state, on the other hand, is the power of the political and economic elites and the capacity of state institutions. Acemoglu and Robinson argue that if you are in the corridor, the fight between the two forces will create a dynamic, which strengthens and maintains the balance between them.

The Acemoglu and Robinson book contains many interesting accounts of the development of different countries and regions in relation to the corridor. It describes how countries in Europe entered the corridor in a way that was good for freedom. The positive development was because one managed to maintain a sufficient balance between the authority of the central authorities and the authority of citizens. Once within the corridor, the system developed further with help from the dynamics between state and society. They argue that the basis of the European societies was the democratically organized tribal societies, while the states were based on institutions and political hierarchies from the days of the Roman empire and the Christian church.

They note that the outcome became quite different in societies which had similar starting points and structures. Large shocks may have different types of effects on development depending on starting conditions. To get into the corridor, you need a society with a balance between strong and centralized state institutions and a mobilized society that can stand up to the political elites.

Acemoglu and Robinson give many examples of how a country can fall out of the corridor and lose its freedom. This happened, for example, in the Weimar Republic, Italy under Mussolini, Chile under Pinochet, and medieval communes in Italy. The exact results depend on the character of the competition between state and society. The corridor tends to be narrower when established interests (like powerful landowners) feel threatened, and this makes it harder to achieve freedom. The problem is aggravated if the political system is incapable of finding solutions and compromises. If there are economic crises—such as the depression of the 1930s or the financial crisis of 2008–2009—there is an increased risk of limitations of freedoms. If there emerges in such a situation a charismatic leader, he may have a chance of taking power. The crisis in Germany of the 1930s depended on the polarization between state and society, inability of institutions to compromise and solve conflicts, and a chock (the depression) which destabilized the system. Acemoglu and Robinson also write a lot about the Swedish model, which grew out of the compromised in the 1930s. The Swedish development is held out as a good example of how a country can stay within the corridor. In Sweden development combined state capacity to handle new challenges and the society's organized commitment, which made sure that power was balanced.

The maintenance of freedom and democracy depends on a complex interaction between state and society, and freedom and democracy can be lost in many ways. After the end of the cold war in the 1990s, many observers, including me, thought we were on track for a more democratic world with increasing freedom for citizens. We also saw that happen in Eastern Europe as well as in the developing world, but in the last decade, the development has been reversed. The V-Dem Institute (2023) concludes in its annual report for 2022 (p. 6) that 'advances in global levels of democracy made over the last 35 years have been wiped out'. They note that 72 percent of the world's population lived in autocracies in 2022 and that there are now more dictatorships than liberal democracies. Other aspects of freedom and democracy such as freedom of expression were deteriorating in 35 countries in 2022.

So, we end this section on a pessimistic note. Democracy is on the decline. Freedom is under threat. From the 1990s onwards I believed that globalization would tie countries of the world closer together and that trade interaction and information exchange would lead to democratic change in most countries. Right now, this prediction has been proven wrong, but I still believe democracy will eventually dominate the world. And despite recent setbacks, I believe that globalization will make a comeback and that this will then be a factor that contributes to the spread of freedom and democracy.

10.4 Is Fraternity Declining?

The fraternity dimension has economic, political, and social components of identity jointly determining the social cohesion of a society. The main economic determinant of the extent of brotherhood or shared identity is economic inequality reflecting types of jobs and incomes. The political component is national identity, that is, a feeling of belonging to a nation. The social component of identity is a feeling of shared cultural values. We have already discussed the economic dimension quite extensively, so we will here concentrate on the two other dimensions.

Populism as we know it today has made a comeback in Western societies over the last few decades. There has been a gradual loss of shared identity leading to less brotherhood or less fraternity. Earlier people generally tended to identify with the society they were living in, but some groups of people have now moved away from this position. They have moved in two directions—towards nationalism/anti-globalism and towards internationalism/globalism. Between these two points, there are of course intermediate positions including the traditional 'social-democratic' form of fraternity.

Collier (2018a) argues that jobs and nation are the key identities, which are sources of self-esteem. Rational individuals get their utility from esteem and seek to maximize that. When inequality was small, the differences in esteem were due mainly to relatively small income differences. Inequality was falling in the North from the 19th century up until the 1980s, when the trend was reversed. Over time, jobs became more important, and complex jobs were better paid. The well-educated thought their job was their key identity, while the less-educated came to think the nation was their identity. Diverging identities made the society increasingly divided.

The loss of shared identity had consequences. As identities polarized into skill and nationality, trust for those at the top began to collapse. Willingness to help others may depend on three narratives: shared belonging to a group, reciprocal obligations within a group, and a link from an action to the well-being of the group that shows it to be purposive. To sum up, 'the part of the population that is skilled and educated has tended to sheer off from nationality as its core identity, leaving the less fortunate clinging to its diminished status' (Collier, 2018a, p. 54). This has weakened the shared identity across the society, and this has weakened the sense of obligation felt by the fortunate towards the less fortunate. This is noted among the less fortunate, which therefore trust their betters (the elite) less.

However, national identities can be damaging. Polities function if the units of political power coincide with shared identity (Collier, 2018a, p. 57). Populists try to build a support base through narratives of hatred of other people who live in the same country. Oppositional identities are lethal for generosity, trust, and cooperation. However, the educated do not offer an alternative basis for a shared identity with the less-educated citizens. 'Unless the divergence between our polities and our bonds is reversed our societies will degenerate, becoming less generous, less trusting, and less cooperative' (Collier, 2018a, p. 62).

One consequence of globalization is that social connectivity becomes increasingly globalized (Scholte, 2008). This may lead to a shift where the elite switches its identity from a national one to a globalized one (Goodhart, 2017). There may also emerge parallel societies where immigrants may retain strong links with their countries of origin, but less so with the country of destination. Therefore, globalization may strengthen global links and solidarity, while undermining solidarity within countries. For example the support for the welfare state may be undermined, if citizens feel less connected with parts of the population. Anti-immigration feelings may thus be driven by economic self-interest of the poorer segments of society rather than by cultural animosity, although that also may be part of the story.

Ingelhart has discussed changing societal values for a long time and has shown that there was a shift towards postmaterialist values in Western societies after World War II. 'The Silent Revolution thesis argued that when people grow up taking survival for granted it makes them more open to new ideas and more tolerant of outgroups (with insecurity having the reverse effect)' (Inglehart and Norris, 2017, p. 443). However, in recent decades, there has been a backlash against postmaterialism—motivating populist authoritarian parties. Insecurity encourages an authoritarian xenophobic reaction in which people close ranks behind strong leaders, with strong in-group solidarity, rejection of outsiders, and rigid conformity to group norms (Inglehart and Norris, 2017, p. 443).

Inglehart and Norris (2017) find that support for populist authoritarian parties is motivated by a backlash against the cultural changes linked with the rise of postmaterialist and self-expression values, far more than by economic factors. The proximate cause of the populist vote is anxiety that pervasive cultural changes and an influx of foreigners are eroding the cultural norms one knew since childhood. The main common theme of populist authoritarian parties on both sides of the Atlantic is a reaction against immigration and cultural change.

Economic factors such as income and unemployment rates are surprisingly weak predictors of the populist vote. Thus, exit polls from the US 2016 presidential election show that those most concerned with economic problems disproportionately voted for Clinton, while those who considered immigration the most crucial problem voted for Trump (Mutz, 2018; Reny et al., 2019).

However, there is both cohort and time effects. Inglehart's and Norris' (2017, p. 447) main point is that decades of declining real income and rising inequality have produced a long-term effect conducive to the populist vote. Thus, although the proximate cause of the populist vote is a cultural backlash, its high present level reflects the declining economic security and rising economic inequality.

The domain of public policy is spatial and predominantly national. However, our identities, and the social networks that underpin them, are becoming less so—because of the skill divide and rising complexity. The citizens of the world are abandoning their national identity. This threatens to undermine the shared identity.

Globalization has had a double effect on fraternity. On the one hand, it has meant that particularly the well-educated have acquired a broadened global sense of fraternity, and this can be said to have been fraternity-enhancing. On the other hand, this group has in a sense opted out of the traditional national fraternity, which means that national fraternity has declined. Since there are two types of fraternity in play, it is harder to characterize the change. The erosion of a shared identity represents a reduction in the utility of citizens or a welfare loss, while the divisions in the population at the same time make it harder to get a consensus to implement policies to enhance the welfare in society. And irrespective of whether you prefer one or the other of the fraternity dimensions, it would be desirable to have a better national cohesion. We will discuss some important policy dimensions in the next section.

10.5 Policy Challenges in the Era of Globalization

Globalization and technical progress (automation) have had positive impacts on society by increasing production and reducing poverty. There has been a problem, though, as to how the gains have been distributed. Unqualified labour in industrialized countries has not received much of the profits of the global economic integration. The gains haves largely ended up in the pockets of capital owners and qualified labour. Also, automization primarily has benefited capital and qualified labour, which has contributed to making income distribution increasingly uneven.

Inequality has also increased because of the deregulation of certain industries, particularly the financial sector. Firm concentration has increased and the risk taking has become larger, and this has increased profits. Firms in certain sectors have become very large because of economies of scale.

Thus, we have seen a combination of (1) economic globalization, (2) automation, (3) growth of the financial sector, and (4) the growth of super large firms. These large changes have had many positive effects, but they have also been bad for equality. Since states have not tried or succeeded in handling the distributional effects, the mistrust against the political institutions has increased. And without the trust for those, their ability to balance and solve conflicts in society is reduced. Polarization increases. Here, I will discuss some policy issues, which are particularly challenging in the globalized world.

We have repeatedly pointed out that the dimension of economic inequality is a political key issue. How it is handled determines in a broad sense where society is heading. The distribution of income in a society is the end result of all the economic processes therein. To address the issue of inequality comprehensively, one would need to understand the mechanisms of the various processes and how one can intervene in them to affect the distributional result (without having too negative effects on the growth of the pie which is to be distributed). There are some more radical proposals in the debate such as Piketty's proposal of basic wealth for everyone in the form of a cheque of money to be received when they come of age. There are also ideas about a basic income for everyone, which may be possible in the long run at least.

Anyway, the question of income distribution policy is hard to delimit. Here, I will confine myself to a sketch concerning distribution in some areas that are relevant from the globalization perspective we have had in this chapter. However, in a companion chapter (Bigsten, 2023), I give a broader review of what kind of policies one could apply to achieve a more egalitarian distribution of incomes in industrialized countries.

10.5.1 Trade

Standard trade theory (with competitive markets in a two-country model) says that both countries gain from an exchange, but it does not say that all groups within a country must gain. It says that the winners gain more than enough to compensate the losers, so that everyone in the end is better off. However, for this to be realized, there must be actual transfers of compensation, and if the political system cannot deliver this, there will be losers from increased trade or globalization. The losers are often spatially concentrated, which means that certain areas may suffer a lot. Moreover, it may well be that it is not enough with financial compensation alone if workers feel that having a job is part of a decent life and their identity or self-respect. What is required in terms of policy is thus measures going beyond compensation such as active labour market policies with re-training, regional development policy, etc.

It is, of course, furthermore the case that trade is not always done in competitive markets. In such situations, it may be possible that a country can increase its welfare at the expense of the partners by using tariffs or other types of interventions. Large countries can benefit from such interventions. However, the implementation of such policies will mean that the total output of the world would suffer, so these interventions are not first best from a global perspective.

Large and influential countries may also use trade measures to achieve their political aims. In recent years, countries in the West have become increasingly concerned about having all or most of the deliveries of certain inputs, for example, coming from a country they do not trust or with which they have a latent conflict. In those cases, many countries are now seeking to de-globalize, that is to move production closer to home. Thus, policy interventions will also depend on the political situation and superpower rivalries in the world. Whatever the case, this is one of the major policy areas when it comes to dealing with inequality issues.

10.5.2 Migration

Migration of factors of production tends to increase global production, but it is not self-evident that it is beneficial for both host and origin countries. Migration is generally beneficial for migrants—otherwise they would not migrate. It could benefit all parties if there was a system of compensatory transfers from the winners to the losers. Still, there is no such transfers in the real world, which means that some citizens in both the origin and destination may lose. In the country of destination, immigrants will share in accumulated assets, thereby reducing per capita ownership of the natives. Immigration also increases congestion in various types of infrastructure and public services. Immigration of unskilled labour tends to be detrimental to earnings of the native unskilled labour, while being beneficial for skilled labour. Therefore, it is reasonable to expect, for economic reasons, differences in attitudes to immigration between the well-educated and the less-educated natives.

As far as the income distributional effect of migration from poor to rich countries is concerned, it is quite conceivable that it reduces global inequality by moving citizens from a low paid job in a poor country to a better paid job in a rich country. At the same time, it is quite likely that the immigration of less-educated workers into rich countries with well-educated population will increase the group of low-income people in the recipient countries, and this would tend to increase national inequality there. Such migration may thus be expected both to increase inequality (nationally) and to decrease inequality (globally). It seems likely in such a situation that globalists are positive to migration, while nationalists are negative to migration. And this seems to be the case in many Western countries.

10.5.3 Financial Globalization

The scope for globalization has meant that some firms can achieve global market dominance and have the ability to reduce their taxation dramatically. Policies to regulate monopolies are national, while there has been little in terms of globalization of regulation. Instead of coordinating taxation and other regulations, countries compete by lower taxes and by deregulating. There is a race to the bottom in terms of taxation and regulation. This process has contributed to the increase in national and global inequality, which may have contributed to the animosity of people towards the elite, who they feel are responsible for the policies implemented.

10.5.4 The Urban–Rural Divide

All countries are increasingly urban dominated. This is where much of the economic growth occurs due to the agglomeration advantages. The economic gains can be seen as an economic rent from exploiting the locational advantage of urban areas (Collier and Venables, 2017; Collier, 2018b). The markets transfer these rents to two scarce urban factors—land and skilled labour. Since these rents are not heavily taxed, their growth contributes to the increase in economic inequality. The elite feels they deserve their income because of their skills and hard work, but the metropolitan rents generate an aversion against the elite among the citizens in non-metropolitan regions. The inflow of migrants to the urban regions further increases the rents of agglomeration benefiting the elites.

This is an area where the need for egalitarian policy interventions is obvious (to economists at least), but they seem to be politically very hard to implement.

10.6 Concluding Remarks

Globalization has had a large impact on the global economy, but this does not mean that all groups have seen their situation improve or at least not improve to the same extent as it has done for the elite. The process of globalization has helped reduce global inequality by helping poorer countries catch up economically at the same time as it has contributed to increasing inequality within Northern countries. There is thus a downside of globalization, which has not been sufficiently addressed. This has contributed to the populism that we now see in the advanced economies (Collier, 2018a, 2018b).

Post-World War II policymakers in Western societies managed to deal with the challenges by using taxation to redistribute consumption and to provide security. However, in recent decades, these societies have become increasingly divided on geographic, educational, and identity grounds. The new urban elite is divorced from the less-educated provincial population. This has paved the way for elite critical populist movements, rather than a mobilization along the classical left–right scale. These groups are anti-globalist and may be able to undermine the liberal global system that helped both the poor South to achieve an economic take-off and the rich North to see continued increase in average incomes. However, humans also need a sense of purpose, belonging, and esteem, which the current paternalistic capitalist societies in the North have been unable to deliver. The challenge is to find development strategies for the North that can bring people together without sacrificing global exchange and collaboration.

The policy challenges are economic, social, and political. Policymakers need to deal with the economic divergences, fragmentation of identifies, and exclusionary nationalism. Higher ambitions in terms of equality may have a cost in terms of reduced economic efficiency, but they may still be necessary for stable and just long-term development. Reduced economic inequalities should also make it easier to reduce social polarization, and by doing so, we would have a better chance of maintaining a (relatively) open global system benefitting development in the South.

So, what are the consequences of this development for our freedom (and democracy)? Many citizens of the industrialized countries have only seen modest economic progress during recent decades, while at the same time the development has made others rich. The political system has not been able to deal effectively with this distribution problem. It did not manage the financial crisis of 2008–2009 particularly well. People faith in institutions has therefore been eroded, and this makes it even harder to find agreement on political compromises. Populism gains strength when the people feel an aversion and mistrust against the elite or when they feel it is not working for their best interest. A strong charismatic leader who says he can represent the people's 'true wishes and interest' can then gain power. He may then seek to eliminate institutional limitations on power, so that he can support the people 'better'. It also means that the society's control of the state is reduced, and you risk ending up in despotism outside the corridor of freedom.

Still, it seems likely that the current trend towards a reduced focus on equity issues nationally and globally will eventually come to an end. Milanovic observes that 'the growth of poor nations will remain of crucial importance' (p. 232) for the evolution of global inequality. He further notes 'that one can hardly overestimate its importance in poorer countries as a means of making the lives of ordinary people better' (p. 232). Rapid growth there may also help reduce the demand for migration.

The basis for the increase of populism in recent years in the West was that a sizeable share of the population felt they had lost or have been disfavoured relatively in the context of globalization-driven economic changes, and there has been a feeling among citizens that the elites have too much power and a lack of faith in institutions. The success of populist movements makes it harder for all parties to compromise and to accept restrictions. The struggle between different parties becomes increasingly polarized, and they fail to solve the conflicts.

To turn this development around, one needs to form a broad coalition of citizens among which one can compromise to be able to roll back the support for populists. This can contribute to a reduction of the base for a more populist development, which in the long term might reduce our freedom, equality, and fraternity.

References

Acemoglu, D., and Robinson, J.A. (2019). *The Narrow Corridor: States, Societies, and the Fate of Liberty*. New York: Penguin Press.
Bigsten, A. (2023). Atkinson on Inequality. In this volume.
Collier, P. (2018a). *The Future of Capitalism. Facing the New Anxieties*. Elcograf: Allen Lane.
Collier, P. (2018b). The Downside of Globalisation: Why It Matters and What Can Be Done About. *The World Economy*, 41, 967–974.
Collier, P., and Venables, A. (2017). Who Gets the Urban Surplus? *Journal of Economic Geography*, 18(3), 523–538.
Goodhart, D. (2017). *The Road to Somewhere: The Populist Revolt and the Future of Politics*. London: Hurst & Co.
Inglehart, R., and Norris, P. (2017). Trump and the Populist Authoritarian Parties: The Silent Revolution in Reverse. *Perspectives on Politics*, 15(2), 443–454.
Milanovic, B. (2016). *Global Inequality: A New Approach for the Age of Globalization*. Cambridge, MA: Harvard University Press.
Mutz, D.C. (2018). Status Threat, Not Economic Hardship, Explains the 2016 Presidential Vote. *PNAS*, 115(19), E4330–E4339.
Piketty, T. (2014). Capital in the Twenty-First Century. Cambridge, MA: The Belknap Press of Harvard University Press.
Piketty, T. (2020). *Capital and Ideology*. Cambridge, MA: The Belknap Press of Harvard University Press.
Pritchett, L. (1997). Divergence, Big Time. *Journal of Economic Perspectives*, 11(3), 3–17.
Reny, T.T., Collingwood, L., and Valenzuela, A. (2019). Vote Switching in the 2016 Election: How Racial and Immigration Attitudes, Not Economics, Explain Shifts in White Voting. *Public Opinion Quarterly*, 83(1), 91–113.
Scholte, J.A. (2008). Defining Globalization. *The World Economy*, 31, 1471–1502.
V-Dem Institute (2023). *Democracy Report 2023, Defiance in the Fact of Autocratization*. Gothenburg: Department of Political Science, University of Gothenburg.

Index

Note: Page numbers in *italics* indicate a figure on the corresponding page.

2008 global financial crisis 12, 28–29, 43–45, 47, 50, 157, 182–183, 198

Abacha, Sani 138
Abel-Smith, Brian 27, 95
Acemoglu, Daron 1, 197–198
Afghanistan 8, 89, 123, 128–130
Africa 28, 138; European colonial powers in 143; extreme poverty in 100
African Americans *see* Blacks in the US
agriculture: African 117; capital investment in 119; commercial 22; European 117–119; Portugal 165
al-Assad, Bashar 138
Alentejo, Portugal 165–166, 167, 168
Alfani, Guido 20
Alon, Titan 45
American blacks *see* Blacks in the US
American Creed 120
American dilemma, the 120–121, 123
American Revolution 5, 21
Amin, Idi 138, 142–145, 148–150
Amnesty International 128, 150
An American Dilemma (Gunnar Myrdal) 8, 120–121, 123
Annales school 29
antidiscrimination law: US 30n1
anti-globalist sentiment 191, 199
anti-immigration policies 197
antiquity 13, 143
apartheid and apartheid system, South Africa 8, 115–116, 118–119, 123–126, 128, 130
Arab-Israeli War 127
Arab royal families, wealth of 139
Argentina 138

Asia 138; average per capita income 118
Asians: expulsion from Uganda of 143; in South Africa 131n1
Åslund, Anders 144
Atkinson, Anthony 6, 7, 12, 28, 61, 62–65, 71n4, 71n7, 95–97, 98–100, 101–103, 104–107, 108–109
Atkinson Index 7, 97–98
Auerbach, Alan J. 72n16
Auten, Gerald 70
automation 161, 201
Autor, David 68, 72n18
Azerbaijan 143

Báez, Buenaventura 143
Bakiyev, Kurmanbek 138, 149
Bali, Azad 175
Banerjee, Abijit 28
Bangladesh 123–124
Bantus 131n1
Bantustans 124
Bashar al-Assad *see* al-Assad, Bashar
Baumol, William 146
Becker, Gary 121
Beijing Convention for Women 1995 49
Belgium 138
Bengtsson, Bo 176
Berg, Andrew 108
Bettio, Francesca 41–42
Bielby, Denise 42
billionaires 141
Black Lives Matter 89
Blacks in the US 127; as American underclass 88; antidiscrimination law and 30n1; Jim Crow laws 119, 124; racial discrimination against 8, 115,

119–125, 127, 128; struggle for civil rights 7; US labor market and 119–123, 131n6
Black South Africans 125, 128
Blanchard, Oliver 2
Boigny, Félix Houphouët 138
Bokassa, Jean-Bédel 138, 144–145, 149–150
Bonnet, Carole 49
Bonnet, Odran 69
Bourdieu, Pierre 23
bourgeoisie 11, 22, 30
Bourguignon, François 98, 101
Boushey, Heather 72n17
Brandt, Osvald 143
Brown v. Board of Education 121
Buddhists 123
Burma 123, 142, 146
Burnham, Forbes 145
Busch, Felix 45
Bush, George W.H. 7, 86–88, 91, 93n13

Cagé, Julia 29
Cairney, Paul 185
Camille See Law of 1880 (France) 37
Cantillon, Richard 22
capital: economic power over women and 45; flow of 10; human 35–36; labor and 5, 10; stocks 12; unequal access to 45
capital accumulation 68, 173
capital assets 6
capital income 3, 6, 59, *65*; labor income and 61
Capital in the 21st Century (Piketty) 6, 29, 60, 65–70; debates following 68–70; 'Regulating Capital' 60; role of capital in 65–68
capitalism 5; agrarian 22; American 92; *American Capitalism* (Galbraith) 77; American Century and Cold War 23; concepts of class and 30; emancipation from 30; enemy of 76; hypercapitalism 108; inequality under 194; laws of 65–68; Marx as critic of 11, 25–26; industrial 21; North Atlantic financial 28; pre-capitalist inequality 19; progressive income tax to remedy 89; unfettered 20; US 82
capitalist mode of production 25–26
capitalists 22; European 117; industrial 117–119
capitalist societies 204
capitalist state 174
capitalist system 84

capital ownership 7
Carnation Revolution of 1974 178, 180
Cassel, Gustav 11
Castro, Fidel 138–139
Cavalcanti, Thiago. 48
Ceauşescu, Nicolae 138, 141, 150
Central African Republic 138, 144
Chanysheva, Lilia 151n4
Chenery, Hollis 101
Chicago School 174
childcare 33, 42, *43*, 45, 49–50
children: Barcelona targets for 49–50; basic income for 106–107; deprived 95; education of 37; employment rates based on number of 41, *41*; segregated schools and black children 121; time spent with 45; women's time and 122
Chinggis Khan 138
Civil Code of 1804 France 37
civilized labor policy 117
Civil Rights Act of 1964 US 121
civil rights, US 8, 120
civil servants, corrupt 147
Civil War: Libya 150; US 119
class: different problematics of inequality and 24–27; inequality and 19–30; French concepts of 5, 21–22, 29, 30; gender, race, and 25; German concepts of 30; as keyword in English-language books *21*; Marxist concepts of 25–26; middle 22; proletarian 11, 175; rise of 21–24; sociology and 23; upper-middle 179, 182; working 179, 183; *see also* elites; functional underclass
class distinctions 158, 162, 167
Cocola-Gant, Augustín 182
cohesion: national 11, 201; social 96, 160, 186, 199
Cohesion and Regional Policy (EU) 159, 161, 164–165
Cold War 23, 28, 144, 198
Collier, Paul 199–200
colonialism: British 126; European 138, 143; Portuguese 181; post-colonial era 123
Colored, as racial category in South Africa 118, 131n1
commodity market 77
Communism 27, 30; Soviet 82
Communist dictatorships 138
Communist Manifesto (Marx and Engels) 22; *see also* Marx, Engels
Congo Free State 138, 195
Corn Laws 22
Corsi, Marcella 47

Index 209

COVID-19 43–45
Crenshaw, Kimberlé 23, 30n1
crimes 129; hate 126; war 150
crimes against humanity 150
crimes of apartheid 128
crony capitalism 141, 144
Cuba 138, 144; *see also* Castro
Curie, Marie 38

Dahlerup, Drude 48
Dalarna, Sweden 163–164, 166, 167
Dalits 8, 123, 126–127
Dauphin, Sandrine 48
Dear, Michael 175
Deaton, Angus 28, 109
directly unproductive profit-seeking (DUP) 144
discrimination 2; American court cases involving 121; consumer 122; as determinant of economic inequality 115–130; effects of 4; existential inequality and 24; legal 121; legal protections against 34; monopsonistic 115, 121–122; pervasive, against women 33, 35; preference-based 115, 121–122; race or racial 8–9, 13; racial discrimination against Blacks in the US 8, 115, 119–125, 127, 128; racial discrimination in occupations 122; racial discrimination in South Africa 115, 116–119; religious 124; statistical 115, 121–122; systematic 124; systemic 115; theories of 121–122; US antidiscrimination law 30n1; women in Afghanistan 128–129; *see also* Dalit; Uyghur
discriminatory practices 6, 51
domestic inequality 12
domestic violence 129, 184
domestic work 33, 42–44, 48
Dominican Republic 138, 142–143, 145
Duflo, Esther 28
Duvalier family, Haiti 138; Baby Doc 142, 145, 149; Papa Doc 138, 141, 145–146
Duvalier, François (Papa Doc) 138, 141, 145–146; 'Essential Works' of 143
Duvalier, Jean-Claude (Baby Doc) 142, 145, 149

Eastern Europe 191, 198; Communist dictatorships 138
EEC *see* European Economic Community
efficiency of markets 11–12, 79
efficiency, government's sacrifice of 146–147

efficiency wages 107
elites 1, 203, 205; economic 198
Engels, Friedrich 174
entrepreneurship, three kinds of 145
environmentalism 75
Equatorial Guinea 138
equity 3; economic 43; growth-equity trade-off 107
equity-efficiency trade-off 108, 162, 192–193
equity policies 51, 197
Erhel, Christine 49
Esping-Andersen, Gösta 47, 49
Estado Novo 179
Ethiopia 138
European Council 49
European Economic Community (EEC): Portugal's entry into 178, 181–182
European Social Fund 50
European Union: childcare in 50–51; Cohesion and Regional Policy 159, 161, 164–165; family policies 50; Lisbon Strategy 50; NUTS nomenclature 158–159, 164–165
Expropriation Act (Portugal) 179

Fadeyeva, Ksenya 151n4
farmers 8, 92; European 117–119; tenant 22
farming, of taxes *see* tax farming
Ferrand, Michèle 39
Ferry, Jules 37
feudal privileges 19
feudal seigneurial rights 19
Finland: childcare in *43*
Fox, Elizabeth 42
France 5, 21–22, 19, 29–30, 36–39, *43*, 46, *46*, 48, 49, 66, 67
free blacks 119
freedom(s): American Creed of 120; feelings of 10; fundamental rights and 125, 128; as good in itself 192; outcome dimension of 191–192, 197–199; political 75; threats to 197–199
freedom of movement 124–125, 127
freedom to work 38
free economic competition 146
free (public) education 37
free market(s) 11–12, 76, 180
free trade doctrine 5
French Revolution 5, 10, 12, 21, 37
Friedman, Milton 11, 81
Frigeni, Roberta 20
functional underclass 87–88, 91

Gaddafi, Muammar 138, 144–145, 150
Galbraith, John Kenneth 6–7, 75–91
Gawon, Yakubu 145
Gaza Strip 127
Gazprom 143
gender: class, race, and 25; race and 23, 30n1
gender apartheid 128
gender discrimination 8, 35: Afghanistan 123, 128–129; global 123; local 123
gender egalitarian welfare states 47
gender inequalities 4–6, 33–51; consequences of 43–47; contemporary issues in women in the labor force 40–43; defining 33; economic crises and 44–45; feminism as response to 21; in French education 36–39; in housing 12; public policies addressing 47–50; women and poverty and 45–47; women's economic emancipation and welfare state and 47–49; *see also* women
gender labor market inequality 1
gender norms 128
gender perceptions of occupations *39*
gender policies 34
gender quotas 34
gender stereotypes 6, 42
genocide 124, 150
Georgia, republic of 143
Germany: childcare in *43*; concepts of class in 30; general lack of interest in inequality in 20–21; OTRAG rocket company 146; poverty risk in *46*; Ruhr 158; West 118, 146; Worker's Party 25
global inequality 7, 10–11; Atkinson on 96, 100–101; global poverty and 100–101
globalization (globalisation) 10, 12, 102, 104, 107–108, 160, 177, 191–205
Global North 28
global patterns of oppression 124
global poverty 100–101, 109; SDGs for 101
Global South 22
global supply chains 125
global tax: on capital 60; on corporations 106
global welfare 109
Glukhovsky, Dmitri 151n4
Goblet Law of 1886, France 37
Goldin, Claudia 1, 28
Goldthorpe, John 23
Google Ngram 20–21
Great Recession 89

Greece *46*
Gruchy, Allan 92n11
Guergoat-Larivière, Mathilde 49
Guizot, François 37
Gypsies *see* Roma people

Haby Law of 1975, France 37
Hague, the 149–150
Haig, Robert 59, 67
Hailie Selassie 138, 149
Haiti 138, 142–146, 148; slavery in 19; *see also* Duvalier family
Haitian Revolution 5
Hamnett, Chris 173, 177
Harrington, Michael 27
Harvey, David 174
hate crimes 126
Hayek, Friedrich 11
Heckscher, Eli 11
Heckscher-Ohlin model 102
Henry VIII 138
Hernes, Helga Maria 48
Heureaux, Ulises 143
hierarchy: Catholic tradition of 19; European 159; executive 84; human 24; occupational 23; power 143; social 21–22, 126
Himmelweit, Susan 44
Hobson, Barbara 47
'homelands' system 118
House of Saud 138, 150
Howlett, Michael 177
Huber, Evelyne 47
human capital 3, 35–36, 160–161; attracting 166–167; investment in 148
human rights 2, 28; abuses of 124; fundamental 109; gender inequality as challenge to 33; upholding 124; violations of 125
Human Rights Watch 128
human trafficking 184
Hungary *43*, *46*, 164
hypercapitalism 108

India 65, 100; castes and caste-based discrimination in 21, 127; Constitution 126; Mughal 138; *see also* Dalits
Indonesia 138
inequality: accidental decrease in US of 71n11; Atkinson on 95–110; class and 19–30; different problematics of class and 24–27; discovery of 19–21; discrimination as determinant of 115–130; economic 59–60, 77, 95, 115–130, 199; examples of, in three

regions left behind 163–166; existential 24; extreme 137–150; fixing 28; Galbraith on 75–91; global 205; global changes in 193–197; globalization and 191; housing and (Portugal) 173–187; income 59; inegalitarian turn and rediscovery of 27–28; overall development in 20th century of 63; overview of and introduction to 1–13; Piketty on 28–29, 30, 59–71; policies to reduce 103–108; regional 157–168; rising 200–201; wage 67; wealth 59, 70, 75; *see also* gender inequalities
inequality index 61
Inglehart, Ronald 200
injustice 127–128; social 2, 173–174; systemic 130; territorial 173
Iraq 89, 138
Iraq War 150
Ireland *43, 46*
Israel: accusations of committing crimes of persecution against Palestine 128; establishment as a state 127
Israeli-Palestine conflict 127–128
Israelis, ejected from Uganda 144
Italy *43, 46*, 138
Ivory Coast 138

James, Laura 177
Jaumotte, Florence 49
Jenkins, Stephen 95, 98
Jim Crow laws, US 119, 124
Johnson, Lyndon 77, 91n1
Johnson, Simon 1
justice 7; advancing or retreating 104; Atkinson on 96, 104; economic 98; ideals of equality and 127; Rawls on 24, 28; regional development and 9, 157, 168; seeking 129; social 3, 12, 19, 28, 33, 51, 127; striving for 126

Karimov, Islam 138
Kazakhstan 138
Kemeny, Jim 177
Kennedy, John F. 77, 91n1
Kennedy, Robert 91n1
Keynesian economics 12, 76–77, 93n14
Keynes, John Maynard 76
Khodorkovsky, Mikhail 143, 150n4
Kim dynasty, North Korea 138–139, 150
Kim Jong-un 139
kleptocracies 141; difficulty of uprooting 150; Russia 144
kleptocratic regimes 9, 13, 140–142

kleptocrats 137–138, 140, 145, 147; violent overthrow of 149
Korpi, Walter 5, 26
Kremlin 151n4
Krugman, Paul 71n1, 71n8
Krusell, Per 68
Kuznets, Simon 31n4, 62, 65, 71n11
Kuznets curve 65
Kuznets hypothesis 194
Kuznets waves 194, 196
Kyrgyzstan 138

labor: attracting 10; bourgeoisie's exploitation of 11; capital and 5–6, 67; compensation of 78; demarketing of 48; domestic 42; division of 33, 42; new money from 59; robots replacing 72n19; wealth and 2; women's 35, 44
labor force: women in 48, 50
labor income 12, 61, 65, 67–68, 70; capital income and 62–63; distribution of 67–68
labor market: education and 92n11; flexibility in 49; trade unions in 77; US 8; women's integration in 43; women's position in 34, 40–41, 47–48
land alienation 116–118
land competition 174
land expropriation 124, 128
landlords 22, 78
land policy 179
Lasalle, Ferdinand 25
Latin America 28, 99, 138
Leopold II of Belgium 138
Levi, Margaret 137
Lewis, Jane 48
Libya 138, 144–145
Lindbeck, Assar 76
Lindert, Peter 71n1
Lisbon, Portugal 165, 183, 185–186
Lisbon Strategy 38, 50
Litvinenko, Alexander 150n4
Lukashenko, Alexander 138

Madrick, Jeff 76, 86
Maduro, Nicolás 138
Magnitsky, Sergei 151n4
Malpass, Peter 175
Malthus, Thomas Robert 78
Manchester, England 174
Mandela, Nelson 118–119
Mankiw, Gregory 72n17
Marcos, Ferdinand 138–139, 141, 145–146
Marry, Catherine 39
Marshall, Alfred 11

Marx, Karl 5, 11, 22, 25–27, 87, 92n3
Marxian tradition, class analysis according to 22–23
Marxism 30n3; Bokassa's conversion to 144; neo-Marxism 5, 26, 173; orthodox 27
Marxist revolution 29–30
Marxists 13; Lasalle and 25
mashup index 100
Maslow's hierarchy of needs *167*
McCarthy, Eugene 91n1
McGovern, George 91n1
Meade, James, E. 61
Meltzer, Allan 71n8
Meulders, Daniele 46
migration 202–203
Milanović, Branko 10, 173, 193–195
Milošević, Slobodan 138, 149
military campaigns against the Rohingya 124
military dictatorships 28
military spending 75
militias 141, 145
Millar, John 22
Mill, John Stuart 11
Mobutu Sese Seko 138–139, 146, 149–150
Mohammed VI 138
Mongols 138
mono-functional housing projects 180
monopolistic: competition 103; power 104
monopolization 142
monopoly 82, 104, 145; local 177; national policies to regulate 203
monopoly privileges 145, 147
monopsonic discrimination 115, 121–122
Morocco 138
Mubarak, Hosni 150
Mugabe, Robert 138, 150
Mughal India 138
Murie, Alan 175
Murray, Charles 88, 91
Myrdal, Gunnar 8, 10, 93, 115, 120–121, 123, 131n7, 160

Nakba 127
Napoleon Bonaparte 37, 138
Navalny, Alexei 137, 150n4
Nazarbayev, Nursultan 138
nepotism 2, 145
Netherlands 19, *46*
New Deal (US) 194
New Generation of Housing Policies (NGHP) 183–185
New Socialism 84
New Welfare Economics 11

NGHP *see* New Generation of Housing Policies
Nguema, Francisco Macías 138, 148, 150
Nicaragua 138–139, 143
Nigeria 138, 145–146
nomad theory 174
nomenklaturas 138, 150n2
Noriega, Manuel 142, 146, 149
North Korea 138, 150
NUTS nomenclature (EU) (NUTS 0, 1, 2, 3, 4) 158–159, 164–165

OAS *see* Organization of American States
Obiang, Teodoro 138
occupational segregation 41–42, 43; horizontal 45
occupations: gender perception of 39, *39*; invidious 87; prestige perceptions of 23; racial discrimination in 122
O'Dorchai, Sile 46
Oesch, Daniel 23
Ohlin, Bertil 12; Heckscher-Ohlin model 102
Ohlsson, Henry 72n15
oligarchs 140, 144, 150
Orange Free State 116
Organization of American States (OAS) 144
Orloff, Ann 48
Ortega, Daniel 138
Ottoman Empire 143

P90–95 group 64
P90–99 group 64, *64*
PAC *see* Pan Africanist Congress
Pacione, Michael 174
Palestinians 8, 127–128
Palier, Bruno 176
Pan Africanist Congress (PAC) 118
Paraguay 138
Parker, Richard 75–77, 82, 86
Pérez Jiménez, Marcos 138, 149
Périvier, Hélène 44, 48–49
Perón, Juan 138, 149
Peters, Guy 185
Philippines 138–139, 143, 145
Physiocrats 22, 25
Piketty, Thomas 1–3, 5, 6, 12, 28–29, 30, 59–71, 98, 100–101
plunder 4; political cliques' pocketing of 141; steps to successful plunder 140–142; taxation and borrowing as methods of plunder 142–144
plunder by the state 13; *see also* predatory state
Poland *43, 46*

Politkovskaya, Anna 150–151n4
poor, the: Galbraith in 77–79, 82, 85–91, 93n13; *Poor and the Poorest* (Abel-Smith and Townsend) 27, 95; coexistence of rich and 19; income gap between rich and 5, 12, 88; inequality between rich and 97–98; outnumbering the rich 3; relation between the rich and 71n2; rich and 1; society as consisting of the rich and 21; subsidy for 86–87; rural 92n6; trickle-down theory and 91, 109
poor white problem, South Africa 117–118
populism 91, 191, 199, 200, 204–205; anti-immigration sentiment of 191, 197; backlash factor of 200; rise of 11
Portugal 10, 163, 165–166, 167, 168, 173–187, *178*
poverty 11; absolute 1; Atkinson's work on 7, 95–101, 103–104, 107–109; economists [by name] who focused on 11; eliminating 87; Galbraith's work on 77–78, 80, 82, 86–90, 92; global 109; Harrington on 27; *Nature of Mass Poverty* (Galbraith) 92; persistent 5; polarizing inequality of 27; *Poor and the Poorest* (Abel-Smith and Townsend) 27, 95; recent evolution of 96; redistribution schemes prolonging 3; reducing 82, 90; women and *45*, 46–47, 50
poverty/discrimination nexus 121
poverty line 86, 108
poverty rate 46–47
poverty reduction 75
poverty risk 43, *45*, *46*
poverty trap 107
predatory state 137–150; defining 8; economic effects of predation 146–148; end of predation 149–150; flexible budget 145; increased informality of 148–149; methods of 9; rationale of redistribution in 139–140; rent creation by 144; state-owned and private enterprise 145–146; steps to successful plunder in 140–142; taxation and borrowing as methods of plunder 142–144; use of foreign aid 144–145
Prigozhin, Yevgeny 151n4
Programa Especial de Relojamento [Special Rehousing Programme] 182
proletariat 11, 175
PRR *see* Recovery and Resilience Plan (PRR) (Portugal)
Putin's Palace (documentary film) 137

Putin, Vladimir 9, 13, 140–141, 143–144, 146, 149; circle and cronies of 141; palace of 137–138
quality of life 9, 123, 158, 167; 'Economics and Quality of Life' (Galbraith) 92n11; regions, inequalities, and 161–163

Quesnay, François 22

Rahmon, Emomali 138
Rakhine State 123
Ravallion, Martin 100
Rawls, John 3, 24, 28
Ray, Debray 72n20
Reagan, Ronald 7, 86–88, 91, 93n13
Recovery and Resilience Plan (PRR) (Portugal) 184
refugees 124, 181
region: defining 159; perceptual 159; quality of life and 161–163; typologies of 158–159
regional development strategies 166
regional inequality 9–10, 157–168; causes of 160–161; key challenges to 158
regional policy, urban-centered 165, 202
regions left behind, three examples of inequality in 163–166
Reichelt, Malte 44
rent creation 144
rent seeking 145, 146
repression 9, 125, 141–142
Reskin, Barbara 42
retornados (returnees) 181
Ricardians 25
Ricardo, David 5, 11, 22, 78
Robinson, James 197–198
Robinson, Joan 122
Rodrik, Dani 2
Rohingya 8, 123–124, 130
Roma people 173–174, 185
Romania 158
Roman Empire 198
Romans 143
Roman use of classes 22
Rosneft 143
Rousseau, Jean-Jacques 20
Royal Swedish Academy of Sciences 1
Rubery, Jane 44
ruler of predatory state 8–9, 13, 137, 139–143, 146–149
ruling class 148
ruling clique 8, 137, 139–142, 144–147, 150
Ruonavaara, Hannu 176
Russia 9, 140, 143–144; *see also* Putin; Soviet Union

Saddam Hussein 138–139, 150
Saez, Emmanuel 62, 70, 72n18, 100
Sandinistas 139, 150
Saudi Arabia 138, 150
Scandinavia 48, 76, 77, 121
Schneebaum, Alyssa 45
Scott, Allen 175
Scott, Joan 35
Scottish Enlightenment 22
Scottish Highland 158
SDGs *see* Sustainable Development Goals
Second Empire, France 37
segregation: educational 118, 121; housing 10, 13; neighborhood 124; occupational 41–42, 43, 45; racial 118–125, 127, 129; residential 131n5; systemic 125; US 119–121, 123–126, 131n5; workplace 122
Selassie *see* Hailie Selassie
Sen, Amartya 3, 5, 24, 26, 28, 103–104
Seron, Carroll 42
Sese Seko, Mobutu *see* Mobuto Sese Seko
Sevilla, Almudena 45
Shah of Iran 138, 149
Simons, Henry 59n67
Six-Day War of 1967 127
slavery 119–120; in Haiti 66
slaves 19; as capital 66
Slovenia *43, 46*
Smith, Anthony 68
Smith, Adam 3, 5, 11, 22, 78
Smith, Matthew 70
Smuts, Jan 118
social class 22
social class distinctions 9
social discord 2
social fragility 28
social housing 10
social identity 29
social inequality 2–3, 24
social injustice 2, 173–174
social justice 3, 12, 19, 28, 33, 51, 127
social mobility 23–24
social norms 34
social protection 48
social welfare 4, 7, 96–97, 192
social work 39
Solow, Robert 71n1, 95
Solow–Swan growth model 62
Somalia 150
Somerville, Peter 176
Somoza Debayle, Anastasio ('Tachito') 139, 141, 143, 150
Somoza family, Nicaragua 138
Somoza García, Anastasio ('Tacho') 150

South Africa 8, 28, 115–116, 117, 118–119, 123–126, 128, 130
Southeast Asia 28
Soviet republics 143
Soviet Union 82, 84, 144, 146
Sowell, Thomas 2
Spain *43, 46*
Stienbaum, Marshall 72n17
Stiglitz, Joseph 1, 28, 62
stratification, sociological 23–24, 173
stratificationism 23
Stroessner, Alfredo 138, 149
Stuart England 138
Suharto, of Indonesia 138, 150
Summers, Lawrence 71n1
Sustainable Development Goals (SDG), on global poverty 101
Sveriges Riksbank Prize in Economic Sciences 1
Swan, Trevor 62
Sweden *43, 46*, 163–164, 166, 167
Syria 138

Tajikistan 138
taxation 2, 3, 7, 9, 22, 59–63, 68, 70, 77, 79, 85, 88, 89, 90, 103, 105, 106, 142–144, 146, 147
Theodoropoulou, Sotiria 44
Tilly, Charles 24
Tinbergen, Jan 102, 194
top-down regional policies 161, 164
top end of wealth distribution 2, 62–68, 70
top income bracket 78, 81
Top Income project 6, 61, 62–65, 68, 100–101
Townsend, Peter 27, 95
Trampusch,Christine 176
Transvaal republic 116
Trujillo, Rafael 138, 141, 143, 145; death of 150
Truman, Harry 91n1
Trump, Donald 89, 200
Tudor England 138
Turgot, Anne Robert 22

Uganda 138, 142–144, 148
Ukraine 158; war in 149, 151n4
underclass 87–88, 91
United Kingdom (UK) *43, 46*, 99
United Nations (UN): International Criminal Tribunal for the Former Yugoslavia 149–150
United Party (South Africa) 118
United States (US) 67, 70, 77, 82, 88, 99, 119–121, 123–126, 131n5, 194

urban–rural divide 203
Uyghurs 8, 123–126, 130
Uzbekistan 138

Van Baar, Huub 174
Veblen, Thorstein 76, 92n2
Venezuela 138
Vivekananda, Swami 3

Waldenström, Daniel 71n3
war crimes 150
Warren, Earl 121
Watt, Andrew 44
Weber, Max 23
Weil, David 72n17
welfare 3; global 109; liberal 48; New Welfare Economics 11; populism impacts of 191; quality of life 161; social 4, 96–97, 192; spatial differentiation of 157; spatial planning and 186
welfare benefits 157
welfare economics 109
welfarindicators 100
welfare reform 75
welfare services 9, 89, 157, 162, 168, 196
welfare spending, US cuts to 88
welfare state 7; Atkinson's work on and defense of 95–100, 102–104, 106–109; changing role of 102; classification of 47; comparative welfare state research 26; expansion of 194; factors shaping 178; Galbraith's support of 76, 87; gender-egalitarian 47; inheritance and 72n15; insurance and 72n15; Portugal as 180; social-democratic 47; strong 76; sustainability of 196; Sweden as 195; tax revenues required by 108; women's economic emancipation and 47–49
West Bank 127

West Germany 118, 146
Wicksell, Knut 11
Williams, Andrea 76
Williamson, Jeffery 160
women: Afghan 8, 123, 128–129, 130; Beijing Convention for Women 1995 49; differential treatment of men and 12; domestic labor and childcare burdens of 42–43; as crypto-servant class 92n6; education of 36–39; industrial-era transformation of roles of 35; lower wages paid to 122; occupational segregation of 41–42; pervasive discrimination against 33; political representation of 34; poverty risk *46*; risk of poverty faced by 45–47; welfare state and women's economic emancipation 47–49; white 30n1; workplace precarity of 40–41
women's labor 35, 44; influx into market of 99; underutilization of 50
women's rights and women's rights movement 5–6, 51; Afghan 129
World Inequality Database (WID) 70
Wright, Erik Olin 23, 26, 30n3

X-efficiency 147
Xinjian Uyghur Autonomous Region 124–125

Yugoslavia: UN International Criminal Tribunal for the Former Yugoslavia 149–150
Yukos oil company 143

Zagóra-Jonszta, Urszula 92n5
Zaire 138, 146
Zimbabwe 138
Zucman, Gabriel 70
Zuma, Jacob 138

Milton Keynes UK
Ingram Content Group UK Ltd.
UKHW031329071224
451979UK00005B/74